OPERATION PIMENTO

About the Author

Adam Hart is a writer and historian from Pembrokeshire in South West Wales. While training to be a journalist at Cardiff University, Adam won a travel bursary to retrace his great-grandfather's escape in the Second World War, inspiring this book. He has also written for *The Times* and *Telegraph*, appeared on the *Antiques Roadshow* and *ITV Evening News* and has spoken on Radio 4 and Times Radio. *Operation Pimento* is his first book.

OPERATION PIMENTO

MY GREAT-GRANDFATHER'S
GREAT ESCAPE

ADAM HART

HODDER &
STOUGHTON

First published in Great Britain in 2025 by Hodder & Stoughton Limited
An Hachette UK company

The authorised representative in the EEA is Hachette Ireland, 8 Castlecourt
Centre, Dublin 15, D15 XTP3, Ireland (email: info@hbgi.ie)

1

Maps and illustrations by Joanna Boyle

A CIP catalogue record for this title is available from the British Library

Hardback ISBN 9781399740135
Trade Paperback ISBN 9781399740142
ebook ISBN 9781399740159

Typeset in Plantin MT Pro Light by Hewer Text UK Ltd, Edinburgh
Printed and bound in Great Britain by Clays Ltd, Elcograf S.p.A.

Hodder & Stoughton policy is to use papers that are natural, renewable
and recyclable products and made from wood grown in sustainable
forests. The logging and manufacturing processes are expected to
conform to the environmental regulations of the country of origin.

Hodder & Stoughton Limited
Carmelite House
50 Victoria Embankment
London EC4Y 0DZ

www.hodder.co.uk

In loving memory of Tessa Holland,
my wonderful grandmother.

1942–2022

CONTENTS

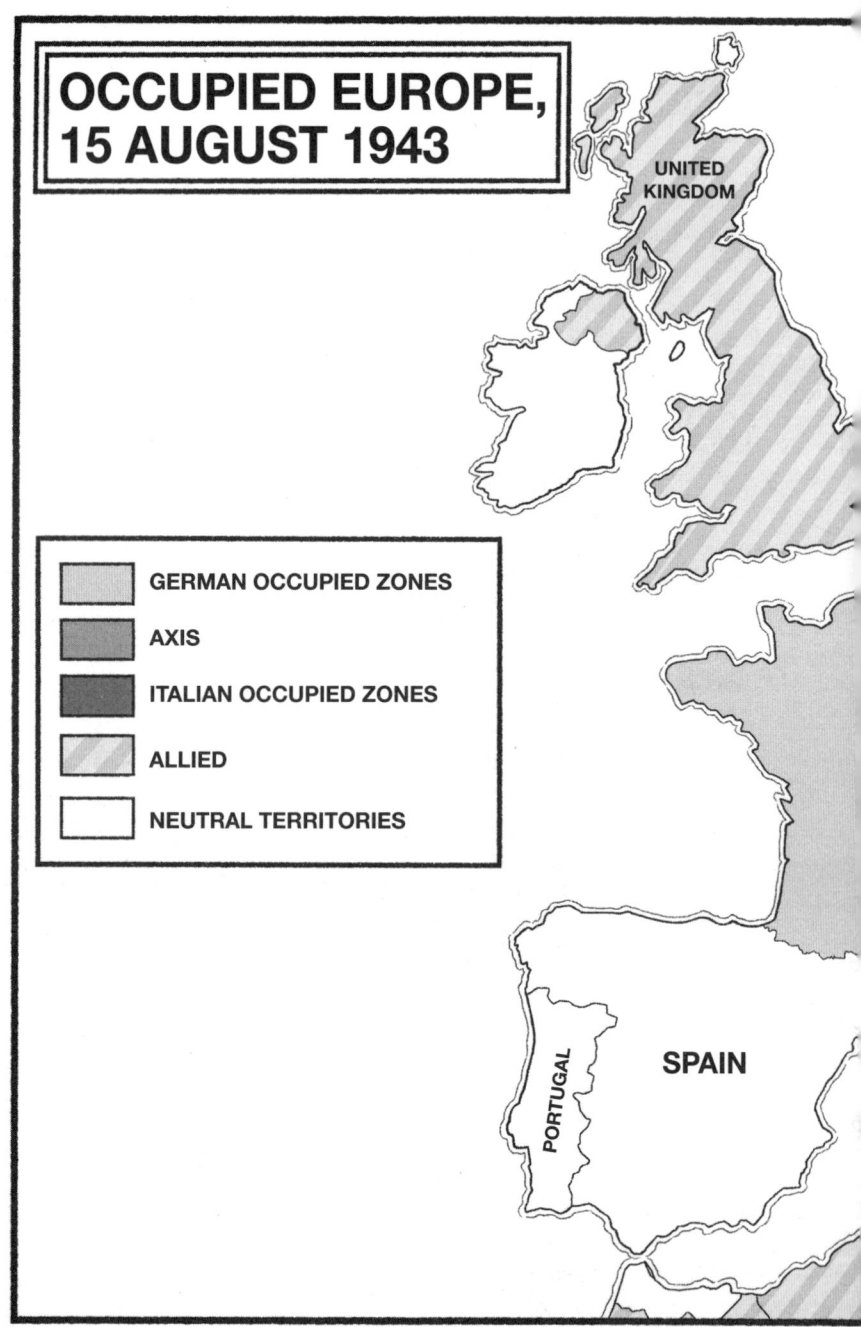

OCCUPIED EUROPE, 15 AUGUST 1943

UNITED KINGDOM

	GERMAN OCCUPIED ZONES
	AXIS
	ITALIAN OCCUPIED ZONES
	ALLIED
	NEUTRAL TERRITORIES

PORTUGAL

SPAIN

The situation in Europe when Frank crashed in France. The Allies had liberated North

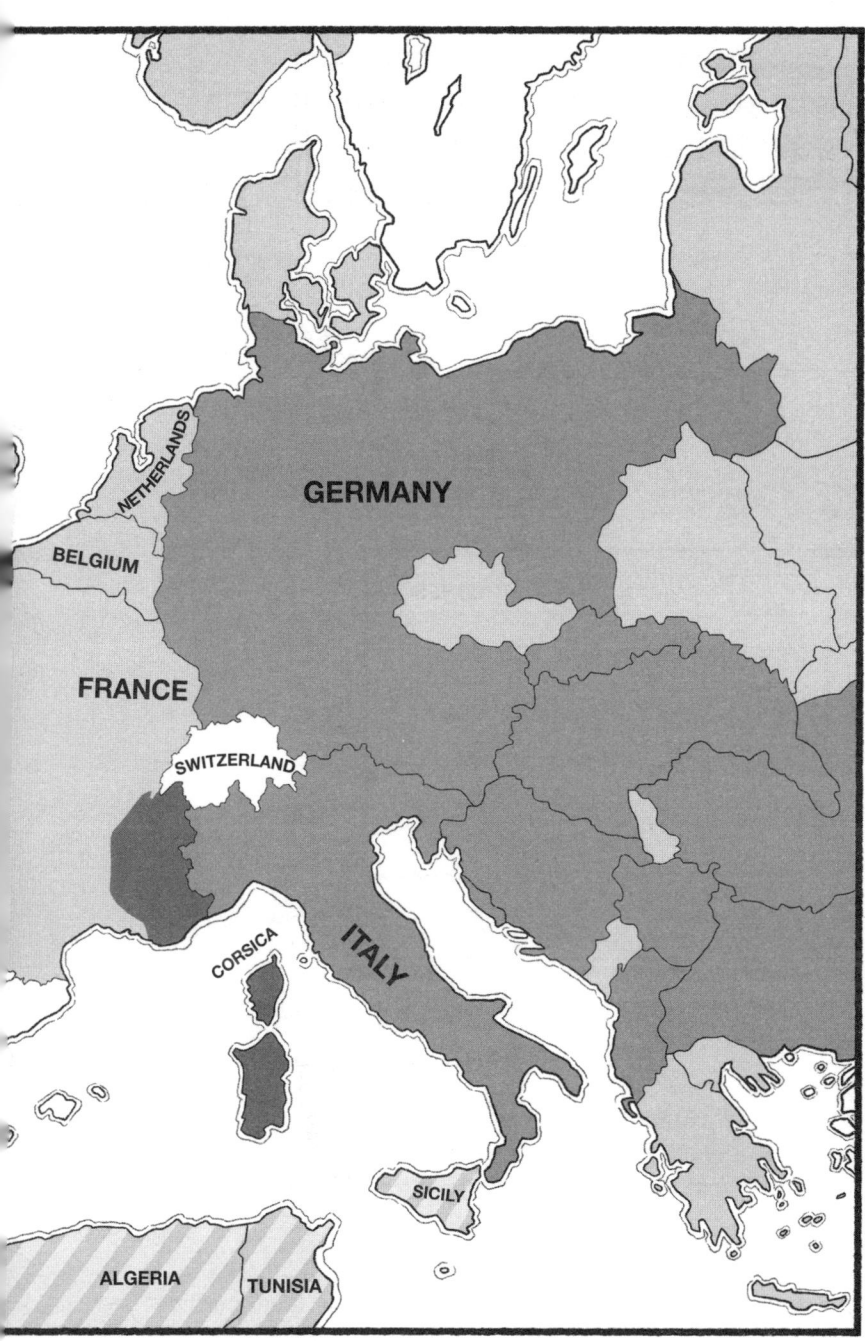

Africa and were now turning their attention to Italy after the fall of Mussolini in July.

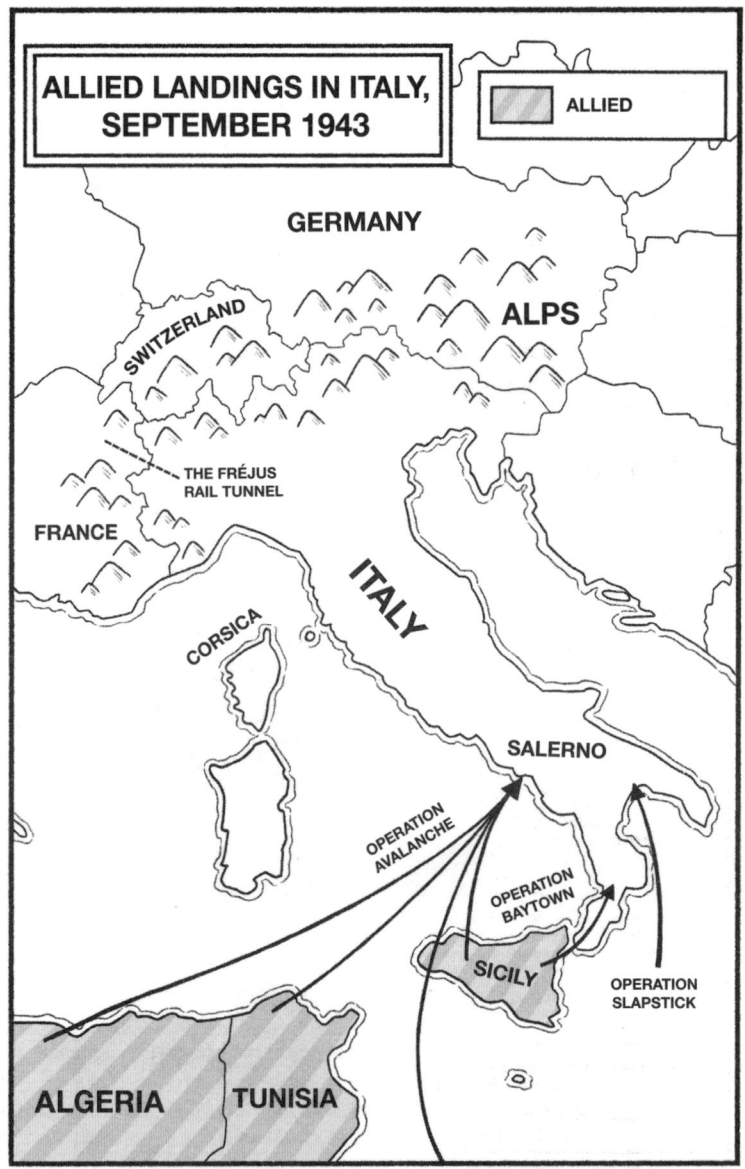

ALLIED LANDINGS IN ITALY, SEPTEMBER 1943

ALLIED

GERMANY

ALPS

SWITZERLAND

THE FRÉJUS RAIL TUNNEL

FRANCE

ITALY

CORSICA

SALERNO

OPERATION AVALANCHE

OPERATION BAYTOWN

SICILY

OPERATION SLAPSTICK

ALGERIA   TUNISIA

Following success in North Africa and Sicily, the Allies planned to invade Italy in what would be the first invasion of mainland Europe of the war. They knew German forces stationed in France would race south through the Alps to meet the invasion once it was launched. Frank was tasked with dropping heavy explosives to French guerrilla fighters for them to blow up a tunnel that ran underneath the Alps. Success would block the Germans' route and buy the Allied armies crucial time to secure a foothold in Italy.

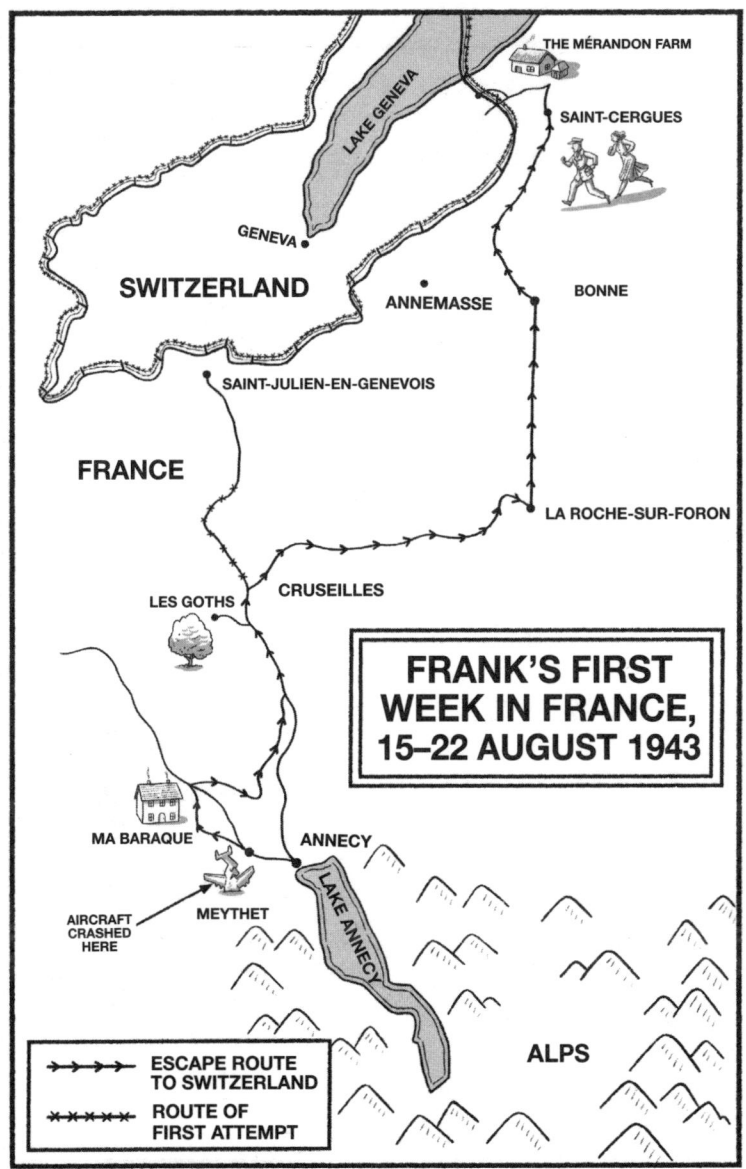

The first few days of Frank's escape following the crash. He managed to cross the French-Swiss border with the help of Colette Périès-Martinez, who pretended to be his lover. The original plan was to be expatriated from Lake Geneva at night by Sunderland flying boat.

FRANK'S ESCAPE:
15 AUGUST–30 NOVEMBER 1943

FOOT
ROAD
RAIL

SPAIN

ALHAMA DE
ARAGÓN

MADRID

SAN
ROQUE

GIBRALTAR

The plans for expatriation from Lake Geneva fell through and so Frank travelled 1,200
rail, although he trekked over the Pyrenees on foot.

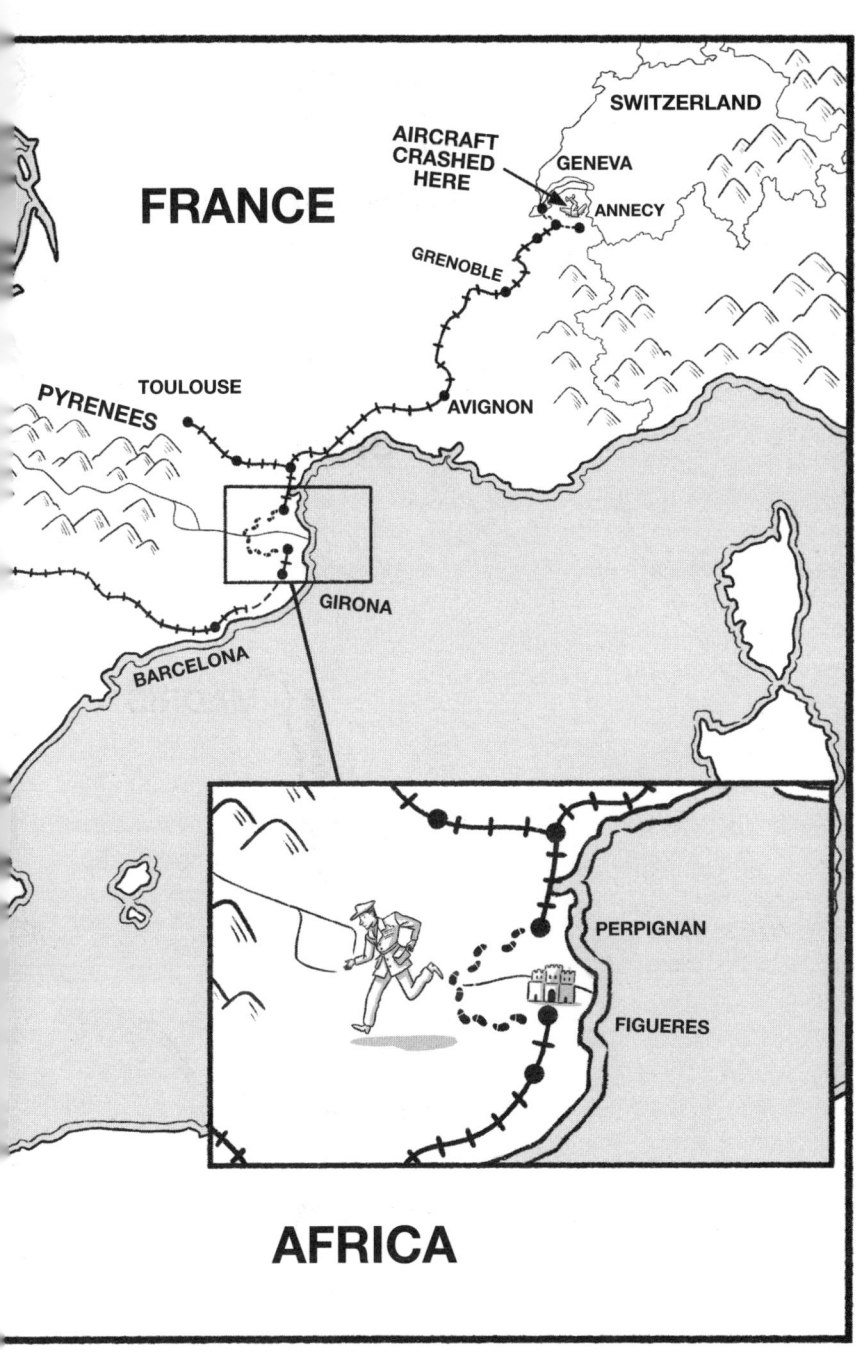

SWITZERLAND

FRANCE

AIRCRAFT
CRASHED
HERE

GENEVA

ANNECY

GRENOBLE

TOULOUSE

PYRENEES

AVIGNON

GIRONA

BARCELONA

PERPIGNAN

FIGUERES

AFRICA

niles southwest across France and Spain to safety in Gibraltar - largely by road and

INTRODUCTION

Frank Griffiths died in 1996, four years before I was born.

Although I never got to meet my great-grandfather, I have heard stories from his life so many times that I feel as though I know him. He is a family legend. A mythical presence whose crisp RAF uniform and daring flying exploits left a heavy impression on me as a boy.

My earliest memories are of my grandmother Tessa talking about her father around the kitchen table in Big House Farm, Carmarthenshire. Between mouthfuls of Sunday lunch, Granny would tell me how Frank used to fly so low, the belly of his aircraft would clip the trees, and when he went missing over Europe, she and her mother did not know whether he was alive or dead for three months.

It was this story that captured my imagination as a teenager. Frank's three-month escape in the autumn of 1943 had the ingredients of a screenplay written by Lord Flashheart himself. The tale differs between the storytellers, however. Characters are confused, details forgotten and loose ends left untied. This is partly what inspired me to retrace Frank's arduous escape: to find out exactly what happened. But there were other reasons.

My generation is the first one unable to hear their ancestors' war stories first-hand. Our understanding of the Second World War is naturally shrinking. By recreating Frank's journey and writing about it, I hoped to prevent his remarkable story from slipping into obscurity while paying homage to my childhood hero, one of the many incredible men and women who fought for the life we enjoy today.

The opportunity arose shortly before my twenty-second birthday. As a journalism master's student at Cardiff University, I applied for a travel journalism bursary offered by the Worshipful Livery Company of Wales. My ambitious pitch was to retrace Frank's 2,400-kilometre journey from the northern Alps to the Rock of Gibraltar, while tracking down as many descendants of his saviours as possible.

After graduating, a summer of planning ensued. Firstly, I re-read Frank's own account of his escape that he wrote in 1981 in a short book called *Winged Hours*. It would be my bible for the journey. He also left an oral history with the Imperial War Museum and a plethora of other written testimonies.

Although a brilliant pilot, Frank was not an author. His book, exciting at times but often hilariously understated, suffers from the fallibility of memory. Written thirty-eight years after the events occurred, I can only guess what details were forgotten or misremembered.

Yet, Frank had a meticulous pilot's brain and the parts of *Winged Hours* that I have been able to cross-reference are remarkably accurate. Others, as these pages will reveal, differ significantly from the memory of others involved.

The main narrative that follows is Frank's escape. It is, in my opinion, the most likely course of his journey, generated from a mixture of his written testimony, and the stories passed down through the families of the people I met on my travels. Frank himself never discovered the full story, or what happened to everyone else. Thanks to the fog of war, the secrecy of the escape networks and the wide use of noms de guerre, no one ever will.

Although often difficult to believe, every event in this book did happen. It is all true. The only 'colour' added are some sections of dialogue to make the story flow. For ease, I have written this dialogue in English, despite much of it being spoken in Frank's schoolboy French.

The second, smaller narrative in these pages is my retracing of his steps seventy-nine years later. Naturally, I could only be so faithful. I would not be crashing a plane into the Alps, but easyJetting into Geneva. There would be no Gestapo snapping at my heels, no amphetamines powering me over the Pyrenees and no jail cell with my name on it in Spain. I also had no wife and baby daughter motivating me to get back home. Many of the places where Frank was hidden – brothels, farm lofts, outhouses and chimneys – are gone, long since demolished or converted.

What remains are the people. While I could not visit many of the physical locations of Frank's escape, I could meet the descendants of those who hid him. Some who, like me, had been told the story by their parents or grandparents a hundred times. Others who could remember what their grandmother's forge was like, how its sooty chimney was just big enough to hide a man. Descendants whose memories held fresh details absent from *Winged Hours*, ranging from the contradictory to the tragic and the downright bizarre.

During these meetings, you would never have guessed we were talking about the events of eight decades ago. As I travelled across Europe, total strangers shook my hand, hugged me or cried in front of me. They bristled with pride, eyes wide and glistening, as I spoke about Frank and their ancestors. They told me it was their family's greatest honour to help him, that they still attend remembrance ceremonies to commemorate this story. Eighty years, I learned, is not really that long.

Considering the stakes for their predecessors, it is no wonder our meetings held such poignancy. Without uniform and the protection of the Geneva Convention, the ordinary civilians of France and Spain who saved Frank were far more vulnerable than he ever was. If captured, he would spend the rest of the war in an officer's quarters in a POW camp. The civilians, however, would be ripped from their homes and families, tortured and deported to concentration camps or, if they were lucky, shot.

Not speaking French, I thought finding these people would be difficult. But using the power of the internet, I was able to track down a descendant of almost every person who saved Frank, arranging to meet many of them in the very place their predecessors had hidden him.

And so, in October 2022, armed with a large rucksack, a map of the Pyrenees, my battered copy of *Winged Hours* and a headshot photo of Frank, I departed for Europe, seventy-nine years after my great-grandfather.

This is our story.

Adam Hart,
November 2024

PROLOGUE

On a hot August evening in 1943, seven men strolled across an RAF airfield in rural Bedfordshire. The heat had gone out of the day and the summer air of England was refreshing, if a little heavy with anticipation. The airmen were walking towards their Halifax, a four-engine heavy bomber, but stopped when they heard the other Halifaxes of 138 Squadron. They watched them taxi into position, surge down the runway and rise into the amber sky.

Each aircraft faced an uncertain future flying over Hitler's Europe, from the fjords of Norway to the foothills of the Pyrenees, and the plains of the low countries to high Alpine plateaus. Meanwhile beneath them, men and women of resistance groups were gathering with signal torches in hand, hiding themselves in hedges, dykes, cattle sheds and forests, where they listened for the sound of friendly engines.

The seven airmen clambered into their Halifax, *O for Orange*. At 9.40 p.m., the pilot, my great-grandfather Frank Griffiths, opened the throttle. The heavy bomber's four engines roared, the aircraft surged forwards and forty seconds later, *O for Orange* parted from English soil. It was the first time the seven had flown together, but they understood their mission was essential. The lives of many hundreds of Allied soldiers could depend on their success. Failure would prolong the war.

O for Orange's crew were of the highest class. With 199 combat missions, two Distinguished Flying Medals, and an average age of twenty-three, they combined experience with youthful fearlessness. Their number included a professional football player from Lancashire, a trainee dentist from the Isle of Skye, and two fathers-to-be from Devon and Essex. At thirty-one, Frank the skipper was the oldest onboard by five years. These men, drawn from different corners of the British Isles, were skilled operators chosen from the ranks of Bomber Command for the job.

After crossing the Normandy coast at 7,000 feet, *O for Orange* entered thick cloud. Rain pelted the aircraft as it cut across France and it looked like the mission might have to be aborted. Near Lyon, Frank watched a Lancaster – one of 140 raiding Milan – tumble from the sky, victim of German flak.

But as *O for Orange* slipped over the Massif Central and into the Rhône Valley, the cloud dispersed and the rain ceased. The operation was on. Identifying Lake Annecy, the skipper flew perilously low while his crew studied the moon-lit fields of the Haute-Savoie for their reception party's lights. Mountains loomed to the front and centre of the cockpit, their snowcapped peaks glowing white under the moon.

It was 2.30 a.m., but no matter how hard the crew searched, no lights flickered. The Halifax, which had been circling with little altitude for nearly ten minutes, was vulnerable. To cover up their activities Frank turned north over Annecy to drop leaflets on the city.

But they had not even cleared the city when the aircraft lurched to port. Glancing out of his cockpit, Frank watched the exhaust fumes of the outer port engine change to white before dying altogether.

This was not the first scrape the skipper had been in. He called up his flight engineer, certain it was petrol trouble, fixable by switching over the fuel tanks. But he received no reply. He called again. More silence.

Frank ordered his despatcher to jettison their load and weighed up his options. He wanted to be near water in case of a forced landing. That meant Lake Geneva twenty-five miles north in the safety of neutral Switzerland, or Lake Annecy which, although only a few miles behind him, was firmly in occupied France.

The skipper bellowed for his flight engineer to contact him as scenarios raced through his mind. Three engines might be enough to coast to Switzerland, thought Frank, so he set course for Lake Geneva, his leg aching from applying right rudder.

But with a terrible shudder, the Halifax's inner port engine conked out and the aircraft jerked violently. *O for Orange* locked herself in a permanent left-hand turn, and what little altitude she had began to dwindle. Buildings leaped up below each wing. A church spire whizzed past, its tiles twinkling in the starlight.

The skipper wracked his mind for a solution. Parachuting was impossible: the aircraft was travelling at 90mph and with less than a hundred feet of altitude. They'd be obliterated before even pulling the ripcord.

With the smell of burning petrol thick in the air, he ordered the crew to crash stations and screamed at the flight engineer to change the fuel tanks. The second pilot, who'd been wrestling furiously with the escape hatch, finally succeeded in jettisoning it.

But it was only a matter of seconds now. He gripped the yoke hard and braced for the terrible impact he knew was coming but could do nothing about.

The flight engineer's voice finally crackled over the radio. 'Okay, skipper, you're on one and three tanks now.'

Petrol surged through the fuel lines. The ground drew closer.

CHAPTER 1

FROM DROPOUT TO RAF ACE

Frank Cromwell Griffiths was born on 1 May 1912, the same month the Royal Flying Corps was founded. Although the youngest of four siblings, Frank was essentially an only child. His brother Leonard was eleven when he was born, and his sisters Constance and Winifred nine and eight. He spent his early years wandering rural Cheshire, sometimes barefooted, often lost, and always in defiance of his mother's rules. This was the age of insular village life, before the motorcar shrank Britain.

Although born in England on the northern tip of the Wirral, Frank was a proud Welshman. His family hailed from Denbighshire in North Wales, and it was here they returned in 1920 after Frank's father had made enough money through his building company. Frank, aged eight, was taught to shoot, ride a horse and hunt a pack of hounds in a privileged, outdoor upbringing.

The same year the Griffiths returned to North Wales, Frank was sent to board at Mostyn House School on the banks of the Dee Estuary. Although intelligent, Frank cared little for the classroom. Sailing had become the first of his many obsessions. As a member of the school's 'wet bobs' club, Frank and his friends spent their weekends sailing to remote spots along the North Wales coast where they built dens, lit fires and dreamed of never going back to school.

However, in 1926, when he was fourteen, the sailing-obsessed Frank was dispatched to Radley College in Oxfordshire, hundreds of miles from his beloved Dee. Little survived from his time there, apart from his accent which morphed from Wirral/Welsh hybrid to English public-school boy. Like most who have come through the boarding system, Frank learned how to fit in amongst a new crowd, when to keep his head down, and how to get away with breaking the rules.

It was adventures in the summer holidays that Frank lived for. In the summer of 1928, he and his friend Jack McQuade hiked ninety-two miles in four days across Snowdonia leading a pony called At Last. The Welsh Cob pulled a ramshackle caravan that Frank had made for the boys to sleep in. Averaging twenty-three miles a day and eight sausages a night, the boys returned home happy and exhausted, their feet coated in tar where their shoe soles had given out.

Frank had just started lower sixth when the Wall Street Crash happened. His father's building company went bankrupt, Radley's school fees went unpaid, and Frank returned home. For his final year of education, he was sent to Kinmel School in North Wales where, on account of his charm, he became head boy. Kinmel taught practical skills instead of the traditional academia, like a modern-day technical college, instilling Frank with a practicality that made him a lifelong 'tinkerer'.

Apart from sailing, hunting and adventure, Frank Griffiths still had no idea what he wanted to do when he left Kinmel. He decided to live on his boat *Olive*, a 23-foot 'Morecambe type' shrimper. After building a cabin on deck, Frank and his dog took to the water in September 1931. Much to his family's disapproval, he spent the next six years sailing around North Wales, sleeping on remote beaches and fishing. He was a young adult living a fourteen-year-old boy's dream, a vaga-bond sailor seeking a different path.

But life on *Olive* was not cushy. In the winters, Frank moored up in the Liverpool Docks and worked for his uncle TJ's business maintaining pubs across Liverpool. 'It was a wonderful six years,' Frank later wrote. 'TJ was a tough boss and I was his lowest paid employee, despite being his nephew. I dropped any pretence of being publicly educated, imitated the Liverpudlian accent a little and survived. I got to know the hardest Liverpudlians, their weaknesses and their amazing sense of humour.'

Frank also used the natural world to supplement his income. On *Olive*, he caught shrimp and ray and sold them in Liverpool's markets, while many dawns were spent shooting ducks and geese in the Dee Estuary before selling them to the butchers.

While his Radley chums settled down across London and the south-east, Frank learned to live with men at the other end of the social spectrum, eking out a meagre existence in the docks. Hardship was commonplace and women were banned from entering.

He recalled, 'The police were always around asking questions of the old salts who lived on the other boats as care-takers, usually if they'd seen anyone nicking anything from their boat; when often the caretaker had pawned it himself. But we didn't pinch each other's belongings and an unusual camaraderie existed among the occupants of the dock.'

Like Christopher McCandless, the young middle-class American who hitchhiked to Alaska to live in the wild, Frank possessed the particular trait that has made many young men with comfortable lives seek a life on the fringe of society.

Danger was never far away. One Sunday in September 1934, Frank was trawling three miles off the mouth of the

Dee, when, hauling up his net and forgetting to put the engine in neutral, he was knocked clean overboard by *Olive*'s boom. Floundering in the water, he managed to grab the trawl rope as it was dragged past him. He tried pulling himself back to the boat, but the force of the propeller slipstream was like a millrace against him and his boots were dragging him down.

The *Olive* had six hours of fuel and was heading for Dublin. Exhausted from clinging to the rope and being battered by waves, Frank was beginning to accept his fate when suddenly he stood up. He was three miles from land, but by some miracle *Olive* had grounded herself on a submerged sandbank, where she was being drowned by the breaking surf.

'At last I got to her,' Frank related, 'clambered over the side, knocked the engine into neutral, dropped the sail and took my boots off. I hauled up the net and to my surprise, it was filled with highly valuable ray! But I'd had enough fishing for one day.'

Frank loved his nomadic, vagabond existence and the freedom that living on a boat afforded someone with perpetually itchy feet. But something was missing from his life on *Olive* and he knew he could not continue this lifestyle forever. The unusualness of his six years' 'adrift' is hard to overstate, however, as gap years did not exist in the 1930s.

Frank's 'Liverpool days' came to an end in 1936, when he was twenty-four. His sister Constance had recently married a farmer from the Isle of Man and Frank wanted to visit them. Flights to the island had just started, so he booked one.

'We roared into the air from Speke Aerodrome in a three-engine Spartan Cruiser,' Frank recalled, 'and the ground disappeared in a couple of minutes as we climbed through murky cloud. Then we burst through the "clag" into the dazzling sunshine. The sky was a brilliant blue and the white woolly stratus cloud drifted below us. I was spellbound. This is what I wanted to do – fly! On the way back to Liverpool I saw a poster of an airman in topee [*sun helmet*] and shorts, standing under a palm tree with a biplane in the background. The poster said: "Join the Royal Air Force and see the World." So I did.'

Training began in Tiger Moths on 8 June 1936 at RAF Desford, Leicestershire. Frank was a natural. He went solo on 24 June after twelve hours in the air. On his second solo, he performed a loop out of sheer joy – an illegal manoeuvre that earned him an 'absolute rocketing' on landing. You can almost sense the reluctance of his instructors as they noted 'above average' in his logbooks, often caveated with comments about 'overconfidence'.

By August, the trainees had been moved to RAF Grantham to learn aerobatics in a Hart. For the first time, Frank struggled. The slow roll had him 'completely foxed', and he vomited at least twenty times, fretting he might lose his career to airsickness. Sheer bloody-mindedness got him through. He passed out of training on 5 December 1936. His instructor wrote in his logbook: 'Inclined to be overconfident.'

Although talented, the RAF was not particularly interested in Frank. He was awarded a short-service commission by King Edward VIII during his short reign. TEMPORARY was stamped in large letters across the top right corner. Frank remembered, 'It was painfully obvious that unless there was a war, my services would not be required.'

Yet fortunately for Frank, war loomed. He was posted to 62 Squadron, who were training new pilots to fly twin-engine Blenheim bombers.

It was a dream come true. War had given him a chance.

There was only one problem. In August 1939, with Britain on the cusp of war with Germany, 62 Squadron were ordered to Malaya (present-day Malaysia) to shore up the Empire in the Far East.

Frank was standing underneath the wing of his Blenheim in the middle of the Iraqi desert when war was declared on 3 September 1939. He was roughly halfway through 62 Squadron's epic journey to Malaya, a trip that took twenty-four days, eighteen stops and forty-seven hours of flying.

For Frank, it was flying 6,500 miles in the wrong direction. 'In a fit of patriotism,' he wrote, 'each of us surreptitiously applied for repatriation to the UK so that we could take part in the war. We were all turned down.'

With Japan not yet in the war, Frank and his 62 Squadron colleagues spent many happy weeks in Malaya sailing up the Strait of Malacca, climbing coconut trees and trying water skiing. But like most young men who had spent hours being trained for a job, Frank wanted to fight.

In early 1940, after just four months in Malaya, Frank's wish to return home came true, but not in the way he wanted. An old back injury flared up leaving him unable to walk, let alone fly. It had happened years earlier in training, when he volunteered to test an experimental parachute with no experience of parachuting. He was strapped to the wing tip of a Virginia biplane in a chair and told to pull the ripcord when the pilot 'throttled back' at 2,000 feet. He 'crumpled up' on landing as briefed, but on tarmac. It took twenty minutes before he could stand up. The damage was done.

The injury's return meant Frank could no longer fly. He wrote: 'This seemed the worst moment of my life. Classified unfit for duties, being sent to England and leaving 62 squadron and my friends after three years.' The Malaya jolly was over. Frank sailed home from Singapore on 29 April 1940.

By the time Frank's ship docked in Weymouth a month later, Hitler's forces had swept into north-eastern France, and more than 300,000 Allied soldiers were being evacuated from Dunkirk. As his ship approached the south coast on 1 June, Frank's first glimpse of Britain in ten months would have been one of chaos, as a flotilla of ships and small boats ferried thousands of troops back across the English Channel.

Frank was sent to RAF Hospital Torquay to be fixed. 'Here my fate was decided in more ways than one,' he wrote. He met a woman.

'One morning I was hobbling down the staircase and noticed a WAAF [*a member of the Women's Auxiliary Air Force*] bending over and dusting the stairs, the same way any man notices a woman doing such things. She turned to look at me and something went "zing". She had a round face, high cheekbones, blue eyes and brown hair wound tightly around her head. This was the woman I wanted to be the mother of my children.'

Ruth Fuller was achingly beautiful. She was six years younger than Frank, had flawless bone structure and perfect, pale skin. She was from London, wore stylish clothes, light make-up and knew about fashion. At the outbreak of war, she and her sister Daphne had joined the WAAF mostly because they liked the uniform. They had been posted to Torquay to help run the medical facility.

Ruth's memory of meeting Frank differed somewhat. 'Frank met me – or saw me – many times sweeping the vast staircase. I didn't notice him. The place was full of young officers, but all in a state of repair.'

Frank began a series of deep therapy X-rays for his inflamed vertebrae. The treatment was working, and soon he was able to take Ruth on their first date, a sailing trip on the River Dart. The pair were joined by Ruth's sister Daphne and a friend Frank had made in hospital, Stuart Robertson. A fellow Blenheim pilot, Robertson had been strafing a German train in the Low Countries when he received a 9mm bullet in the backside.

Through June and July, the Fuller sisters stuffed their gas-mask bags with sandals and skirts and headed out on the Dart with Frank and Stuart. As they romanced in the Devonian sunshine, Luftwaffe planes droned overhead. The Battle of Britain had begun and Hitler was preparing to invade England.

In October 1940, after four months' treatment, Frank was passed fit for flying. 'The repair must have been good for it gave me another 4,000 hours of flying,' he recalled, 'and let me carry on doing the things I love most: skiing, sailing and riding.'

On 16 November, Frank received a new and fascinating posting. The flying would be dangerous, secretive and highly challenging. It would be the most important work of his life.

With 900 hours flying on thirteen different aircraft, Frank's skills and experience were desperately needed across the RAF as it expanded rapidly in late 1940. Fighter Command, fresh from victory in the Battle of Britain, was recruiting heavily to replace the pilot losses it had incurred repelling the Luftwaffe. Bomber Command, the most natural fit for Frank, badly needed more aircrews to escalate its campaign over Europe. Coastal Command, who had the vital job of escorting shipping across the Atlantic and deterring German U-Boats, was also operating at maximum capacity.

Despite the dire need for experienced pilots across the board, Frank had been selected for an even more crucial job. He was to become a test pilot in the Telecommunications Research Establishment (TRE).

Based at RAF Christchurch near Bournemouth, the TRE was a truly cutting-edge organisation. It existed to keep the upper hand over the Luftwaffe, and it did this by pioneering, testing and perfecting aviation technology. Radar, for example, was a product of the TRE. The early warning system had played a crucial role in the RAF's success during the Battle of Britain.

Christchurch was unlike any other RAF Station: it was dominated by civilians. Britain's leading brains had gathered here – physicists, engineers, mathematicians, academics, cryptographers and chemists – united in a mission to beat the Luftwaffe. And amongst this epicentre of innovation were twenty-or-so pilots, guinea pigs to test the boffins' experimental equipment. They would not only test whether the scientists' inventions worked, but judge if an average airman could operate it.

These pilots represented a handpicked elite, chosen for the job on account of their skill, technical knowledge and ability to work with civilians. With 4,000 pilots in Bomber Command and another 1,000 in Fighter Command to choose from, these men were the crème de la crème of Britain's aviators.

Frank arrived at RAF Christchurch on 16 November 1940. 'There were 1,000 men and women employed at TRE, from boffins to bottle washers. It was a most unusual station. We RAF found some of our new colleagues very strange in dress and manner, and at times mirth-provoking, but we had great respect and admiration for them.'

The next morning, Frank completed his first sortie as a test pilot. The boffin accompanying him was testing airborne radar because ground radar, the type in operation for the Battle of Britain, had a range of only sixty to eighty miles. If successful, airborne radar would be fitted to all RAF fighters, meaning the benefits of radar could be harnessed anywhere a fighter could reach.

'I was surprised to find my passenger, who was wearing his helmet the wrong way round, had never flown before and had received absolutely no instruction regarding flight preparation, use of parachute, etc.,' related Frank. 'Yet he was mad keen to get airborne and test his so-called "breadboard". As the flight proceeded, the colour drained from his face and eventually he was sick over his breadboard, which short-circuited and started a small fire. This was extinguished and obviously, we returned to base.'

Despite the humorous first outing, this secretive, unglamourous job far from the frontlines contributed far more to winning the war than an average fighter or bomber pilot.

Months after arriving, Frank personally tested the first airborne radar with Robert Watson-Watt, aka 'the father of radar', on board. Through winter 1940 and spring 1941, he helped to develop groundbreaking navigational aids such as Gee and Rebecca/Eureka, which vastly improved bombing accuracy and navigation, particularly at night or in poor weather. As the war progressed, these aids became ever more important to the RAF's strategic bombing campaign and, ultimately, the breaking of the German war machine.

As Churchill said: 'The effects of our bombing were seen in the very crumbling of the German economy. The destruction of the German industrial machine and the decimation of the enemy's transport and communications systems were vital to our strategy.'

Frank enjoyed the TRE's streamlined, anti-bureaucratic nature and the fact that with so many civilians around, rank and uniform meant little. His logbooks reveal how test-piloting allowed ample opportunity for individualism and, when necessary, encouraged pilots to ask questions and contribute to the research. There was never a dull moment and Frank would have known he was contributing to the war effort without having to be shot at by German flak.

When he was not test-piloting, Frank spent much of his spare time with Ruth, who had been posted from Torquay to Christchurch. Their romance continued on the Dorset coast and one day in the late spring of 1941, nine months after meeting, Frank proposed.

Their wedding, held on Saturday, 30 August 1941, involved a short service in the Christchurch village church with no choir and no bells (as bells ringing would have signalled a German invasion). Afterwards, the newlyweds left in a canvas-topped Austin 7 for their bungalow, the first of thirty-six homes they were to live in together. In it their friends had laid on buns and tea, but the wedding cake, though it looked real, was made of cardboard.

After the tea party they drove to Swanage for their honeymoon, stopping to climb Corfe Castle and let the kippers tied to the car exhaust get cold. 'We went to our hotel and handed in our ration coupons for a rather lonely dinner,' Ruth recalled, 'where we chose bread or pudding. We went for a walk after dinner, then bed.'

On Sunday they drove back home. 'We should have had the next day to ourselves, if for no other reason than to get to know each other!' said Ruth. It had been a typical wartime wedding – married Saturday, honeymoon Sunday, work Monday.

By May 1942, Frank and Ruth had spent the best part of a year living at RAF Christchurch. But British top brass had realised how vulnerable the airfield's position was on England's south coast. So, the TRE was relocated to RAF Defford, near Malvern in Worcestershire. On 25 May, Frank flew a Hudson to Defford with Christchurch's twelve hens on board. To his surprise, all laid eggs on the journey thanks to the reduced atmospheric pressure.

It was a timely move. The Luftwaffe bombed Christchurch a week later. German intelligence documents retrieved after the war revealed: 'We never thought the British would be stupid enough to have such a valuable base so close to France.'

Although he may not have looked it as he surveyed RAF Defford for the first time, clambering out of his Hudson with an armful of fresh eggs, Frank was one of the RAF's most valuable pilots, perhaps one of the most versatile in the world.

In eighteen months test-piloting at Christchurch, Frank had flown 442 sorties in more than fifty types of aircraft, including Lancasters, Spitfires, Hurricanes and Stirlings. He had taken his total flying time to 1,502 hours, which at the time was more than Douglas Bader and Leonard Cheshire, two of the RAF's most famous pilots, albeit in less hazardous circumstances. His ability to get on with everyone had made him a lynchpin between RAF types and the scientists, who knew nothing of military tradition.

But there was no time for self-congratulation at the cutting edge of aviation. Frank and his colleagues were immediately reengaged in their next project – Oboe. This bomb-aiming system, tested by Frank over the summer of 1942, used two radar stations to track an aircraft and pinpoint the location it should drop its bombs.

Oboe helped birth the RAF's famous 'Pathfinder Squadrons'. It was their job to locate bombing targets and drop flares on them before the main force arrived. With Oboe onboard, the Pathfinders achieved unprecedented accuracy. In August 1942, when the Pathfinders formed, just 25 per cent of RAF bombers got within three miles of their target. By 1945 that number had risen to 95 per cent, largely thanks to Oboe.

In the autumn of 1942, Frank was moved from Oboe to a new, more pressing project, the development of depth charges to counter the German U-boat menace. The Battle of the Atlantic was reaching its zenith as 'wolf packs' of German submarines pounded Allied shipping on the arduous journey from America to Britain. Coastal Command needed better means of fighting back. For Frank, this meant piloting flying boats like the Walrus, Sea Otter and Catalina over the Irish Sea, an area he knew well from sailing along the North Wales coast and in the Dee Estuary.

It was his most enjoyable work to date. One day, he was flying a Walrus over the mouth of the Dee when he recognised a trawler from his days in the Liverpool Docks. Fancying some fresh fish, Frank landed his Walrus alongside the vessel, fastened a rope and bought three buckets of fish from the skipper, pouring them into the bilges of his aircraft as he had nowhere else to put them. The dying fish were still flapping when he landed at Malvern hours later.

Later that winter, Frank was carrying out trials on Loch Foyle in Northern Ireland when his Walrus was approached by a man in a rowing boat offering eggs. He negotiated the sale of 432 eggs, which the man rowed ashore and duly brought back to him. The process was repeated for days afterwards, to the delight of the personnel at RAF Ballykelly.

Frank and Ruth's first child, Tessa, arrived on 30 December 1942. She seemed to have little effect on her father's daredevil spirit. Still flying mostly over the Irish Sea, Frank often used Anglesey, an island off the north-west coast of Wales, as a navigational aid. But he also used it for entertainment, specifically the bridge connecting it to mainland Wales over the Menai Strait. If the tide was low and the conditions good, Frank would bring his Walrus in line with the Menai Strait, descend to a hair-raising altitude and thunder below the magnificent Menai Bridge, through a clearance of 100 feet. Of course, there was a war on and silly bravado like this was deeply frowned upon. But for Frank, life was not worth living without it.

In April 1943, the depth-charge trials finished. Frank returned to Malvern, where he was soon awarded the Air Force Cross, a gallantry medal for non-operational flying. It was a reward for accumulating a staggering 1,842 hours of flying on nearly sixty aircraft, the Dakota, Mosquito and B-17 Flying Fortress being the most recent. He had a proven track record of testing some of the biggest aviation breakthroughs of the war.

Frank's personal success mirrored that of the Allies. The last six months had seen the tide turn against Axis forces. In North Africa, Montgomery had reversed British fortunes at El Alamein, driving Rommel's forces west. Pearl Harbor had finally brought the United States into the war, and on the Eastern Front, Germans were being killed 'unit by unit' around Stalingrad. After years of German ascendancy, momentum was finally shifting.

Aged thirty, and with a four-month-old at home, Frank could have remained at Malvern as a test pilot and spent the rest of the war in relative safety. But something drove him down a different, more perilous path.

'I'd been in Singapore for the start of the war and I didn't get back home until after Dunkirk,' he remembered. 'Then I'd been working as a test pilot, so I thought it time I got cracking operationally. So I applied to join a Squadron.'

Perhaps it was a fear of missing out. Maybe it was a desire to fight. Either way, Frank chose to go to war.

He was going operational.

CHAPTER 2

O FOR ORANGE

Given his versatility, Frank could have applied to be posted to any of the famous RAF squadrons, but his heart had settled on a highly unusual outfit based at a small airfield in rural Bedfordshire.

No one in Malvern knew what went on there, only that it was a 'bit odd'. Rumour had it that you could not land there during certain phases of the moon. If you did, you had to sign the Official Secret Acts and were not allowed to leave until operations were concluded. Frank, who had tested some of their highly specialised aircraft, heard that they were involved in cloak-and-dagger operations requiring low-level night flying.

Frank arrived at his new base on 21 April 1943. The boggy, overgrown airfield, dotted with barns, sheds and machinery, looked like a working farm. Jasper Maskelyne, a famous magician in the 1930s and a leading member of Britain's deception campaign in the Second World War, had designed it this way to conceal it from German reconnaissance. Hedgerows were painted across the runways, for example.

Even after Frank joined the base, he struggled to get anyone to tell him what he was going to do at this mysterious farm-cum-airfield. Little did he know, as with all new recruits, that he had begun a week's close observation by the authorities for his personal habits, his alcohol use and his likelihood to blab secrets. All personnel knew the rule of leaving new recruits in the dark until the station commander considered them 'safe bets'.

There were very few airmen around for Frank to question anyway. Most of his new colleagues left for operations at about 9 p.m., only returning at 3 or 4 a.m. Exhausted from tense, dangerous sorties into occupied Europe, the crews slept most of the morning, rising at midday to eat. Then it was straight into briefings for the coming night's mission.

Finally, after a week, Frank was summoned to the station commander's office to swear an oath of secrecy. Group Captain Edward Fielden, captain of the King's Flight in peacetime, explained that if he broke it he would be instantly dismissed, court-martialled and possibly imprisoned. Then he told him what went on at RAF Tempsford.

Tempsford was home to 138 and 161 Squadrons, two top-secret, elite outfits engaged in clandestine warfare. They owed their existence to the Special Operations Executive (SOE), another secret British organisation formed in June 1940 to conduct espionage, reconnaissance and sabotage in occupied Europe. Churchill had ordered the SOE to 'set Europe ablaze', believing resistance to occupation would tie up German resources, undermine morale and 'rot the buggers from within'.

The SOE, nicknamed 'the ministry of ungentlemanly warfare', did this by supplying resistance fighters in Europe with weapons, money and supplies to conduct guerilla warfare. They also infiltrated highly trained spies to recruit more partisans, teach them sabotage and espionage, and when D-Day came, lead them in battle alongside the Allies' conventional forces. These spies were often accompanied by a radio operator (referred to as a 'pianist'), who could organise for more supplies to be dropped to their resistance unit at a pre-arranged location.

But the SOE needed a means of getting their arms and agents into Europe, which Churchill called 'bringing fire and blood' to Europe. He needed a way of infiltrating the Continent with his 'secret army'. This was 138 and 162 Squadrons' *raison d'être*. To deliver the SOE into Hitler's Europe.

These 'Special Duties Squadrons' would fly thousands of missions over occupied Europe, dropping everything from Sten guns and highly trained agents to messenger pigeons. To avoid detection, all operations had to be flown at night, often at terrifyingly low altitudes to avoid German radar detection.

Bernard O'Connor, author of *RAF Tempsford: Churchill's Most Secret Airfield*, wrote, 'Old hands in the RAF had a saying: "Birds and fools fly by day. Only fools fly by night!" These young pilots at Tempsford possessed hawk-like vision, brilliant combat records and unparalleled courage. Flying their sorties only on nights of the brightest moonlight – between the quarter wax to the quarter wane – they were prey to every sort of enemy attack.'

And it was not only flak and German night fighters posing a threat. Telephone wires, water towers, treetops and clouds full of mountain could all spell disaster for a Tempsford aircraft flying low over unfamiliar terrain in the dark, often with an exhausted crew onboard.

Some of the Second World War's most famous spies, such as Violette Szabo and Nancy Wake, were dropped into Europe from Tempsford by the 'moonlight squadrons'.

These spies, known as 'joes' to Tempsford airmen, were often recruited from professions such as acting before undergoing rigorous training in Britain. If they passed, they would be transported to Tempsford and kitted out with all manner of items, including false identity papers, a knife, handgun or garrotte, escape tools, perhaps also a fake moustache or wig, a miniature lock-picking set, a silk map concealed in a pack of cards and, if they wished, a cyanide pill to avoid torture. Then it was down to the aircrews at Tempsford to infiltrate them into Europe via parachute drop or rapid landing.

Secrecy was of the highest importance. The Tempsford aircrews were forbidden from talking about their jobs. Some would complain later in life of the shame they felt having to pretend to fellow pilots in the pub that they had been promoted to a desk job.

Frank joined 138 Squadron as a squadron leader in April 1943, the army-equivalent of a major. His rise through the RAF had been quick, spurred on by the war. Aged thirty and vastly experienced, he was at the peak of his powers. Although unconventional, he was a 'winner type', useful in war when the traditional rigmarole of military life was cast aside.

But until now, his flying had been conducted over the relative safety of Britain. He did not normally have a crew depending on his leadership, cool headedness and skill to keep them alive. Tempsford was different.

Not only would Frank be venturing into the jaws of Hitler's Europe, flying at low altitudes in the dark, he would also have several lives relying on him to get them back home again. Test-piloting was over, this was proper war.

But first Frank needed a crew. Low-level night flying required superb navigation, and the most successful aircrews were always the ones who had spent the most time together, operating as a cohesive team. It could be argued that navigators were more important than pilots, as they directed the aircraft and kept it out of danger. The captain was simply the taxi driver.

Luckily for Frank, he had found just the man, Warrant Officer John Charrot. 'Johnnie', an insurance broker from Palmers Green, joined the RAF in 1940 aged seventeen, because he 'fancied flying'. He wanted to be a pilot, but failed his training when he crashed his Tiger Moth, so retrained as a navigator.

Young, well-spoken and ambitious, Frank took to him immediately. Now at the experienced age of twenty, Charrot had already flown nine operations from Tempsford, including navigating for one aircraft on Operation Gunnerside. That operation saw 138 Squadron drop Norwegian commandos into southern Norway, who then successfully destroyed the Vermork heavy water production plant, a vital facility driving the Nazis' nuclear weapons programme. The Norwegian commandos' exploits were immortalised in the film *The Heroes of Telemark*.

'When Frank came to Tempsford,' Charrot recalled, 'we met in the crew room and immediately he said, "Let's go out in a Halifax." He threw it about the sky like I've never seen a Halifax flown before. We landed and he said, "Did you enjoy that?" I said, "Yes, sir!" I knew I'd found the pilot for me. You could tell he had a lot of skill and I was soon to have the utmost faith in him.'

Frank also recruited Sergeant Jack March as flight engineer, Pilot Officer Robert Peters as wireless operator and Pilot Officer Terry Elderton as rear gunner. Various despatchers accompanied the crew into Europe, whose job it was to look after the cargo – material and human – during the sortie and help it out of the aircraft when it had reached the drop zone. Second pilots occasionally came too, but it was these five men who morphed into an effective, tightly knit crew over the next three months, saving each other's lives on numerous occasions.

Writing in his logbook in red ink to signify operations, Frank began to record his sorties over Europe. His first, on 13 May 1943, involved a 'slight contretemps with flak ship'. Two days later, they were 'engaged four times by light flak' and 'had pitched battle with an E-boat on return'. The E-boat had been sheltering on the surface beside the Cherbourg peninsula in northern France.

Johnnie Charrot remembered, 'Frank just had time to scream "E-boat under the port wing!" before it opened fire. All hell was let loose, but Frank's warning was just sufficient for Terry to swing his turret round and open fire. There is no doubt that four Brownie guns from 200 feet handled by an experienced gunner can be devastating to a lightly protected vessel.'

The following night, on a six-hour flight deep into France, Frank reported his Halifax was: 'Holed by a 303 [*German anti-aircraft gun*] in No. 4 port tank.' Two days later on 18 May, Frank was heading south through the French countryside with a full crew of seven and four joes (spies) on board, when a flak train opened fire at his Halifax, riddling it with bullets.

Frank yanked the aircraft out of danger and sent his despatcher to see if anyone was hurt. 'It looks like an abattoir in the back!' called the despatcher, on account of one agent whose ear had been shot off. Two others had suffered flesh wounds. Miraculously, the crew were unhurt. Frank, who had just been told by his flight engineer that 'the fuselage looks like a colander', abandoned the operation and nursed the stricken aircraft home.

Back at Tempsford, an orderly found the ear in the back of the aircraft, put it on ice and sent it to the agent's hospital, where it was sewn back on.

In his first week in the new job, Frank and his crew had been attacked by anti-aircraft guns, an E-boat and a flak train. It had taken until 1943, but war had truly arrived in Frank's life.

Thankfully, his next three moon periods dropping over Belgium, the Netherlands and France were quiet and successful. As was one particularly unusual drop over North Wales.

It was May 1943 and orders had come through from Frank's aunt to find a mangle – one of those heavy Victorian contraptions for squeezing water out of clothes – and deliver it to her home at the end of an isolated valley near Ruthin, in Snowdonia. Frank found one in Bedford and persuaded the parachute team to wrap it in sponge, fasten a parachute and load it into his Halifax.

'The skipper found the valley without any difficulty,' recalled navigator Charrot, 'but when the rest of us saw this narrow valley with the hills rising to 1,700 feet on either side as well as at the end, we began to wonder if our journey was really necessary. However, Auntie came out into the garden waving like mad with neighbours on either side. It has to go in Auntie's garden, says the skipper, so watch the drift, we will do a dummy run first.

'The crew moaned. We set off up one side of the valley, the mountains rising above us just away from the wing tip, the end of the valley approaching fast . . . no way are we going to pull up over that . . . suddenly the Halifax is tipped violently on its wing, and we seem to scrape the hillside and tear down the other side over Auntie's garden.

'"OK, Johnnie," Frank called. "Got the drift, have you?" All any of us had at the time was fright! "I'd rather fly over a flak train," came a voice from the rear turret. "Give me an E-boat in the Channel any time," from the engineer.

'The manoeuvre is carried out again – up one side, across the top, down the other side, red light, green light – and the despatcher pushes the mangle out. We come out safely, climb rapidly to 2,000 feet and watch the parcel drift gently down, landing safely in Auntie's garden. "Great," said Frank, "now when we get back, enter this in your logbooks as an air test!"'

But just as Frank's crew were truly gelling, they dispersed. Three members, including Frank's favourite navigator 'Johnnie' Charrot, had completed a tour of operations (thirty missions) and were heading home for a rest period.

Elderton, the rear gunner who had held off the E-boat attack, never made it home. Days before his leave, he was cycling back to Tempsford when his wheel got stuck in Sandy railway crossing. He fell, hit his head on the tracks, and died on the crossing.

'Having survived two tours of operations, one with Bomber Command and one with Special Duties, Terry's death was hard to take,' said Charrot. 'Our highly successful crew was truly broken up. With Frank as skipper we had operated on fourteen nights during May and June, eleven of those being successful delivering all agents and packages safely. I shall always be more than grateful to "The Skipper" for walking into the crew room on that day in April 1943 and asking me to join his crew. He was an extraordinary pilot and someone who could always bring the best out of his crew. We all had confidence in his ability to bring us back home. Without his flying skills, I would not have survived.'

Once again, Frank was crewless. To compound matters, he had just received orders for a vital mission. Operation Pimento.

It was 14 August. In twenty-six days, on 9 September 1943, the Allies were launching Operation Avalanche, a huge invasion of southern Italy at Salerno. With 190,000 British and American troops taking part, the Salerno landings would be the biggest invasion of the war to date, and the first of mainland Europe. It was obvious that once the invasion began, German reinforcements in France would be sent to Italy to meet the Allied armies. But to get there, the Germans would have to pass through the Alps. The fastest route was through the Fréjus Rail Tunnel, which starts near

Modane in south-east France and ends in Bardonecchia in north-west Italy.

Operation Pimento's end goal was the destruction of this tunnel. Frank and his Halifax, *O for Orange*, would be dropping heavy explosives to guerilla fighters near Modane for them to blow it up. It was imperative the guerillas succeeded to allow the Allies to gain as much of a foothold in Italy as possible.

The second, less important element of Pimento, involved dropping several containers of Sten guns, money, food and cigarettes for a French Resistance unit near Annecy, fifty or so miles north-west of Modane.

With most of Frank's crew dispersed, Pimento would have to be executed with a 'scratch crew'. As Frank recalled, 'Scratch crews were always regarded as unlucky, particularly when they consisted of men just finishing a tour of operations.'

Frank's first recruit was navigator John Congdon, a 26-year-old from Totnes in Devon, who had already completed a full tour with Bomber Command and won the Distinguished Flying Medal (DFM). Having flown twenty-nine missions with 138 Squadron, Congdon was only one short of a second full tour, which would lead to another period of leave, further medals and likely promotion to a desk or training job. It would have been a timely promotion as Congdon's wife Mary Lake, whom he had married in November 1942, was pregnant, although neither of them knew that when he joined Frank's crew.

The next new recruit was 22-year-old Flight Sergeant Frank Pollard, who was a professional footballer at Bury FC before he joined the RAF as a rear gunner. Pollard had flown twenty-eight missions, two short of the magic thirty.

Frederick Davies, from Middlesbrough, was aged twenty-five and joined Frank's crew as flight engineer, having completed a full tour with Bomber Command in a Wellington.

Finally, twenty-year-old John Maden from Accrington would come as despatcher.

They joined Frank's last remaining crew member, Pilot Officer Robert Peters, who was twenty-two and from Saffron Walden, Essex. Peters had flown a full tour in Bomber Command as a wireless operator, winning a DFM. The achievement also saw him granted a posting to Tempsford to be nearer his wife Phyllis Tarrant, whom he had married five months earlier. Like Congdon, Peters was unaware his wife was pregnant.

After assembling his crew, Frank attended a lecture on 'escape and evasion' in one of the hangars. He wrote, 'I thought it was an interesting lecture, but of course it would never happen to me.'

As the lecture finished, a young flying officer called Roderick Mackenzie approached him. The 22-year-old, a keen golfer from the Isle of Skye who was training to be a dentist, had just arrived at Tempsford and got wind of Frank's mission. Eager for experience, Mackenzie implored Frank to take him as a second pilot. 'He was a keen type, so he came along,' remembered Frank.

With 199 combat missions between them and an average age of twenty-three, Frank's crewmates blended experience with youthful fearlessness. They had two DFMs and an AFC (Air Force Cross) between them. Three had wives. Two were expecting children.

All were depending on Frank.

At 10.30 p.m. on 14 August 1943, *O for Orange* crossed the Channel and began heading south through France. The crew scoured the night sky for danger, but their Halifax remained

undetected as they climbed over the Massif Central and dipped into the Rhône Valley, their moon shadow racing below them.

'How are we getting on?' Frank asked his navigator John Congdon on the Halifax's radio.

'Half an hour to the first drop zone, skipper,' he replied. 'You should see the Alps any minute now.'

Frank stared ahead for a few minutes until he spotted some large, jagged outlines, the tallest of which were snowcapped and glowing eerily white. He flew *O for Orange* as low as he dared, rising over forests and telephone wires like a stone skimming on water.

At 2.30 a.m., *O for Orange* arrived at the first drop point near the city of Annecy. Frank and his crew scanned the shadowy earth for their reception party's torches or bonfires.

'Anyone see any lights?' asked Frank, circling back up the Alpine valley.

'Nothing, skipper,' from the rear gunner Frank Pollard.

'Same here,' said John Congdon, checking his navigation charts again.

O for Orange thundered over Lake Annecy, its water twinkling in the starlight. Mountains loomed on either side. We're sitting ducks, thought Frank.

'Despatcher, drop the leaflets as we pass over Annecy, please, then we'll head on to Modane. I don't like being at the bottom of this valley.'

But they had barely cleared Annecy when the aircraft lurched to port. Glancing out of his cockpit, Frank watched as the exhaust fumes of the outer port engine went white, spluttered and then died altogether. He trimmed the aircraft, applied right rudder and gave full throttle on the other three engines.

Then he called up his flight engineer. 'Freddie, can you switch over number one and three tanks please? Petrol trouble.'

Nothing.

'Freddie, are you there?'

Silence.

'Despatcher, prepare to jettison our load – we've got engine trouble,' said Frank.

Options raced across his mind. If a forced landing was imminent, he wanted to be near water, and that meant Lake Geneva in the safety of neutral Switzerland twenty-five miles north, or Lake Annecy only a few miles south but in occupied France.

'Freddie, are you there?' shouted Frank. 'I need you to change the fuel tanks now!'

More silence.

O for Orange was performing reasonably, even gaining a little height, so Frank set course for Lake Geneva. But the Halifax shuddered again, this time more violently, as the inner port engine conked out. *O for Orange* was now in the bottom of an Alpine valley with two dead engines on the same wing in the middle of the night.

'Despatcher, jettison everything, we've lost both port engines,' ordered Frank, killing Operation Pimento. 'All crew to crash stations immediately. Where the hell is Freddie?'

Losing altitude fast in a permanent left-hand turn, Frank watched buildings approach below each wing. They belonged to Meythet, a small village nestled in the northern French Alps.

For the people of Meythet, *O for Orange*'s arrival began as a distant droning. But as the Halifax neared, the droning intensified, the deep throb of its four Rolls-Royce Merlin engines rattling the windowpanes.

Rising from their beds, the villagers went to their windows to see what the noise was about. Pulling back the curtains, they saw 22 tonnes of burning aircraft tearing across the sky towards their village, parachutes billowing out behind the Halifax.

For 69-year-old Marcelle Rosay, it was the last thing he would ever see. His heart stopped and he fell down dead.

Sylvain Donzel recalled, 'I was woken by the sound of the Halifax and went out onto my balcony to watch. A huge plane flew over us on fire and at very low altitude, so low it shaved the tops of the walnut trees in front of our house.' Another witness, Pierre Dupont, still hears his mother scream, 'It's coming straight for the house!'

Roderick Mackenzie, the young Scot who had begged to come along as a second pilot, wrestled with the escape hatch as the Halifax lost height.

'For god's sake sit down, Mackenzie!' bellowed Frank over the struggling engines. If he did not think fast, they were all about to die. His leg ached from applying full right rudder. The smell of burning petrol was thick in the air. It was seconds to go.

The flight engineer's voice crackled over the radio.

'Okay, skipper, you're on one and three tanks now.'

It was too late. Frank clicked his safety harness to 'taut' and gripped the controls hard. At last, Mackenzie jettisoned the escape hatch.

Then the port engines clipped the first house, the Villa du Fier. Pietro and Erminia Della-Vedova lived there with their two children, Olivier, one, and Serge, three.

'In the rubble of Villa du Fier,' recalled Sylvain Donzel, 'were the charred remains of Mrs Erminia Della-Vedova. One of her children was in her arms and the other, the youngest, was still in his cradle.'

Her husband Pietro told Annecy gendarmerie, 'When the plane hit I ran to the room, but I couldn't get in, the door was blocked with debris. I tried to break it down, but soon I was surrounded by flames, coming from the room my family were in. I ran away, barefoot, just in a shirt.'

Upstairs, Ernest Maritano, a 51-year-old father whose family were away on holiday, was also trapped by the fire. He jumped from the first floor to escape burning alive and crumpled on the ground unconscious. He was taken to Annecy Hospital, but died of his injuries before he got there.

Half a second later, the trailing tail of *O for Orange* smashed into a bakery called the Maison Rey-Grange, killing flight engineer Freddie Davies and rear gunner Frank Pollard instantly.

John Maden, the twenty-year-old despatcher, was flung from the aircraft onto the pavement. He crawled a short distance, but was later found dead, badly burned.

The Krattinger family lived in the bakery. Pierre had already got his wife Alice and son Roger out of the house before the Halifax hit. But thinking Annecy was being bombed, he returned to salvage some family possessions. Pierre was hurrying through the bakery when the plane hit, crushing him to death against his own oven.

'I had just arrived in the yard when I heard an explosion and then I was immediately surrounded by flames,' recalled Alice. 'I was burned on my right leg and face. I didn't know where my husband was or whether he had got out of the house, because all I could see was the wrecked plane and burning debris where our house had once been.'

The Halifax's impact on the bakery was so violent that it split the aircraft in two. Knocked unconscious by the impact, Frank was catapulted from his cockpit still attached to his seat. His seat collided with several telephone wires as it soared through the night sky; they became entangled with the metal hooks underneath his cockpit seat. The unconscious Frank hung limply from his seat suspended above the ground, held in place by only his harness.

Behind him, the trail of destruction was not over. With the tail and rear fuselage buried in the bakery, the Halifax's forward fuselage slammed into a small shoe shop, demolishing it instantly.

'We lived about a mile away from our shop,' Francois Jouvenod relates, 'and my father, awoken by the noise of the plane crash, went to investigate and found his workshop completely destroyed. In the debris of the shoe shop, three charred bodies [*Roderick Mackenzie, John Congdon and Robert Peters*] were found, who clearly didn't have time to get to the back of the aircraft.'

'Everything was on fire,' recalled Sylvain Donzel. 'Francois Jouvenod's shoe-making shop was completely destroyed by the front part of the plane, possibly the cockpit. There was an airman inside, but he was charred. I still remember him, with a red scarf around his neck, which hadn't burned.'

Francis Faes, another neighbour, thought Meythet was being bombed and rushed from his house with his mother and sister. 'I remember it as if it was yesterday,' he said in the 1980s, 'exiting the house and seeing the terrible fire, the mangled aircraft sticking out of the house, the charred bodies of airmen on the ground. The air reeked of burning flesh for days.'

In seconds the Halifax fireball had claimed eleven lives: six airmen and five civilians.

The crash had destroyed three homes and torn families apart. Wireless operator Robert Peters, the veteran of a full tour with Bomber Command, would never meet his baby Linda. Nor would navigator John Congdon, whose daughter Helen was born in May 1944. Pietro Della-Vedova lost his wife and both his children.

This was war at its most indiscriminate, its most cruel.

Only one member of the crew had survived the crash, my great-grandfather Frank Griffiths.

Regaining consciousness in the telephone wires, he thrashed in a panic before realising his seatbelt was holding him in place. He flicked the release lever, fell to earth, broke his right arm and wrist and knocked himself out again.

Coming around for the second time, he felt the heat of the Halifax fire behind him and staggered off in the opposite direction. Two shapes appeared at the end of his tunnel vision – crew members, Frank hoped, unaware they were either dead or burning alive.

But the shapes were Italian soldiers, who occupied this area of south-east France. They grabbed Frank and began marching him to a military lorry that had just arrived.

Suddenly there was a terrific explosion as one of the petrol tanks went up with 1,500 gallons left in it. 'Sheets of flame and rubbish went over my head and the two soldiers yelled something about bombs and ran.' Frank limped in the opposite direction. He made it a hundred yards before passing out in a ditch.

He awoke at the feet of an elderly lady, who was crying her heart out. 'She was very old and I remember her face very clearly, as it showed up well in the light of the fire.' She paid no attention to him when he got up. A throng of anxious onlookers had gathered around the raging fire.

Frank began walking uphill. He had no idea where he was going, his only ambition being to get away from the terrible fire. Running his hand through his hair, he realised it was wet with blood. He felt his scalp and found a cut oozing blood, matting his hair and running down his neck, under his shirt, and along the grooves of his shoulder blades and collar bones.

He managed a few more steps before bending over to be sick. Blood drooled from his mouth and bits of teeth flecked his vomit. The fire hissed and crackled behind him as another section of a house collapsed.

A boy on a bicycle appeared from the shadows in front of Frank.

'Are you English?' he whispered.

'Yes, where are the Boche?' Frank replied.

'There aren't any around here. They're all Italians. I will hide you; get on my bike.'

On 10 October 2022, I alight at Annecy train station and begin searching for Frank's crash site.

Cycling north out of the beautiful city, I head towards Meythet, my eyes flicking right and left down every road I pass, scanning for a memorial I know exists but have never visited. On the Route de Frangy, I glimpse something in the distance and instantly realise it is what I have come for. Waiting at a traffic light, I feel I must keep looking at the memorial, as though it might vanish if I turn away. The light changes and I pedal forwards hard, matching the speed of the traffic, my lungs burning.

I indicate, stop and stare. A short, stone path bends gently through a neatly mowed lawn. It leads to a Halifax tail, cut from granite and inscribed with golden letters that are difficult to read unless you are standing very close. Behind the memorial is a gently sloping bank covered in sycamore trees. The first leaves of autumn lie at the base of the memorial, a mosaic of browns, yellows and oranges, like haphazard wreaths. It is set back from the busy road and if you were not looking for it, you would probably never notice it.

I stand and read the names of the dead inscribed on the memorial several times. I reach out and run my hand down the thick, curved granite, cool and smooth to touch. It is smaller and dirtier than I had imagined, but it is set back just

far enough from the road to hear the birdsong, which Frank
would have liked. I notice there are notes left by the plaque,
long since smudged by the rain, and I wonder who wrote
them. In the distance, the magnificent Plateau des Glières, a
famous bastion of the Resistance in France, rises above the
Meythet rooftops.

I compare 1943 with 2022. The Villa du Fier, where
Erminia and her children perished in the flames, is now the
office of a personal trainer. The Maison Rey-Grange, where
Pierre Krattinger was crushed against his oven, is a burger
restaurant. Jouvenod's shoe shop was never rebuilt. The
memorial now stands in its place. The telephone wires that
broke Frank's fall when he was catapulted from his cockpit
have gone.

The buildings have been completely refurbished and are
now surrounded by a car park serving Meythet's industrial
estate. Meythet itself is no longer a village, but a bustling
suburb of the city of Annecy. The area has changed so much
that I struggle to imagine Frank staggering away from the
burning wreck of his Halifax. Where was the elderly woman
who wept so much? Presumably uphill of the crash, as Frank
remembers the fire illuminating her face perfectly. Frank
admitted the fire haunted him for the rest of his life, that he
suffered nightmares about it for decades afterwards.

Just beyond the memorial I find a deep gorge with a trickle
of water in it. If the Halifax had maintained a few more feet of
altitude, it would have missed the Villa du Fier and the Maison
Rey-Grange, saving the lives of five civilians. On the other
hand, it would have plunged into this gorge and surely killed
Frank.

I have stood by the memorial for nearly an hour now, feeling obliged to walk around the car park a bit. No one has
walked up to the memorial, which annoys me. Everyone has

earplugs in and hurries by. I want someone to come and ask me about it, to tell them that it was my great-grandfather's aircraft and this is the starting point of my journey retracing his footsteps, but, of course, no one does.

To them it is just a forgotten corner of a boring industrial car park.

CHAPTER 3

INTO THE MAQUIS

René Fontaine, the boy on the bike, gestured at Frank to get on. He was going to push him up the hill to his mother Angéline's house.

But there was a problem. Each time Frank tried to grip the handlebars, breathtaking pain shot up his right arm. His wrist was hanging limply and he knew it was broken. With the fire seething behind them, René folded Frank over the handlebars and began pushing, but Frank was semi-conscious and kept slipping off the bike. To add to his pain, a small nut in the centre of handlebars was boring a hole in his sternum, jabbing the bone each time the bike passed over a pothole.

His cries alerted another figure in the gloom. It was René's friend John D'Aujourd'hui. He ran over, grabbed hold of Frank's leg and backside and began pushing. Fortunately, the trio did not have far to go. At the top of the hill, the fourteen-year-olds aimed the bike straight for René's house. They hoisted Frank off the bike and helped him into the kitchen.

As he entered, Frank heard shrieks of surprise from around the room. His vision was blurred, but he could sense a crowd had gathered. He felt someone press a drinking glass into his hand. He swigged it clumsily and felt the tingle of strong alcohol on his lips, the warm burn as it passed down his throat into his chest.

The kitchen belonged to René's mum, Angéline Fontaine. Despite her angelic-sounding name, Angéline was a typical Savoyard woman – physically strong, fiercely independent and the owner of an enormous heart. Her husband had died before the war, so she had raised three children by herself while running the family forge. She had been a resister to occupation at a time when Allied victory was a very distant prospect. Now she had a British pilot in her kitchen, bleeding over her floor, shaking uncontrollably.

Gently, Angéline ushered Frank into a chair and encouraged him to finish his drink. The sharpness of the liquor seemed to restore his vision momentarily. He saw several faces looking at him intently, almost lovingly. Behind him, he felt Angéline bathe the various abrasions to his head with cool water. He began to talk rapidly about what had happened in half-French, half-English, only his sentences did not seem to finish themselves. They lurched from Lake Geneva to his crew to his own family.

'I didn't give a damn if I hadn't a possession in the whole world,' Frank wrote. 'I was alive and I had a wife and child in England whom I might one day see again. I confided this to the folks in the room and for some reason the women started weeping.'

The drink wore off and Frank fainted again. Angéline barked at the men in the room to hold him in his chair while she filled another bowl with water. Consciousness returned in drabs. He recalled, 'I thought I was in the mess playing that game where we jump on each other's backs, only I couldn't work out why the linoleum was spinning so much, and why everyone was talking in a foreign language.'

Bursts of gunfire started from the direction of the blazing Halifax. Angéline dealt orders, and the two Frenchmen holding Frank in his chair began to assist her in undressing him.

Frank resisted, but he had not the strength to stop them. Angéline threw his English clothes into the kitchen fireplace. The men bundled him next door and into the main chimney of the forge. 'Italians,' they whispered. 'No talking.'

The soldiers who had run when the aircraft's fuel tanks detonated were closing in. Frank assumed they were shooting at his escaping crew. But they were actually letting off a few rounds into the nearby woods, hoping to flush out any survivors who might be hiding there.

Long minutes passed as Frank waited in the dark, dirty chimney in his underpants. He could hear movement in the house, hurried footsteps and snatched French, until he felt hands clasping his armpits and lifting him out into the light.

There were new faces in the room this time, which could not hide their surprise at the wide-eyed pilot emerging from the chimney, his mostly naked body smudged with soot and matted blood. The new faces were members of the local Resistance group. After unloading Frank, René had immediately pedalled off into the dark to rouse them. They had come in a lorry to pick him up.

Frank was dressed quickly in French clothes. As he put on the shirt, one of the men took Frank's service revolver from the chair beside him, cocked it, and put it in his breast pocket with a reassuring pat. Then he led Frank outside to a lorry.

Driving away from the forge, Frank saw the terrible glow of his blazing Halifax in the wing mirrors. Once the lorry had climbed out of the valley, the driver shut off the engine and headlights and let the vehicle coast, snaking around hairpins in moonlit meadows.

The pain in his wrist and arm increased steadily, along with his various cuts and bruises. A punishing cold gripped him as his adrenaline ebbed.

Where am I? he thought. Who are these people? Can I trust them? What happened to my crew? If they're dead, who's going to tell their families what happened? How is Ruth going to find out what's happened? How can I tell her I'm alive?

Seventy-nine years later, I meet the granddaughter and great-grandson of Angéline Fontaine in the town square of La Roche-sur-Foron, a few miles from the crash site.

I had tracked them down via a Facebook post that Annecy city council had published three years earlier, commemorating the seventy-fifth anniversary of the Halifax tragedy. The post turned out to be a goldmine, as the comment section was littered with local people's recollections of the event or, in the case of Marie-Annick and her son Samuel Fontaine, their family's heroic role.

It is obvious that the Fontaines are still the same 'good people' who saved Frank in his hour of need. Marie-Annick, wearing a large bead necklace and thick glasses, glows with pride as we begin chatting about her grandmother Angéline and her uncle René.

'It was René who heard the plane first,' says Marie-Annick, sitting down at a café table opposite La Roche's pink town hall. 'He worked in a garage, so when he heard the engines he knew they were struggling. He knew something was wrong. He went outside to look and thought he saw several people jump out of the aircraft with parachutes. Of course, it was containers and not people. When he saw the plane crash, he cycled straight there.'

She has brought a large file of yellowing newspaper articles from the time, her mother's certificate of thanks from the RAF, and most pleasingly to me, postcards from Frank scrawled in his schoolboy French. A light breeze stirs and rustles Marie-Annick's collection of forgotten documents.

It is deeply moving to see how attached she and her son Samuel are to the story. Samuel, barrel-chested, bearded and still wearing his work overalls, has blagged the afternoon off work to meet me. Being a mechanic, he still has oil on his hands. He orders a beer and I join him.

Like a historical detective, I cross-reference Frank's story with the one passed down to them from their grandmother and great-uncle. It reveals some fascinating discrepancies.

Until his dying days, René maintained that he had cut Frank out of the telephone wires with his penknife, as opposed to Frank releasing his seatbelt, falling to earth and being arrested by the Italians. The telephone wires certainly broke Frank's fall and saved his life, but did they suspend him in his chair as he remembers? Perhaps momentarily, before they collapsed and René arrived and cut him out?

As for the Italian soldiers, could Frank have mistaken René for one as he led him away from the wreck? Could René, a fourteen-year-old boy, have exaggerated his heroic role? Perhaps when the Halifax's fuel tanks exploded, René ran for it and returned on his bike. As it was the Italians who had brought down *O for Orange* with small-arms fire, it seems likely they would have been on the scene quickly.

I listen in shock as Samuel tells me that Frank was undressed so the Fontaines could burn his English clothes. Likewise, how he was hidden in their forge chimney in case the Italians arrived. These details had been forgotten or omitted from the story Frank passed down. Having sustained a massive head trauma and slipping in and out of consciousness, Frank could have misremembered. During traumatic events, our brains struggle to process information as our flight-or-fight response goes into overdrive.

What everyone recalls equally is the terrible fire. 'The fuel from the plane ran straight into the River Fier nearby,' says Samuel looking grave. 'The whole river was on fire for hours through the night.' Samuel sits upright, gesturing flames and destruction as his mother nods.

I ask him, 'What was the balance of resister to collaborator in Meythet when Frank crashed?' Samuel translates for Marie-Annick and then answers, 'About half the town. You have to understand people were scared for their families. At the start of the war it made no sense to be a resister. Britain was going to lose.' If true, half of Meythet would probably have turned Frank away, either because they were collaborating with the Italians or, quite understandably, were too afraid to be caught sheltering an Allied airman.

Samuel returns to how shaken and distraught Frank was, something largely skimmed over in Frank's account. 'He came into the house . . .' Samuel says, before gesturing tears and shaking hands, 'really upset, crying. He was terrified and badly injured. He talked a lot about his crew and his family.'

Then it is my turn to talk. I tell them a little of Frank and I feel their attention focus on me, undivided. I show them photos of Frank. 'He looks like you,' says Marie-Annick earnestly and I cannot help but feel proud. Samuel falls on my well-worn copy of Frank's memoir *Winged Hours* and to my amazement, apart from the first few days in France, he and his mother know very little about Frank's mammoth escape across the entire Iberian Peninsula. '*Espagne*?' Marie-Annick says, pointing at the page with Frank's escape route map.

Samuel begins devouring the book, his leathery finger underlining the sentences and leaving light oil stains across the page as he translates for his mother. But there is not time for him to read the whole book, and I need it for my journey, so we order the bill and start to gather our belongings.

'Have you seen my photo of Frank?' I ask, flicking through Marie-Annick's newspapers. It must have blown off the table. Embarrassingly, Marie-Annick and Samuel leap to their feet and begin searching the town square, crawling on hands and knees to see under cars. After a few minutes, Marie-Annick finds it on the other side of the street. 'That's the second time we've saved him now!'

Despite my protests, Marie-Annick pays the bill and we kiss goodbye. Samuel crushes my hand in his vice-like grip. Over three hours of continuous talking, the pair barely took their eyes off me. Samuel often touched his massive chest when I asked him about his predecessors. With Marie-Annick, we did not even share a language, and yet for three hours we held each other's attention.

This was my first flavour of the tenacious people of the Haute-Savoie, a region I later learned was autonomous until 1860. It was also the first region of France to liberate itself from fascist occupation in the Second World War, without the help of the Allied armies. After meeting Marie-Annick and Samuel, this comes as no surprise.

From the cab of the lorry, Frank could see a large building appearing out of the darkness.

He was led to the back door and taken straight upstairs to a room that smelled heavily of perfume. In it stood a four-poster bed with lacy upholstery, a white canopy and a first-aid kit laid out on the mattress. A crowd stood around the bed, and one member began tending to Frank's wounds.

Frank had arrived at Ma Baraque. This three-storey building was something of a *maison de rendez-vous*, or brothel, often entertaining Italian soldiers and occasionally Gestapo agents in the bar downstairs and the bedrooms upstairs. This made it the perfect focal point for the local Resistance, who often hid their compromised soldiers or, in Frank's case, escaping airmen in the rooms upstairs.

The aim was twofold. Firstly, to get visiting Italians and Germans intoxicated in the bar and listen to their drunken conversations. Secondly, by serving their enemies, Ma Baraque would be the last place to be suspected of spying, harbouring fugitives or organising a secret army. Ma Baraque embodied the saying: 'Keep your friends close and your enemies closer.'

A short, middle-aged woman wearing a nightdress burst in. Standing at barely five foot, Hélène Bastin was in stark contrast to the crowd of male onlookers, yet her entrance commanded attention. Frank realised quickly that she was the boss.

Hélène, whom everyone called Pépette, set about cleaning the gash in Frank's scalp with trembling hands. As she worked, Frank's eyes darted about the room. The people in Ma Baraque were different from those at the Fontaines' forge.

In the dimly lit bedroom, he could make out men in khaki uniforms with the Croix de Lorraine embroidered on their shirts over their hearts. They were armed. Two girls also entered the room wearing silver Croix de Lorraine brooches and carrying daggers. Frank would later discover that Pépette carried a tiny, six-chambered .22 revolver in her apron. These people were members of the French Resistance, also known as the Maquis.

As Frank retold his story, his eyes focused on one maquisard at the front of the crowd. Pat was the leader of the local Maquis, a young man of only about twenty-two, but he could speak excellent English and was a born leader, brave to the point of foolhardiness.

Pat began to reply to Frank, but he stopped and lifted both hands. The room fell quiet.

There was a rumbling of engines like distant thunder and it took Frank a moment to work out why everyone looked so pleased.

'It was the noise of Bomber Command returning home after raiding Milan,' he remembered. 'We all had a drink on the strength of it. Pat told me they always sat up when Bomber Command went over and toasted to the boys' good fortune. I only wish the crews aloft could know of the joy they bring the French when they go over.'

But for Frank, the noise of Lancasters and Wellingtons depressed him. 'Main Force would be home in two hours and I was stuck in France,' he bemoaned. 'Even with the best of good fortune, I didn't have a hope of seeing England for weeks.' The thought was only brief, for Frank felt the walls closing in on him, and he just had time to be violently sick before passing out again.

'I must have been out for quite a while this time, as they all seemed rather concerned when I came to. I had brought up some blood and they thought I was hurt internally. But I knew the blood came from my mouth where the oxygen mask had damaged my gums.'

Pépette revived him with another glass of marc, a rough spirit made from the skins and seeds of grapes, and finished dressing his wounds. Then she kissed him on the forehead and barked at two young maquisards in the corner to help the stricken airman to bed.

'Pat, do you know what happened to my crew?' Frank asked, as he was hoisted from his chair.

'We have found two bodies, I'm afraid,' Pat replied, 'but we think the other four are on the run. I have men out looking for them.'

'What about the people in those houses?' said Frank.

'Only Italians and Germans lived there, not French people,' lied Pat, as he turned for the door. 'I have to go out now and see what's going on. Try to rest. I'll see you in the morning. *Bonne nuit.*'

It was now past 4 a.m. and Frank was desperately fatigued. His body craved rest, but every time he felt himself sliding into sleep, his brain jolted him back to the present. Lying in his bed, he watched the flames from his Halifax flicker against the ceiling and wondered which members of his crew were dead. He replayed the events in the air. Could he have made Lake Geneva when the first engine conked out?

He was the one who made the call to continue, and that may have sent his friends – and civilians – to their graves. But how could he have known that engine number two would give out as well? He tried to focus on this point.

A young maquisard arrived. Seeing Frank's agitation, he held his arm softly and said, 'I will sit with you. Don't be afraid.'

Pépette returned at dawn. She dismissed the young man and handed Frank an enormous bowl of real coffee she had acquired on the black market and a lump of bread that he could not eat.

Pat poked his head around the door.

'I'm sending out more men to look for your crew,' he said, 'and a doctor will come later to see you.'

Then began a stream of visitors. Everyone wanted to see the man who had walked away from the Halifax inferno. Frank explained, 'They were thrilled with my arrival and despite the tragic ending to our mission, it had raised the morale of the district to know that we hadn't forgotten them in England.'

At 10 a.m., a tall man with a grizzled face entered and introduced himself as 'the doctor'. After applying antiseptic to

Frank's abrasions, the nameless doctor summoned two of the broadest maquisards from downstairs and instructed them to hold Frank in his chair. Then the doctor began to set his arm, without anaesthetic.

Arm realigned, the doctor lashed it to three bits of wood and said, 'Keep it this way for thirty days. I'll be back to check on you.'

It was Pat who returned first.

'How did it go?' Frank asked.

'We think your crew were all killed,' replied Pat. 'We found more bodies in the rubble this morning. I'm sorry. We want to hold a funeral tomorrow morning in Meythet Cemetery.' Then he said, 'The Italians are searching for you with dogs, but you will be safe here. We've made sure all the bitches on heat are around Ma Baraque to distract the dogs. We will move you to Switzerland soon,' he added, before closing the door behind him.

Frank thought of twenty-year-old John Maden, the handsome despatcher who had been calm to the very last moment; of John Congdon, his navigator flying his last mission before completing a second tour of operations; and most acutely, he thought of Roderick Mackenzie, the 22-year-old Scot from the Isle of Skye, who had begged to come along.

Gunfire rattled in the valley below Ma Baraque. Its steady, staccato bursts grew louder and closer until Frank was in an absolute panic. Pat entered and said, 'Don't worry, you won't be taken alive.'

'This wasn't very reassuring,' Frank wrote, 'but what he meant to say was "have no fear, they will not take you while one of us is alive".' What was reassuring was the sight of Pat ordering his maquisards into position. In a matter of moments, they had every window covered, fingers resting on safety catches as they peeked between the curtains.

Frank thumbed for his own revolver under his pillow, but doubted whether he would have sufficient strength to fire it. It was another hot August afternoon and despite no more gunshots, the atmosphere remained charged. Patrols of Italians kept whizzing past in cars and lorries, 'but apparently it was too hot for them to go scrambling through the countryside.'

Then a patrol car pulled up at Ma Baraque and a group of Italian soldiers unloaded into the bar for a drink. Upstairs, Frank and the maquisards ceased all movement and listened to the Italian chit-chat drifting up through the floorboards. It was unbearably hot. Frank lay in his bed like a mummy, not daring to wipe the sweat from his brow for fear the springs of his mattress might squeak.

Every time another Italian wandered into the bar, Pépette's enormous black Labrador, Bobby, barked his head off. Bobby had absorbed his owner's fear of Italians, the same way a child will absorb the fears of its mother. He was an excellent early-warning system, but his barks cut through Frank like a knife scraping on a china plate.

Another warning system in place at Ma Baraque was the calling of an imaginary cat called 'Polly'. If someone entered who was untrustworthy, one of the barmaids would go to the door and call for 'Polly'. On hearing the call, the maquisards upstairs would cease playing cards and smoking, gently pick up their loaded guns, cover the windows and wait for the all clear.

Frank came to notice these things, as any sick person lying in the same place all day would. Despite the lace and the perfume, the room was pleasant, with a view of Mont Blanc to the south. It allowed Frank to see what was going on outside. 'I soon tired of this,' he recounted, 'because it gave me an inferiority complex to see the enemy dashing about.'

Exhausted but unable to sleep, Frank lay in bed all after-noon in a stupor, adrenaline ebbing and flowing every time he heard the enemy outside his bedroom window. He was suffer-ing intense pain in his mouth, whiplash in his back and neck, and discomfort in his broken wrist and arm. His persistent headache and bouts of nausea were almost certainly concus-sion-related. He had to be helped to the bathroom.

Pat entered. 'Frank, could you show me where you think you dropped your containers?' he asked, holding out a map. Several locals had seen the parachutes floating down behind the Halifax, mistaking them to be members of the crew.

The two men located the dropping point on Pat's map and a plan was hatched for a search party to leave as soon as dark-ness had fallen.

'I dropped into a doze that evening,' wrote Frank, 'but awoke soon after midnight to find a terrific commotion going on. I thought the Italians had come for me. All the maquisards were dashing around with Sten guns and manning the windows. Once they were in position, silence reigned until Pat burst in and said breathlessly, 'It was an ambush – the Italians were waiting for us – they have your containers. We nearly walked right into it, but managed to get away without firing a shot.'

Pat continued, 'We'd heard some of your weapons were being stored in the police station, so went there instead and forced them to hand over the guns. But the gendarmes chased us on bicycles. We must guard Pépette's tonight in case of attack.'

A maquisard was already perched on the windowsill. It took Frank several hours before even a wink of sleep came to him. 'Anyone attacking Ma Baraque that night would have had a mild surprise, as there was practically a man and a woman in every window with a Sten gun,' he remembered.

The next morning, 16 August, grim silence returned to the upper level of Ma Baraque, thanks to a gendarme who spent most of his day off getting drunk in the bar. At one point a plainclothes Gestapo man even came in, but he stayed for only one drink.

Late in the afternoon, the gendarme went outside to his car, where he stood for about quarter of an hour. Frank recalled, 'I felt like leaning out the window and saying, "Okay, I'll come quietly." After all, I had got out of the most terrific crash alive and why should I risk getting shot now? If I gave myself up, I would have a guarantee of coming out of the war alive.'

Frank assumed that he would be sent to a POW camp, where he would sit out the rest of the war. But there were other cases, particularly when escaping airmen had been given civilian clothes and were embedded within the local Resistance, where escapees were executed, tortured by the Gestapo, or sent to concentration camps.

Two things dismissed the idea of surrender from Frank's head. Firstly, the fear of interrogation at Stalag Luft. Secondly, the fact that for helping him, Pépette, Pat, and all the men and women of Ma Baraque would be thrown in jail, where torture, deportation and execution were likely. With darkness falling, the gendarme finally returned to Annecy. Pat swept into the loft with a stranger by his side.

'This man was in a bar in Annecy a short while ago and a gendarme said to him, "If I were you, I would move your friend. The Italians know where he is and they are coming for him at ten o'clock tonight." That gives us half an hour to get out. I'll come and dress you in a few minutes, then we will leave for the mountain.'

'I think I can walk ten miles,' replied Frank, overestimating his abilities. 'Shouldn't we set off sooner in case they come early?'

'Don't worry,' Pat shot back, 'the Italians are always late.'

Ma Baraque was like a beehive. Great hunks of black bread and cheese were being loaded into rucksacks alongside ammunition magazines and bottles of wine. Frank was dressed into 'civvies' stolen from a second-hand clothes shop.

Pépette kissed each man on the cheek as they filed out the back door of Ma Baraque. After a few hundred paces uphill, Frank realised that ten miles was beyond him. Having not eaten for two days, he was weak and breathing raggedly.

The whole hill was covered in dense scrub in which the Maquis had built a network of passages. It was possible to travel over the entire hillside without being seen. The Italians were too afraid to enter the scrub, because it was so easy to surprise them and bump them off. This scrub was called *maquis* at the time, hence the Resistance movement's moniker.

Near the top of the hill, Frank had a 'bedroom' allotted to him, which had been cut out of the bushes. It had netting stretched between four bushes and was covered in hay, 'making a marvellous bed'. Lying in his lair, Frank revelled in the cool mountain air, so refreshing after the hot, brothel bedroom.

Pépette arrived sometime after midnight to see how he was getting on. She had climbed all that way to bring him water and an extra blanket.

'That woman looked after us as though we were her own children,' Frank recounted. He tried to thank her, but she shrugged it off.

'*Non, non. Merci beaucoup, Pépette,*' persisted Frank, taking hold of her hand.

She looked at him square in the eyes and said, '*C'est pour la France.*'

No attack developed that night, but the bar had been crawling with Italian soldiers. Pat reckoned they were afraid to attack and losing interest in the war. Their leader Mussolini had been arrested three weeks earlier and replaced on 26 July by Marshal Pietro Badoglio. Although publicly committing Italy to continue fighting alongside Germany, Badoglio had begun secret armistice talks with the Allies. Many Italian soldiers sensed it was only a matter of weeks until their country officially surrendered.

Early next morning, 17 August, shards of sunlight infiltrated Frank's lair, filling it with a hundred tiny searchlights. The dawn chorus boomed across the hillside. For the first time, Frank had slept soundly. In the Maquis, he knew he could make a run for it. In Ma Baraque, he knew he was trapped.

Pépette arrived with her girls. They had brought flasks of coffee to soften the bread that had gone hard overnight. Frank emerged from his nest, sat down in a clearing and using his good arm, brought a bowl of coffee to his mouth. He looked around at his newfound comrades. Half had begun cleaning their weapons, stripping and reassembling them 'with a loving care that would put the Home Guard to shame'.

The gentle clinking of metal, the softly spoken French, the pleasant temperature, the safety of the scrub. The warm bowl of coffee in the cool mountain air. Frank was with the Maquis in the *maquis*. Slowly, morale began to return.

From their mountain eyrie, the men watched the sun arc into the sky. A bell tolled in the valley way below and a maquisard turned to Frank and said, 'That is for your crew. Their funeral is happening this morning.'

Pépette returned at midday with a two-gallon can of water that she had lugged up the hill. She spent an hour in the bushes, mostly talking to Pat, whom she clearly adored. 'It is safe. Please come back down for lunch,' she told him, and he relented. Fried eggs, boiled potatoes, bread, cheese and wine were waiting for them on the table.

After lunch, the chief of the secret army in the Haute-Savoie arrived to a flurry of salutes. Colonel d'Oisa was of average height and build, but he commanded attention. 'D'Oisa was in mufti when he arrived, but no Air Marshal could have had a more respectful reception,' Frank recorded. The colonel turned to him and spoke with a voice loud enough for the room to hear.

'Your crew were buried in Meythet Cemetery today,' said d'Oisa.

'Yes, we heard the bells from up on the hill,' replied Frank.

'I should tell you, something rather extraordinary happened during the funeral. The Italians – they wanted to bury your crew without a crowd – but the locals had crowded around Annecy hospital, demanding to hold a military service. They believe your men died for them. But the Italians refused.

'They loaded the coffins into a lorry and set off for Meythet cemetery. But they had to drive slowly because there was no room for the gravediggers in the truck, so they had to walk in front of the lorry. Every house the procession passed, people came out and followed, demanding the Italians let them bury your men themselves. The streets were lined with people.

'When the Italians arrived at the Pont du Tasset [*the bridge connecting Meythet with its cemetery*], they stationed two soldiers and said, "Do not let anyone past." But word was spreading like wildfire and the crowd was building on the bridge, shouting to be let past. The Italians raised their weapons, but there were too many people and they did not have the guts to shoot civilians.

'Hundreds of people went down to the river, took off their shoes and waded across. Then they practically ran to the cemetery, where the Italians were yelling at the gravediggers to dig faster. They were handling the coffins carelessly, tossing them around like sacks of potatoes. Even the Germans wouldn't have done that.

'They were plain coffins too, with no military honours. The crowd really hated that. They began edging closer, ignoring the Italians' warnings. Everyone was shouting abuse at them – you could feel the tension swelling. It was electric. I thought the soldiers were going to fire into the crowd and cause a stampede. We started chanting *Vive la France! Vive l'Angleterre!* and *Vive la libération!* The Italians knew they couldn't do anything. We sung "La Marseillaise", belting out the chorus several times. It was deafening. I've never seen anything like it.

'As soon as the coffins were in the ground, the soldiers retreated to their trucks while we booed and whistled and shouted, "Shame!" When they left, the crowd flooded the cemetery and covered their grave with flowers. People are still there now, arranging the flowers and building a proper cross. Your men won't be forgotten in Meythet.'

Frank wished he could convey this story to the families of his dead crew members.

The colonel continued, 'We have arranged for you to travel to the Swiss frontier in a car at 5 p.m. today. A motorcyclist will check for controls ahead. If you're stopped by anyone, start moaning and the driver will say you have fallen into a threshing machine and he is rushing you to hospital. We didn't have time to forge any papers for you.'

Frank nodded, nerves bubbling inside him. Could he not spend the rest of the war on this scrubby hillside being fed by Pépette? She had just appeared with a trilby hat and a huge pair of dark glasses. Taking care to avoid his cuts, she slid the arms of the glasses over Frank's ears and pulled the hat low over his forehead. '*Voilà!*'

Frank checked himself in the mirror. 'All I had to do was dab my nose with a handkerchief and I looked vaguely normal.

No one would have guessed I had recently been catapulted from a Halifax cockpit.' The party remained at the lunch table rehearsing the plan.

At 4.50 p.m., sixty-two hours after the crashlanding, Frank crept out of Ma Baraque and hid in the bushes alongside the road. A car drove slowly past ten minutes later. All he had to do was nip out and get in.

But just as he stepped out of the bushes, Pépette rushed out of Ma Baraque, threw her arms around his neck, kissed him on both cheeks and burst into tears.

'It rather upset our predetermined plan, but fortunately I was able to get aboard without anyone seeing,' wrote Frank.

With the trilby pulled low over his face, Frank stole a final glance of Ma Baraque in the wing mirror before the car turned a bend and disappeared into a fold of Savoie countryside.

Switzerland approached.

Leaving the crash site, I head east towards Meythet Cemetery on the same route the villagers took eight decades ago. On the Pont du Tasset bridge, I stop and look at the River Fier below, imagining the mob of locals wading across and surging up the far bank. I realise this was the same stream that *O for Orange*'s fuel had set alight just forty-eight hours before the funeral.

It is only a mile along the Chemin de Grèves until the cemetery appears on my left, guarded by two large yew trees. I heave the heavy, black gates open and step into a sea of grey. There is not a blade of grass and every gravestone is made from stone or concrete. The effect is forbidding. But nestled in the top right corner, I spot two rectangular head-stones with curved tops, distinctive in their light grey, Portland stone hue.

Here lie navigator John Congdon and rear gunner Frank Pollard. Their graves are bare and I feel an idiot for not bringing flowers. Pollard, only twenty-two, was the same age as me when he was killed, which makes me feel strange, even guilty. The lad from Middlesbrough had almost certainly never visited the Alps. I think of the wonderful cycling and skiing trips that I have had here.

I turn away from the graves and look up at the magnificent Plateau des Glières dominating the horizon. Great buttresses of rock glint in the sunlight, backed by candy floss clouds and a brilliant, baby blue sky.

It is fitting how Frank and John face the plateau. The supplies they were carrying to France were almost certainly destined for guerilla fighters living up there in the high Alpine meadows.

CHAPTER 4

THE DOGHOLE

The journey to Switzerland was hot, slow and uncomfortable. The car kept stopping to allow a motorcyclist to go ahead and check for enemy controls. Italian soldiers whizzed past in troop trucks. Everyone's hands groped for their revolvers. Sweat trickled down spines.

At Saint-Julien-en-Genevois, a Swiss border town, Quino the driver turned to Frank and said, 'Go lie in the bushes up there. It might take a while for the motorbike to check the border.' Frank did as he was told, but after twenty minutes the motorcyclist returned shaking his head.

'It's hopeless trying to get through today,' he said, 'there are too many checks. We'll take you somewhere else, somewhere quiet, safer than Ma Baraque.'

Quino turned the car around and headed south back into France. Frank could not help feeling disappointed. From under his trilby, he watched the sun fade into the horizon, breathing pink and orange streaks into the cirrus clouds above. Quino steered the car down a very steep hill, bringing it to a halt in a tiny village.

Frank had arrived in Les Goths. This hamlet, nestled deep in a valley somewhere north of Annecy, was nothing more than three chalets and a disused sawmill. Frank, Quino and the motorcyclist approached the nearest house – Le Petit Coin – and knocked.

A small, timid-looking woman half-opened the door and a hushed, rapid conversation in French followed, none of which Frank understood. After a minute or so, the young woman looked Frank up and down with her big round eyes and gestured for him to come in.

The trio entered and Quino formally introduced Frank to his new host, Madame Pallud. 'Please, call me Mimi,' she said. Frank smiled and nodded as Quino began to explain that he would stay with Mimi until arrangements had been made for him to be transported into Switzerland.

As Quino spoke, Frank's eyes were drawn to the corner of the room, where a baby stirred in a cot. He walked over and gestured to Mimi if he could hold the baby. She agreed. 'Josette,' she said quietly, as Frank lifted her from her cot. 'She's six months old.'

Staring into Josette's eyes, Frank could see Tessa looking back at him, his baby girl back in England, who was just two months older. He told Mimi about Tessa and her mother Ruth and how he wished he could let them know he was alive.

In return, Mimi told Frank about her husband John, who was away working on the railways, and her brother-in-law André, who lived with her. André was a Resistance fighter in hiding. He had been injured in 1940 in the Battle of France, but escaped capture. The Resistance was his way of getting back at the Germans.

Like Pépette of Ma Baraque, Mimi Pallud was a no-nonsense, passionate Savoyard woman, who loathed Italians and Germans. She was more softly spoken than Pépette, preferring not to be the centre of attention and keeping to herself. Because of her baby Josette, she felt the pressures of war more keenly than most. She and her brother-in-law's actions carried the threat of torture and deportation if they were caught and who knows what that would mean for her only child.

Frank, tired from the day's events, was shown to a bed, where he slept like a corpse until late in the morning. Emerging for breakfast on 18 August, his fourth morning in France, he found André at the table. The young man leaped to his feet and shook Frank's hand vigorously, chattering about what an honour it was to meet him and how the pilot who walked away from the Halifax was all the locals were talking about.

Frank liked André. He was of average height and build, had dark hair and intense eyes that were never first to break contact. Having been on the run for most of the war, Frank could tell he was a serious operator, capable and deceptive. André's contempt for Italians and Germans was almost frightening. He made Frank feel safe at Le Petit Coin.

So too did the design of Le Petit Coin and its sheer isolation. Situated deep in a valley, Frank recalled: 'You could hear if a vehicle was coming down the escarpment above you. If you needed to hide, there was an outhouse out the back standing over the dried-up Rivière Les Usses. I could see everything that was going on from that outhouse through the gaps in the planks. If anyone approached, it was easy to pass through planks and drop down the nine-foot bank to the riverbed along which escape was easy and cover excellent.' Like his bed in the scrub behind Ma Baraque, Frank did not feel cornered in Le Petit Coin.

It was another beautiful summer's day in the Haute-Savoie, so after a long conversation with André, Frank went into the garden. Beside the riverbed, underneath a Victoria plum tree, he found a long deckchair and before he knew it, he was asleep again. The toll of the crash and his body's attempts to heal itself were still weighing heavily.

After a few hours André dropped a plum into Frank's lap. 'Let's walk,' he said. Despite Frank's limited French, the pair wandered for a few hours up the Usses valley chatting about France's leader, the collaborator Marshal Pétain, Frank's containers and the war in general. Trout darted for the bank as the two men's shadows fell over the water. Rounding a corner, a heron fled from the shallows, squawking unhappily. The flicker of morale Frank felt in the *maquis* behind Ma Baraque was growing.

That evening, for the first time since being shot down four days ago, Frank ate a full meal. The perennial fear was waning. Sadly, it did not last. At 2 a.m., Frank was awoken by terrible, piercing screams. 'I broke into a sweat of fear right away and thought the Italians had caught Madame Pallud and were torturing her,' he recollected. 'I tried to cock my revolver, but couldn't manage it with one hand.'

Frank headed for the window to jump out, but stopped when he heard a scream from right below him. 'In the full light of the moon, I could see a woman throwing her head back and making all the noise.' A few confused, heart-pounding moments later, André burst into the room shouting, '*C'est bon! C'est bon!*' He quickly explained that the woman was mad and often came round screaming when there was a full moon.

It was several hours before Frank's pulse calmed enough for him to fall back asleep.

The next day, Frank's third at Le Petit Coin, was to be his last. Napping after lunch, he awoke to find an attractive young woman sitting at the end of his bed, and a room full of people. Quino the driver was there, along with André and a man called Marcel Fournier.

Quino spoke first. 'We have a new plan. Our contacts know of a place where you can get across the border without having to go through checks. There's a hole underneath the border fence you can wriggle through.'

'It's called "the doghole",' added the new man Fournier, with a grin. 'A whole class of Jewish schoolchildren went through it the other night. Right under the Italians' noses.'

'Yes, but we need to get you there first,' said Quino. 'We will drive you some of the way, but there are vehicle checks everywhere, so our plan is for you to walk to the border with Colette.' Quino motioned to the woman at the end of the bed. 'If you pretend you're lovers just walking in the countryside, the Italians will leave you alone. Make sure you hold hands and stop regularly to chat, sit down even. We'll give you some clothes that'll make you look like a local. If anyone comes near, blow your nose with a handkerchief so they can't see the cuts on your face.

'Oh and whatever you do, do not run,' added Quino. 'The Italians know we'll be trying to get you to Switzerland. It's essential you look like lovers going for a casual stroll. Don't make a dash for the border when you get nearby. The Italians will shoot first and ask questions second.'

I meet Mimi Pallud's grandson Nicholas Buzaré in a car park in Cruseilles, a town about three kilometres away from Le Petit Coin.

'Please, call me Nico,' he says, shaking my hand gently. He is a tall, haggard-looking Frenchman with bloodshot eyes and a large beard that gets increasingly grey near his chin. Dressed in a grey greatcoat and a woolly hat, Nico looks like a shepherd, rugged and windswept, with deep folds in the skin around his eyes and forehead. He could be anywhere between fifty and seventy. His smile is a picture of kindness.

He speaks exceedingly softly, telling me in good, slow English that he will drive me to Les Goths and show me Le

Petit Coin before taking me to the cemetery where his grand-mother Mimi is buried. I notice his hands shaking slightly as he lights a cigarette with his leathery, yellowing fingers. He drives at a snail's pace.

In Les Goths, we stroll leisurely in the crisp autumnal air. In 1943, this hamlet was nothing more than 'three houses and a disused sawmill'. It is not much bigger today. There is a riding school, a small cluster of pretty houses, and a communal picnic area beside the Rivière Les Usses – an idyllic clearing in what is otherwise a heavily forested valley.

Walking silently, we listen to the river gurgling as it bends its way past moss-covered rocks thick with decomposing leaves. Jays and woodpeckers call warily from above. Acorns fall into the river with voluptuous *plops*. Stately oaks groan in the breeze. The place feels timeless, and I wonder if Frank was able to enjoy these few moments, or whether he was too caught up in his own perilous predicament.

'Le Petit Coin,' murmurs Nico, gesturing to a three-storey, typically French chalet about fifty metres from the river. It was sold years ago and is currently empty, the garden unkempt. No one remembers the outhouse. A small concrete wall has been built between the house and the river and the place does not fit with how I had imagined it.

'That's the window Frank was going to jump out of,' says Nico between cigarette drags, referencing the incident of the mad woman wailing outside the house in the middle of the night. Frank recreated this moment for a photo in 1979. I do the same.

We return to Cruseilles, where Nico buys me lunch. Over our baguettes, he tells me about his visits to Wales as a child, living with my mum, aunt and uncle for weeks on their farm in Carmarthenshire, and of how he and his brother Dominique attended the weddings of Frank's younger children. This shocks me greatly. I knew Mimi Pallud had managed to contact Frank through the RAF Escaping Society in 1973, but I had no idea they became close family friends afterwards, exchanging grandchildren for many years.

All this happened through the 1970s and 1980s, before social media and mobile phones made it easy to keep in touch. As the grandchildren grew up, the families drifted apart and the connection fell dormant. No contact had been made for at least twenty years. Until now.

After lunch, Nico takes me to meet his mother Josette, Mimi Pallud's daughter, who was a baby when Frank visited in 1943. Aged eighty, Josette Buzaré is the only person who features in Frank's escape who is still alive, albeit as a six-month-old. She has only moved three kilometres from Les Goths. Her flat is incredibly neat and roasting hot. As I enter, she rises from the sofa with hands clasped to her mouth, tears collecting in her eyes, gasping quietly, as though my visit is a surprise. She hurries next door and re-emerges with a folder bursting with yellowing newspaper articles and correspondence.

Leafing through Josette's impressive collection, I ask about her mother Mimi. 'My mother often told me the story of the British pilot who came to stay during the war when I was a child,' begins Josette. 'She always talked about how much Frank liked to hold me because it reminded him of his own baby back home [*Tessa, my grandmother*].'

I show Josette a photo of eight-month-old Tessa being fed on a train by her mother Ruth. 'On the back,' I say, 'Ruth has written: *Tessa 8 months. On the train to* [RAF] *Tempsford to pick up her father's bike and belongings after he crashed and was sole survivor. We were unaware that he was alive for about 3 months.*'

The photo is dated August 1943. 'I think it would have been taken while Frank was in Les Goths with your mum,' I explain, 'as Ruth would have received the "missing" telegram by that point and gone to retrieve Frank's things.'

Nico translates my words and Josette gasps, hand over her mouth, at almost every word. She asks how Tessa is now. I tell her she died a few months ago. She begins to cry. She shows me a photo of herself as a baby taken on the lawn of Le Petit Coin, just after Frank's visit, and the heat in the flat makes my eyes sweat.

On 20 August at 4 p.m., a car left Le Petit Coin and headed north for Switzerland. In the back sat Frank and Colette, the sweating, fretting Welshman contrasting sharply with the nonchalant, 22-year-old blonde. The car was propelled by gasogene, a wood-burning apparatus, which meant great bags of fuel were jammed in alongside the unlikely pairing.

Climbing out of the Usses valley, their tyre burst. Marcel and Quino, the two Resistance members in the front, spat terrible French curses as they changed it, sweat dripping from their noses. A few miles later, at La-Roche-sur-Foron rail crossing, the motorcyclist escort went over the tracks just before the barrier started dropping.

'Wild shrieks on the horn from Marcel persuaded the railway man to stop winding down the barriers and we shot under them with a few inches to spare,' recalled Frank. Several miles later, the car pulled into a small lane, stopped, and everyone got out. They were stood on the lip of a small, shallow valley, the far side of which was Switzerland.

'This road goes right up to the border,' Quino said to Frank, pointing at the track unfurling away from them. 'Once you've crossed that railway in the bottom of the valley, turn right into those fields. Keep walking uphill until you reach that farmhouse, can you see it?' Frank nodded. 'Make sure you take it easy. You are lovers, remember,' added Quino with a reassuring smile.

Frank straightened up his outfit. He had discarded his sling in favour of a light jacket, the pockets of which held his RAF wire cutters and revolver. With the jacket button done up, he could hook his thumb over it and support his broken arm. In his other hand was his handkerchief, ready to be pressed to his scar-ridden face if anyone approached. A trilby completed the disguise.

Colette looked at ease in a long summer dress. She was only fractionally shorter than Frank. Her blonde hair matched her pale skin. Frank could tell she was different from most of the French men and women he had encountered so far. Her clothes and the way she spoke betrayed a more privileged upbringing.

'We'll go and buy cigarettes from the border guards to keep them busy,' said Quino. '*Bonne chance.*'

Hand in hand, Frank and Colette began their stroll to Switzerland. After crossing the railway, they entered the first field. One of the French farm labourers turning over hay with his pitchfork stopped and looked at them. Pitchfork in one hand, he held up the other and made a 'V for Victory' sign with his fingers.

'My faith in my disguise was somewhat shattered,' Frank remembered, 'but we carried on. The frontier looked so close now. I was determined to get across.'

Sensing Frank's agitation, Colette gave his clammy hand a few squeezes. She talked about the most mundane things – the weather, lunch – anything to appear like they were chatting. He croaked a few replies, but his mouth was so dry it was becoming painful to speak. Grasshoppers leaped around their feet as they strolled through the hay. 'It was ghastly, worse than crossing the Dutch coast at nought feet on a moonlit night.'

As the farmhouse loomed on the horizon, Frank could make out a barbed-wire fence just beyond it. The border. Only a hundred yards from safety, he thought. He desperately wanted to make a break for it, but could feel Colette's hand wrapped around his, like an anchor holding a boat.

The pair arrived at the farmhouse. The door opened as they approached, so they walked straight in. Immediately the temperature dropped five degrees, and for the first time in what seemed an age, Frank drew breath.

'*Bonjour, les Anglais,*' boomed a voice from behind them. The man finished locking the door and approached, one hand outstretched to Frank.

'What an honour! An RAF pilot in my farm!' he said.

'This is Monsieur Mérandon,' said Colette, as Frank tried to take in what was happening.

'*Non, non,* call me Léon,' protested the stout figure. He was six foot tall and his overalls were having a fair job holding back his sizeable belly. Frank noticed Léon's rolled-up sleeves hugging muscly, tanned arms. Despite being fifty-six, Léon's face, complete with a large scar below his jawbone, looked much older. It betrayed a lifetime of outdoor work. It was clear he was not the sort of man you would want to bump into in a dark alleyway.

Not that Frank was worrying about that – Léon was grinning ear to ear. He could not believe a British pilot was in his kitchen. He set a glass of fresh milk on the table for Frank and began to grill him about his crash and the war in general, Colette diligently translating for the enthusiastic Frenchman.

As they chatted, Frank looked around the idyllic farmhouse kitchen. The first thing he noticed was two clocks above the mantelpiece. One had 'French Time' below it and the other, an hour ahead, was labelled 'Enemy Time'. Seeing he was looking at it, Léon launched into a rant about the Italians patrolling his farm. He clearly despised them and said so, loudly. When an off-duty Italian walked past the farmhouse on the road, he opened the window to make sure the man could hear his tirade.

With two hours till darkness, Léon insisted Frank come and see his horses in the back garden. 'You are an Englishman, you must know about horses,' he said. Frank really wanted to remain hidden in the house, but felt he had better satisfy his host, so went along. Soon he was roped into seeing the wretched heifers and pigs too, creeping from barn to barn with his trilby pulled low.

Darkness was now falling, so the pair came back inside. Léon sent his daughters to go and check on the border guards, while Colette and Frank rehearsed their plan. A clap of thunder rumbled from the direction of the Alps, only a few miles east. Rain pattered on the windowpanes.

Léon's daughters returned and said most of the Italian soldiers were going into their huts because of the rain. 'Okay, let's go,' said Colette rising from the table. She and Frank slipped out of the back door into a patch of sunflowers. They began crawling, Frank one-handedly.

At the edge of the sunflowers, they stopped to watch the border guard marching up and down the nine-foot-high fence, only thirty yards away. 'This diminutive Italian was the only remaining obstacle between me and freedom,' recounted Frank. 'My mind was filled with rather violent thoughts, for he didn't know we were there and I had my revolver cocked.'

The light was fading. The rain intensified. Another growl of thunder fractured the air behind them. The guard looked up at the sky, about-turned and marched off to his guardhouse seventy yards away, closing the shutters behind him.

'Now,' said Colette.

They ran from the sunflowers to the fence. Colette lifted up the wire and Frank realised why it was called the doghole. He fell to his knees and wriggled underneath the same way a dog would. With his good arm, he lifted the wire for Colette who slipped through rather more easily.

Tucking the wire away, the pair set off across the field into the gathering darkness of Switzerland, the smell of rain thick in the air. '*Libre!*' Colette whispered.

Frank could not reply. 'I just took her hand and squeezed it.'

Another crackle of thunder sounded as they ran. After thirty seconds, the edge of the first field appeared, flanked by a row of trees and a ditch. Frank jumped it.

As he was regaining his balance, a cold, sharp edge of a bayonet pressed into his throat.

'*Halt!*' called a German voice from the darkness.

Finding Frank and Colette's crossing point into Switzerland is one of the most rewarding and satisfying parts of my journey. I know they crossed near the town of Saint-Cergues thanks to a map that Frank left behind. Sitting by its Mairie (*town hall*), I pore over Frank's account of his walk and, with a map in my other hand, plot his route out of France.

Setting off from Saint-Cergues into a shallow valley, I soon arrive at a railway line, where I am pleasantly surprised to find a footpath snaking to the right. I take it, pushing my bike up a gentle hill towards Switzerland, past the point where the farm labourer made the V for Victory sign at Frank. The temptation to think *sod it* and make a break for it must have been unbearable.

I crest the slope, spot Mérandon's farmhouse and approach. It is big and untidy and the garden is filled with bits of wood and pipes that have been gutted from the house in a renovation project.

Behind the farmhouse, where the sunflower patch would have been, is now a small building site, but the border has not moved and is still a stone's throw away. I walk towards it, trying to imagine nine feet of barbed-wire fence.

I cross into Switzerland, walk across the first field and stop at a ditch. It must be the same one where Frank found a bayonet pressed against his throat. Pulling out my baguette, I settle down for lunch, looking out over the field at the Jura mountains north of Lake Geneva.

A farmer in magnificent denim dungarees enters the field in his tractor. He waves as he trundles past me in his ancient tractor and I wave back. This process is repeated fifteen times as he sprays the perimeter of his field, only stopping when he is too far away to wave. I wonder if he knows the story of his field.

Looking south-west, Mont Salève looms over Geneva. Behind me, the northern fringe of the Alps rises steeply from the earth. Ahead, a single sunflower with an enormous bumble bee on it sways in the breeze.

I feel underwhelmed and overwhelmed. Apart from some stones emblazoned with a large, red S, there is no way of telling this was the border. The scene of an exhilarating escape. The spot where my great-grandfather, arm broken and face criss-crossed with cuts, escaped his Italian and German pursuers, guided by a young, attractive Frenchwoman amidst an Alpine thunderstorm.

It is just an ordinary field – flat, green and distinctly unremarkable.

Returning to the vacant farmhouse, I meet Bernadette and

Laëtitia Mordal, granddaughter and great-granddaughter of Léon Mérandon. They live in the small bungalow next door. I am a total stranger, but they welcome me into their home like a returning hero. I feel embarrassed at the reception I am given.

Laëtitia's boyfriend and Bernadette's husband are both there too, and a history teacher friend of theirs who speaks English. Bernadette pours coffee into my mug and pushes a plate of madeleines at me. She is a typical elderly Frenchwoman, elegant, confident and effortlessly stylish.

Unlike other descendants I have met so far, Bernadette and Laëtitia have very little by way of photos and documents. But Bernadette is full of memories of her grandfather. She confirms he was indeed a fiercely passionate man, known for his enormous personality and for laughing in the face of danger. 'Léon always said it was the honour of his lifetime to have helped a British pilot escape in the war,' she explains.

But Frank was not the only person the Mérandon family helped to escape persecution in the Second World War. Bernadette glows as she tells me about the Jewish schoolchildren, French Resistance fighters, spies, documents and money that her grandfather passed in and out of Switzerland through the doghole.

'The Italian soldiers actually visited the farm sometimes to buy produce,' she says. 'Once they heard the noises of the Jewish children playing upstairs, but Léon said it was his wife who had TB and the Italians didn't check.' I learn that after the war, Israel tried to bestow Léon with a Righteous Among the Nations award (an honour for non-Jewish people) but he turned it down out of modesty.

These stories are being recounted to a series of gasps and nods and oos from around the room. But it was not just Léon who helped run the doghole. His sons Jean (twenty-two), Raymond (eighteen) [*Bernadette's father*], and his daughter Huguette (thirteen) all assisted. Indeed, Raymond was already a wanted man and had to flee to Switzerland to avoid arrest shortly after Frank's visit. While in self-exile, the Germans sentenced him to death.

All this was happening while the family were caring for Louise Mérandon, Léon's wife, who had cancer. She died eleven days after Frank's visit, aged fifty-two. She had been upstairs when he was there, but he had never realised.

We get up and head outside to poke around the farmhouse. I sense it is painful for Bernadette to see her family home gutted like this. I believe there had been a falling out in the family and someone had forced the sale of the house.

Bernadette takes out a picture of the border fence, and we recreate the photo. She tells me Léon really hated this fence, as he had fought in the First World War and could not stand the sight of barbed wire. He despised the Germans because one of their shells had lodged some shrapnel in his jaw, and they had taken him prisoner.

We arrive at the spot of the doghole. 'How many people were passed through here?' I ask. Bernadette has no idea.

'*Beaucoup*,' she says, '*mais un seul pilote.*' But only one pilot.

We go back inside and I get out my photo of Frank and his book. I open it to the relevant page and hand it to the history teacher, who begins to read it in French. The room's attention falls undivided onto him, and I have a sudden irrational fear that Frank may have written something rude about their brave ancestors.

They hang onto every sentence, clapping occasionally, laughing often and asking questions. But there is not enough time to read the whole book. As I am preparing to leave, I ask Bernadette if she has a photo of Léon. She appears with a tiny, stamp-sized headshot printed on paper. It is the only photo in existence of him. Léon scowls back at the camera. He looks like a tough old bugger, but under the hard exterior there was clearly an enormous heart.

After another round of firm handshakes and cheek-kissing, I get into my car and drive away, grateful for having met such a wonderful family.

CHAPTER 5

A BRAVE DECISION

The voice from behind the bayonet called something in German, which neither Colette nor Frank understood.

'*Was machen Sie? Wer sind Sie?*' Frank felt the bayonet tip in his chest now. '*Ziehen Sie sich!*' ['Move!'] growled the voice, as a single arm grabbed Frank's shoulder and began marching him away from the ditch.

After a couple of paces, Frank peeked over his shoulder. The man had come out of the shadow of the tree and Frank could just make out a grey uniform. This was it, Frank thought, POW camp for the rest of the war. What will happen to Colette? Rain pounded down around them and lightning crackled overhead, lighting up the Alps and Lake Geneva.

Frank thumbed for his revolver and set it to safe. They were approaching a guardhouse and he did not want the German to find it on 'fire'. The soldier banged on the wall as they went past one corner and the door flung open. Frank and Colette stepped into the light.

Another soldier dressed in grey stood before them, smiling. In an instant, Frank knew he was safe, as the buttons on the soldiers' tunic were emblazoned with Swiss crosses. The soldier with the bayonet must be a Swiss who only spoke German.

'English, eh?' asked the Swiss soldier. 'You must be that pilot who crashed at Annecy and got away. We've been expecting you,' he said gleefully. Frank simply stood there blinking, dripping rainwater onto the floor. 'I'll call up Geneva. A car will come pick you up.'

'Can I have a drink please?' asked Frank, surprising himself with his own voice. The man got up and left for several minutes. The moment the door closed, Colette said, 'Don't answer any questions. Wait until Geneva. Victor will sort everything.' Rain hammered on the tin roof.

Who is this Victor? Frank thought, looking around the hut. It consisted of nothing more than one window, one light, one chair and a desk holding a telephone and a few papers. In the corner there was a rack stacked with rifles and an umbrella.

The door opened and the smiling guard handed a bowl of milk to Frank. He restarted the questioning, taking no offence at Frank's shrugs and smiles and non-replies, until the car arrived. 'Well, *bon voyage*, aviator,' announced the man, 'and *bonsoir, madame*. Enjoy Geneva.'

As the car pulled away from the guardhouse and into Switzerland, Frank knew he had finally made it. Although it was only 20 August – a mere six days after the crash – 'it seemed like six weeks since my arrival in Annecy.'

There were five security stops between the border and Geneva, but at last the car arrived at a grand place called the Hotel Bristol. It was well past midnight and Frank fell into bed, not stirring until late next morning. While breakfasting with Colette the next day, two smartly dressed men walked in.

The English-looking one was Victor Farrel who, in King's English, explained that his job as a 'passport control officer' involved handling all SOE affairs in Geneva. The other man, a Swiss intelligence officer called Clement, searched Frank's stuff. He confiscated the revolver, but left the remains of Frank's escape kit.

Victor told Frank he would be taken to a nursing home to receive proper medical attention.

'After you've recovered properly,' he continued, 'you have a choice. Firstly, to be interned with the other Allied airmen who've parachuted into Switzerland. You will go into a system, fingerprints, ration cards, a bunk with your name on. They will interrogate you in the camp, but you will be looked after, better than a POW camp. But make no mistake, you will be in Switzerland for the rest of the war.'

'And the second option?' asked Frank.

'Try and get back to England,' said Farrel. 'Most airmen who land here are arrested immediately and interned. The Germans occasionally let the Swiss send airmen home in return for Luftwaffe crews who've baled out over Switzerland. But as you've made it here by yourself, you aren't part of this trading game. As far as the Swiss and Germans are concerned, you don't exist. Not yet anyway.'

'How would I get back to England?' replied Frank.

'Leave that to me. While you decide, you can assist me in Switzerland. I'm trying to establish dropping zones across the country to receive war materiel and agents, something I gather you know a bit about.'

Victor and Clement shook Frank's hand. 'There's no rush to make a decision,' added Victor. 'It will take some weeks to organise repatriation for you. Besides, it looks like those scars won't be healed for a while.' He turned and left.

Colette got up to leave. Frank pulled out his compass. 'Have this. Please.' She blushed, accepted, kissed him on both cheeks and left, bound for the doghole.

'It was impossible to express my thanks to Colette adequately for the help and risks she had taken,' Frank remembered.

So began weeks of clandestine life in Switzerland. Once he had received proper medical attention, Frank split his time between the luxurious Hotel Bristol, and the flat of a couple he had been introduced to by Victor.

As Resistance members, Joan and Félix Fournier were also living a clandestine lifestyle. Their flat was a hive of under-ground activity. Total strangers slept on the floor most nights – couriers coming through the doghole at Mérandon's farm – who brought with them secret documents, money and coded messages.

While Joan hosted these couriers, her husband Félix was out raising money from his Swiss friends to buy weapons and uniforms for the Maquis. Félix would then run these weapons and uniforms into France, often on his own back through Chamonix on skis, where high altitudes meant permanent snow.

Although not in immediate danger, Frank had to remain a ghost in Geneva. He could not let the Swiss authorities discover his true identity. Disguised as a British diplomatic official, he toured the Swiss countryside with Victor, scouting potential drop zones for the SOE should Switzerland be invaded by Germany. Victor asked him to write an account of his time in France to be sent to England 'in the diplomatic bag', meaning it would not be censored.

'During those days,' said Frank, 'I went through a traumatic period of self-analysis. I was now fairly fit and while my facial scars showed, they didn't look too recent. If I wished, I could be interned with the other aircrews in Switzerland, but I knew it was my duty to get back to England and carry on with the war. But there was another reason that far transcended this call to duty and that was the strongest force in man; the desire to get back to a certain woman . . . and she was in England.'

Frank chose escape.

Nineteen days after Frank entered Switzerland, General Eisenhower announced that Italy had surrendered to the Allies. Hitler responded by taking over the Italians' occupation of south-east France, encircling Switzerland with the Wehrmacht in the process.

For Frank, this meant the next stage of his escape would involve evading highly motivated German troops, not the lacklustre Italians.

Victor created a new identity for him: Monsieur Victor Burnier of 7 Rue du Lac, Annecy, born 1908. This made Frank older than he was, necessary to explain why he had not been called up for forced labour in Germany. If asked about his scars, he would say he had been injured in the Fall of France in 1940. He now 'worked' for the Todt organisation, the Nazi company responsible for a range of engineering projects, which should let him travel freely.

Meanwhile MI9, a secret British organisation that assisted Allied forces escaping from behind enemy lines, worked up an audacious plan.

On any night in October, the BBC would broadcast a coded message that Victor's men would listening out for. When they heard it, Frank would be rowed from Geneva to the French section of Lake Geneva, where he would await the arrival of a Sunderland flying boat. Once the Sunderland had landed safely, he would clamber aboard and be flown home.

The hitch, it seemed, was not landing a gigantic Sunderland on Lake Geneva under the noses of the Germans in the middle of the night, but the fact there simply were not any available. The Battle of the Atlantic was still raging, with 88,000 tons of merchant shipping and two warships being sunk in September 1943 alone. Every available Sunderland was needed to escort Allied shipping, deter U-boat attacks

Frank briefing scientists and RAF airmen at RAF
Christchurch, Hampshire, where he was a test pilot
from November 1940 to April 1943.

RAF Tempsford, Churchill's secret airbase disguised as a farm in rural Bedfordshire. Frank was posted here in April 1943.

Senior officers of RAF Tangmere, Sussex, in 1943. Tangmere was the forward operating base for Special Duties Lysanders flying to and from occupied France; Tempsford was the 'home' base.

Frank doing what he did best.

Frank's flak-damaged Halifax bomber on the runway at RAF Tempsford
after a midnight mission over France.

The crew of Halifax JD180 – Codename 'O for Orange' –

Flying Officer Sydney
John Congdon, DFM.
Age 26. Navigator.

Pilot Officer Robert William
Peters, DFM. Age 22.
Wireless Operator.

Sergeant John Maden.
Age 20. Despatcher.

killed on *Operation Pimento*, 15 August 1943.

Flying Officer Roderick Alexander Mackenzie. Age 22. Second Pilot.

Sergeant Frederick Ronald Davies. Age 25. Flight Engineer.

Flight Sergeant Francis Pollard. Age 22. Rear Gunner.

An Italian soldier surveys the devastated *Villa du Fier* where Erminia Della-Vedova and her two young children perished in the flames.

Two Italian Alpini soldiers stand amidst the destruction. A corporal in the Alpini Mountain Infantry had downed Frank's low-flying Halifax with his Beretta while guarding Annecy barracks.

Opposite page left: The smoking ruins of Frank's Halifax after it crashed into a rural French village, killing all six crew and five civilians.

René Fontaine, the 14-year-old French boy who pushed Frank from the burning Halifax on his bicycle.

John D'Aujourd'hui, René's friend who helped get Frank to safety.

Angéline Fontaine, René's mother. She gave Frank first aid before hiding him in her chimney.

and recon the open seas. After weeks of back and forth, the plan was abandoned.

'No matter,' reasoned Victor to Frank in mid-October, 'we have worked up a new plan. We've organised a Lysander pickup for you somewhere in northern France. When London says so, we'll put you across the border in a town called Annemasse. There's a wall we've put people over before. The top of it is Switzerland, the bottom France.'

Victor continued, 'Once you're over the wall, walk into Annemasse with a handkerchief in your left hand. A gendarme will see this and come out to greet you. The gendarme will give you a first-class ticket to a town in northern France, via Paris. When you reach this town, go to the Café de la Paix, order a drink and pay for it with a 20-franc note with the number 4711 written on it in pencil.'

'The number on the cologne bottles?' quipped Frank.

'Exactly,' replied Victor. 'It's a Resistance café. A waiter will deliver you to your final destination, presumably a field somewhere. I don't know myself, only London does.'

'When do I go?' asked Frank.

'In the next few days,' said Victor.

Frank knew from his Tempsford experience that this new plan was going to be a close-run thing. There was only a day or two left of the moon period before the nights would be too dark for pickup in a Lysander aircraft, which he knew would be carried out by his friends in 161 Squadron back at Tempsford.

And that was assuming he would make it to this field somewhere in northern France.

Plenty could go wrong before that.

On 20 October, sixty-one days after Frank arrived in Switzerland, *La Bise* arrived. This northerly wind starts on the Swiss Plateau, blows south-west across Lake Geneva, strengthening between the Jura and Alpine mountains, before hitting Geneva squarely and infecting its residents with an end-of-summer melancholy.

Frank knew the Lysander plan inside out. It relied on several people executing their role. If one failed, the whole chain would be broken and Frank would be stranded. No single person in France knew the plan in full, only officials in London.

Leaving the Hotel Bristol for the final time, Frank walked to the British consulate where Victor worked. It was 5 p.m. and a soft rain was falling. He looked through people's front windows at men returning to their wives after work, with children cavorting around in front rooms. In the consulate, two young men were leaning against the counters talking in French. They nodded at Frank as he closed the door behind him. He nodded back.

Victor swept in. 'Hello, gentlemen,' he announced. 'I trust you're ready for France?'

'We're all going together?' asked Frank.

'Yes, last minute change, I'm afraid,' replied Victor. 'No need to discuss plans. It's all in hand.'

But Frank was annoyed. He was not told he would be smuggling himself back into France with two young men. Who were these blokes? He was sure they would attract more attention as a trio.

'I've got an address for you in case things break down in Paris and you need a bed,' said Victor, passing Frank a piece of paper. It had a long French phrase – presumably a password of some kind – underneath an address.

'This is a café near the station. Speak these words to a waiter and they'll know what to do. I'm sure you won't need it. Follow me.'

He led the trio outside to his car and got in the passenger seat while Frank and the two men got in the back. Pulling away from the consulate, Victor turned to face them.

'Here's 25,000 francs each,' he said, passing a small stack of notes over his shoulder. 'You'll be going over the border in a place called the Two Poplars. There'll be a Swiss border guard waiting for you. Remember, handkerchief in your left hand, Frank. You two, coats over your right shoulders.' The two men nodded.

Forty silent minutes later, the car stopped about 500 yards from a large country house. Just beyond it Frank could make out the border wire. It was more nerve-wracking crossing the border in this direction. At least there had been the promise of Switzerland when he went through the doghole, and he had greater belief in Colette than he had in these two men.

'Okay, chaps, walking from here,' said Victor. 'Go to the far wall of this house. Someone will be waiting for you.' There was a round of handshakes before Frank and the two men stepped out into the gloaming.

Frank thought he may as well ask these boys their names, as they were about to go over the border together. 'Joe' and 'Freddie', they replied, exchanging a few pleasantries while they waited beside the house. Fog was collecting in the garden, smothering what little light was left in the day.

A man arrived. 'See that guard over there?' he said, pointing to the bottom of the garden, where a figure stood by two large trees, his silhouette just visible. 'Go to him. Keep your heads down.' The trio crouch-jogged across the garden. The fog made Frank feel secure, more hidden, but his mouth was terribly dry.

They arrived at the two trees. The guard, in a thick German accent, said, 'In this place, between these two trees, is the border. There is a small wall you must climb down into France, so be careful. The German patrol just went by, so they will not return for another fifteen minutes. *Bon voyage.*'

Joe and Freddie went first, dropping into the foggy twilight of France. Frank followed, but he did not expect such a drop. The moment his feet hit the concrete – his first touch of French soil in almost three months – his legs crumpled. Pain fired up his spine into his neck and shoulder blades. His back injury meant he was no good at jumping off things. Joe and Freddie crouched over him for several minutes before he could stand up. Hardly a great start, thought Frank, as he hobbled into France.

After fifty yards the road turned a corner and the men walked straight into a gendarme standing outside a sentry box.

'Papers, please,' said the gendarme.

Frank handed over his *carte d'identité*, trying to remember to respond to the name Victor Burnier. The gendarme opened it. Frank's stomach dropped. The *carte d'identité* stared back at them, empty. It had not been filled in.

But the gendarme clearly knew what was going on. He handed the papers back to Frank and said, 'Thank you, sir. You better get that filled in.'

Joe and Freddie handed theirs over, telling the gendarme they had been visiting their sister in Saint-Cergues.

'*Merci. Bonsoir,*' said the gendarme, handing their papers back. They continued walking, Frank squeezing his handkerchief like a boxer does to his hand wrap.

Tense minutes passed as the trio walked on into the fog. Will my contact be put off by the sight of three men instead of one, thought Frank. Can they even see me in this fog? Could I walk all the way back to the doghole before dawn? He felt the piece of paper with the Paris safehouse address in his pocket slowly burning a hole into his leg.

'*Halt!*' called a voice firmly from somewhere nearby in the fog. 'Turn out your pockets.'

The sharpness of the syllables betrayed seriousness, but Frank realised they were being directed at two youths on bicycles off to their left. A pair of German soldiers were frisking the two lads. Walk normally, Frank told himself, remembering Quino's advice for his walk to the doghole with Colette. The Germans will shoot first and ask questions second.

The fog thickened. The light faded. After fifteen more minutes wandering, Frank broke the febrile atmosphere.

'We've only got half an hour before curfew. I say we cut the wire and head back into Switzerland.'

'Have you heard of a place called the "Garage Savoie"?' Freddie replied. 'I've heard it's friendly. Let's try to find it before giving up.'

Joe agreed and so it was decided two to one.

Joe and Freddie both spoke French, so they began asking civilians for directions to the Garage Savoie. But not everyone had heard of it, and the ones who had were giving differing directions. It was now twenty minutes until curfew.

'I'm going back to the border. Are you coming?' said Frank.

'Okay, sure, let's do it. We must have missed our contacts in this fog,' replied Freddie.

The trio began retracing their steps, but had barely made it ten yards before a different gendarme stepped out of the shadows.

'*Bonsoir*. Papers please.'

Joe and Freddie handed theirs over. Frank, turning away from the gendarme slightly, put his Paris address note in his mouth and prepared himself to swallow. This one seemed like he meant business.

'Where are you going?' he asked.

'Garage Savoie,' from Freddie.

'Where have you come from?'

'Saint-Cergues, my sister's house.'

'I don't believe you,' said the gendarme. 'You've just crossed the frontier, haven't you?'

Frank swallowed the piece of paper.

'My mouth was bone dry and I just don't know how it went down,' he recalled. As the edges of the paper scraped down his throat, Freddie and Joe protested their innocence loudly at the gendarme. To their great surprise, he handed back their papers.

'Okay, okay,' he said. 'The Garage Savoie is about three kilometres that way. You'll have to be quick if you want to make it before curfew.'

Hearts pounding, the three men power-walked back to Annemasse. It was almost completely dark. Off-duty German soldiers wandered around the streets. Freddie asked more civilians for directions, but none of them knew the Garage Savoie.

'Only ten minutes to curfew,' Frank said. 'I'm walking back to Switzerland. Are you coming?'

'Let's go,' said Joe to Freddie. 'No one knows where the Garage Savoie is and our contact has obviously failed to show.'

Freddie looked as though he was about to agree, but fixated on something over Frank and Joe's shoulders.

'Has that man on a bike been following us?' he asked.

Frank turned slowly, realising this was not the first time he had seen this shadowy figure either. But no one had time to say anything further, as the cyclist was approaching. He stopped a few feet in front of them, fog swirling around the tails of his overcoat.

'Are you looking for the Garage Savoie?' said the man. His scarf muffled the question so it was barely audible.

'Yes,' replied Freddie. 'Do you know Victor?'

'Yes, I know of him,' said the man. 'You'd better come with me.'

The man got on his bike, gave a half-turn of the pedals and slowly slid away into the fog.

'What do we do?' whispered Joe.

'Follow him,' Freddie reasoned. 'If he knows Victor we'll be fine. It's not like we've got a lot of options.' He was a natural leader, Frank thought.

The trio set off in pursuit of the bike. After a few hundred yards, the man stopped outside a block of flats, secured his bike in a basement and with the men following, climbed to the fourth floor. He rang a doorbell. A short, anxious-looking woman opened the door and hurried them all inside, before closing the door firmly.

As it swung shut, Frank saw two gendarme uniforms hung on the back of the door. *Trapped.*

But something about the woman did not fit. 'The enthusiasm on her face . . . it's something you can't explain, but you just know they're on your side,' remembered Frank. She hurried the trio into her kitchen, where the man on the bike was taking off his overcoat, revealing a full gendarme uniform underneath. *What on earth was going on?*

'*Bonsoir.* I am Monsieur Roche,' said the man, extending a bony, delicate hand.

'Don't worry, I'm on your side. At least I think so. You've just crossed the border, correct?'

Nobody reacted.

'Well, I think so. When I was coming off duty tonight, a colleague told me he'd seen three men wandering around asking for the Garage Savoie. I went home and put this coat on and came to see if I could find you. I thought you might shoot me if I kept the uniform on,' he said, smiling. Roche explained he needed to cross-examine everyone before they could all have dinner. He turned to Frank first.

'I'm RAF,' he explained. 'I crashed near Annecy two months ago . . .'

Roche leaped to his feet and began pumping Frank's hand like a carjack. 'You are the pilot who survived! What an honour! I can't believe you are in my flat. You're the hero who's been bringing weapons for our fighters! Thank you!'

The gushing went on. Eventually Frank cut in, 'Thank you, thank you, that's very kind – but I was supposed to go to Paris tonight and go back to England via pickup tomorrow.'

'Not possible,' replied Roche. 'I'll need to arrange new transport, but I can't do it in time tonight. Stay here tonight, we'll have dinner and sort something out.'

Frank turned to Joe and Freddie, who both had funny looks on their faces.

'Does the word "Samoyède" mean anything to you?' Freddie asked.

Frank made the link immediately. Samoyède was the name of an operation he had flown a few months ago. These boys must be agents. Not only that, they must have been dropped by the Tempsford Squadrons.

Over the next few minutes, the men worked out that Frank had dropped supplies to Freddie's resistance unit 400 miles away in Belgium, before he had been compromised and forced to go on the run.

Joe, the quieter of the two until now, interrupted, 'When I came over my pilot dropped me seven miles from my target. I had to spend the night lying under a hedge in the rain sipping my brandy ration. It was hell – because of you lot!' The atmosphere was convivial. 'And why do you have to go round and round the reception party, waking up the entire area? Everyone knows we're coming before we even leave the aircraft.'

Frank tried to explain how difficult low-level night flying was, and that if they strayed from their planned route just a little, they would get a bellyful of flak.

'You can't just turn a Halifax round like a jeep. It's a bloody big aircraft.'

Monsieur Roche sat smiling. He had a British pilot and two spies in his flat. Soon everyone was sat around Madame Roche's table, tucking into a wonderful meal made with ingredients she had procured on the black market.

The Roches were Corsican, anti-Italian, and lived off black-market trade between Switzerland and France. Frank liked them enormously. They told the trio how tense Annemasse was currently and what a bad time it was to cross the border. Colonel d'Oisa, the Resistance leader in the area who had visited Frank in Ma Baraque, had been captured three days earlier and imprisoned with some other guerillas in the Hotel Pax just down the road.

Hundreds of Resistance fighters had since come down from the mountains ready to attack the hotel. This had reached the ears of the Gestapo headquarters in Lyon, who upped their presence in Annemasse. Their leader, SS Officer Klaus Barbie, who was building a reputation for personally torturing French Resistance members with barbaric methods, was in town.

Suddenly the Tempsford joking seemed very silly. Although no one said it, Joe, Freddie and Frank knew Monsieur and Madame Roche would be brutally tortured by Barbie if they were caught harbouring them.

The next morning, the trio awoke to find no one at home. A man entered without knocking and introduced himself as Girard, 'one of Victor's men'. Girard explained the Paris plan was out of the question. The trainline from Annemasse to Paris was too risky. It kept getting strafed by Allied fighters for a start.

The new plan, Girard revealed, was to head south, away from Britain, to the Pyrenees Mountains separating France from Spain. His best courier was coming up to Annemasse in a few days' time. She would need to meet Frank first, but if he passed her vetting, she would deliver him to the Pyrenees. Joe and Freddie would have to stay behind, though. She only dealt in bona fide airmen, not the shadowy world of espionage.

During their stint in Annemasse, the trio ate most of their meals in the little café opposite Roche's flat. It had all been fixed and the café was Resistance-aligned. The food was good, but Frank was totally unable to enjoy it. He had to remain silent while Joe and Freddie talked in French. Worst of all was trying to remember all the tips the two agents had given him for 'eating, ordering and paying like a Frenchman'.

On Frank's third day in Annemasse, a hush fell over the café as the trio were finishing their lunch. 'We heard the tramping of feet outside and about twenty men and women walked past handcuffed together with a gendarme at either end,' recalled Frank. They were being taken to the Pax Hotel – the Gestapo headquarters – to face Klaus Barbie and his murderous cronies.

'As the procession went past, all conversation in the café ceased and each man seemed to say a prayer to himself,' wrote Frank. 'There was a terrible loathing in their eyes, and I felt that I would hate to be a German on the day of liberation.' A few minutes later, a German NCO lurched into the bar and ordered a round of schnapps. He looked around the café and spotting the three men, cried, 'Friends, drink with me!'

Joe and Freddie, trained in espionage, chatted politely to the slurring drunk, shielding Frank from conversation. Eventually, some of the soldier's colleagues entered and he lost interest in the trio. Frank, Joe and Freddie tipped back their schnapps, wandered to the door and stepped outside, breathing heavily.

It was a beautiful clear day, only marred by the fact the streets were filled with off-duty Germans. Frank wanted to sprint as far as he could in the other direction, but followed Joe and Freddie's lead, walking slowly back to Roche's flat.

That night, Frank lay awake. 'I was thinking of those poor wretches in the Pax Hotel.' Untold horrors were happening in its cellars, which had been adapted as cells. All the usual methods of torture were being used to extract information.

The desire to get out of Annemasse burned a little brighter.

CHAPTER 6

THE QUEEN OF THE PYRENEES

After five days in the Roches' Annemasse flat, Girard returned with the courier.

Leaning heavily on a cane, she hobbled into the kitchen where Frank, Joe and Freddie were sat around the table. She heaved an enormous bag onto it with a thud. The stench of cigarette smoke – and was that cheese? – followed closely behind her. A straw hat laden with exotic feathers and fake fruit teetered on her head.

'Which one of you claims to be RAF?' she barked, revealing two large, yellowy front teeth.

Frank lifted his hand a few inches. A mangy black cat padded into the room and brushed against the woman's leg. Ignoring Frank, the elderly woman turned to the cat and said gently, '*Mifouf!* Clever boy! Would you like some water?' She was still wheezing from climbing the stairs.

Frank watched as she went to a cupboard, took out a bowl, filled it with water and put it on the ground, stroking the mangy Mifouf with two arthritic fingers, whispering softly. She must be in her sixties, Frank thought, and she did not shake my hand. Returning to the table, the woman opened her bulging bag, took out an ivory cigarette holder, placed a cigarette in it and lit it. She took a couple of deep drags.

'What is your name? Where have you come from?' Her

breathing was ragged. 'Who have you been in contact with so far?' Freddie translated the questions into English.

'My name is Frank Griffiths,' said the Welshman. 'I'm a squadron leader. I crashed near Annecy two months ago.' Usually this sparked a reaction, but there was no warm reception this time, no pumping handshakes or cries of '*Quel honneur!*'

Frank continued, 'I got away to Switzerland and spent time with Victor.' He hoped the magic name might ease fears that he was a German stoolpigeon.

But she looked unimpressed. 'How did you re-enter France?' she snapped. 'What squadron were you in? Where were you based?'

'I can't tell you that,' said Frank. All RAF aircrew had been trained to only give their name, rank and number.

'I said what squadron! Where did you fly from!' thundered the woman, her voice deep from years of tobacco smoke.

Frank looked around the room for support. Was this really happening? Freddie and Joe looked perplexed and Girard, the man who had organised the meeting, merely stared at his feet.

There were a few moments' silence before the woman grunted, shrugged aggressively, snapped her bag shut and departed without so much as a word, Mifouf in toe.

'What the bloody hell was that about?' asked Frank, after the door closed behind her.

Girard smiled. 'She's cautious. We'll try again tomorrow.'

Françoise Dissard was no ordinary woman.

The next morning, 22 October, Girard returned with Françoise, and a slab of a man whom she did not introduce. While she sat at the table, the beefcake stood in the corner eyeing Frank.

'If you want my help, tell me the number of your squadron,' said Françoise. She was wearing an enormous shawl covered in cat hair and looked nothing like the eccentric aristocrat of yesterday.

'I told you yesterday, I can't. We're not allowed.' The beef-cake blinked.

'Where is your base?' she said sharply.

'All I can tell you is my name is Frank Cromwell Griffiths, my service number is 37967 and my rank is squadron leader. *Commandant,*' he added, somewhat desperately.

It suddenly dawned on Frank he had not shown her his identity discs. 'Wait,' said Frank, seeing Françoise was about to fire back. He undid a shirt button and leaned forward so she could see them hanging around his neck.

Françoise balked. 'Who gave them to you? Did you steal them from someone?' Frank felt the temperature rising. This was hopeless. The beefcake would not stop looking at him.

Joe intervened, 'But he came out of Switzerland with us.'

Françoise snorted. 'So? That means nothing.' She removed her cigarette from the corner of her mouth and leaned forward, staring into Frank's eyes.

'Are you married?' she asked. Her breath reeked of tobacco and coffee and her eyes were heavily bloodshot. Frank nodded. 'What was the date of your marriage?'

Frank paused, it was not a military question, and things were pretty desperate.

'Thirtieth of August 1941,' he replied.

The moment the words left his mouth, a smile spread over Françoise's face and she extended a hand to him. All tension evaporated. 'Obviously she had been in touch with England and asked for some security check so she could ensure I wasn't a stoolpigeon,' recalled Frank.

Girard laughed easily and even the beefcake cracked a smile. Françoise dismissed him. She explained to Frank she had brought the man to rough him up if he gave the wrong answers. Madame Roche entered and, sensing the convivial atmosphere, produced a bottle of marc, pouring drinks for everyone despite the fact it was 10 a.m.

Françoise turned to Frank. 'You will now be going back to England via the Pyrenees and Spain. This afternoon we will catch an overnight train to Toulouse, first class. I have guides who will take you from there over the mountains. Don't forget your toothbrush.'

Already Frank was beginning to realise why Girard thought her the best in the business. This elderly woman, who yesterday had looked like an eccentric grandmother, had transformed herself overnight into a recluse covered in cat hair. He would learn later that she was called 'The Queen of the Pyrenees' by American airmen escaping France.

'We will take the slower Tarascon Junction route to avoid Lyon,' continued Françoise. 'I will pay you no attention and you will do the same to me. We don't know each other. If you're questioned, I will not help you. If you're arrested, do not look at me. There's nothing I can do at that point anyway. All you need to do is follow my lead and don't be an idiot.'

What a marvellous character, Frank thought. Only ten minutes ago she had been raking him with fierce cross-examination, her thug ready to beat him up if he failed to pass muster.

'As for you two,' she said to Joe and Freddie, 'Girard has a plan for you. My organisation helps only RAF and USAAF – no exceptions.'

Girard returned after lunch with Frank's ticket to Toulouse and a copy of *Le Signal*, a pro-German magazine designed to deter train passengers from speaking to him. Frank approached Monsieur Roche to pay him for his board and lodging.

'I can't thank you and your wife enough ...' he began, thrusting 500 francs on him.

'No, no. Absolutely not,' replied Monsieur Roche, pushing the money back. 'You go back to England and kill some more Germans for me and I'll be more than satisfied.'

There was nothing left but to say goodbye to Joe and Freddie. After his initial mistrust, Frank had grown to enjoy their company and had utmost faith in them. Apart from their physical appearances, Frank knew precious little about them. Their names were almost certainly fake. This was probably the last time he would ever see them, he thought, shaking their hands and turning to leave.

It was time to catch the train. Leaving the Roches' flat, Girard and Frank strolled towards the station, milling amongst throngs of off-duty German soldiers. Frank could see a gendarme checking papers in the main entrance to the station, but Girard was already steering him to some other entrance. Slipping down a back alley, Girard ushered Frank into a side door that led to a small room at the back of the station buffet.

'In half an hour we'll go sit at that table,' announced Girard, pointing to one right out front. 'Another gendarme will come and sit with us. Pretend to talk for a while, then when your train arrives, he'll escort you to your seat so no one will come asking questions.'

Frank's watch hands seemed to race the next hour. At 5 p.m., his train arrived. Girard, the gendarme and Frank got up and waited outside their carriage. Françoise arrived and, without taking a blind bit of notice of them, boarded the train, muttering curses about travelling conditions, her bag and life in general. She drew all attention onto herself.

Frank followed her onto the train and into a carriage compartment, where he took a seat in the corner. He just had time to take in the purple upholstery, the luggage racks overhead and the two sliding windows before another passenger opened the compartment door. As instructed, he put his head in his right hand, rested both against the window and pretended to fall asleep.

'I didn't want anyone to ask me any questions,' he explained. 'French people are so chatty ... It can be difficult to stop them confiding their entire family history to you when travelling.' Eyes shut, Frank counted the door slide open another three times. He felt the cushion depress as someone sat next to him. *Trapped.*

Peeking between his fingers, Frank saw the platform swarming with German soldiers, many of whom were demanding passengers open their luggage. But Germans were not Frank and Françoise's main concern. From the sea of passengers, he could see several blue tunics and navy berets bobbing in the crowd, patrolling the platform like sharks in the shallows. Milice officers.

These men belonged to the Vichy government's fascist paramilitary arm. It was the Milice's job to hunt down Jews and Resistance fighters for the Germans. They were often more effective than the Gestapo. As native Frenchmen, Milice officers spoke local dialects, knew more about the towns and countryside and had informants in the local population.

After what seemed an age, the train lurched away from the platform. Frank could hear Françoise sucking on her ivory cigarette holder, muttering to herself like a batty old lady. Others chatted in the carriage – *two women and a man,* Frank clocked. He was beginning to build a picture of them when the train stopped and he sensed Françoise get off.

What is she doing? He hurried after her, keeping a distance while she struggled with her bag. La Roche-sur-Foron, read a sign. She boarded another train and soon they were heading south towards Annecy, the town Frank had lost his first engine over. He desperately wanted to check with Françoise that everything was okay. She had not acknowledged his presence once.

At Annecy, Frank sensed her leave again. He opened his eyes and went to get up, but realised just in time that her enormous bag had stayed put. He relaxed, but it was too late. An old man in the corner saw he was awake and asked, '*Annecy?*'

'*Oui*,' Frank replied, cursing himself the moment the word left his mouth. He had broken a golden rule. The old boy began questioning Frank in French, none of which he understood. *Please come back, Françoise . . .*

The compartment door slid open. Frank looked up gratefully, but instead of Françoise he saw a blue tunic entering their compartment. A Milice officer. 'Better a carriage full of Germans than this viper,' Frank recorded, 'who being local was likely to spot I was phoney.' At least the old boy had fallen silent at the sight of the blue tunic.

Seconds later, Françoise entered. She must have seen the Milice man and hurried back, Frank thought. Grumbling audibly, she reached up to her bag and took out Mifouf, her mangy cat. The distraction allowed Frank to pretend to go back to sleep. But every sense was firing on full alert. Remaining still and lifeless was agony. Frank was sure the Milice man was going to hear his heart pounding on his ribs.

The door opened and Frank heard multiple pairs of shoes enter the compartment, accompanied by children's voices. A family? The train pulled away.

'Does anyone mind if I switch off the light?' someone said, presumably the Milice officer. There was a general murmur of agreement and Frank sensed the carriage fall dark from behind his eyelids.

For the first time in two hours, Frank opened his eyes. With Françoise, the Milice man and a family of three, the compartment was full. Françoise brushed her foot against Frank's. It felt terrific to be acknowledged. He stretched his legs and arms and peered into the blackness enveloping the countryside. Poor night for flying, he thought.

By 11 p.m., everyone was asleep. The child next to Frank, asleep in his father's arms, parked his legs on Frank's chest. He was delicately manoeuvring the limbs when Françoise gave a mighty snore. 'She made such a racket I thought she might be ill and I was seized with fear that she might die in her sleep,' remembered Frank. 'At the rate she smoked cigarettes, I didn't think she'd last long.'

The door slid open. 'Tickets please.'

Shafts of light spilled into the compartment like searchlights. The only one awake, Frank had his ticket ready first. The controller took one look at it and said, 'Why didn't you go on the Toulouse Express via Lyon?'

Frank swallowed. Whatever answer he gave, the Milice officer would be listening closely.

'I'm for Toulouse too,' Françoise said quickly. 'I missed the train in Annemasse and they said this was the quickest way via Tarascon. Were you the same?' she asked Frank. He nodded. *Saved.*

The controller bought it and clipped the tickets. Frank glanced at the Milicien, but he was too groggy to care. The ticket man left and Françoise followed him.

Grenoble approached, the most dangerous point of the journey owing to its many checkpoints. It was past midnight. Frank's eyelids drooped, but adrenaline kept him awake. Françoise's nose was firing on all cylinders. Frank was counting the seconds between snores when the door was flung open and the light turned on, revealing the bulky frame of a German NCO.

'*Cartes d'identité, s'il vous plaît,*' said the German crisply. So this is the dreaded German control, thought Frank. He forced himself to yawn and take a long time searching for his card.

My name is Victor Burnier, he told himself. My name is Victor Burnier.

The NCO checked the family's cards, chatting ably in French. He turned to Frank, who held out his card. *Don't let your hand tremble.*

The fat German stared at it for a while, handed it back, said, '*Merci,*' and switched off the light. *That was it!* Françoise brushed her foot against Frank's. He felt like jumping up and kissing her.

At 3 a.m., the train pulled into Grenoble. On the dimly lit platform, Frank could make out a German officer in full uniform with a majestically dressed woman wrapped around his arm. Disturbingly, they walked towards the door nearest their compartment. A muffled argument broke out in the corridor. The controller seemed to be telling them there were no more first-class seats available.

The door was wrenched open.

'Tell two of them to give up their seats then,' demanded the officer to the controller. Frank feigned sleep, but Françoise was having none of it.

'Where do you think you are!' she roared. 'Berlin?'

Frank opened his eyes. No one could pretend to sleep through this. The officer looked taken aback, but his lady, dressed in thick furs and lavish jewellery, was outraged.

'We paid for these seats and we were here first,' Françoise growled at the controller, daring him to move her.

Why must she argue? thought Frank. They can have my seat. I don't care, just no questions please . . .

The fur-clad woman seethed and a bitter argument ensued. Frank, being eyed by the Milice officer, scratched his chin with his copy of *Le Signal.* The controller stepped in.

'Madame, Monsieur, please have my bunk in my compartment,' he said. 'It is more comfortable anyway.' Grudgingly, the German couple withdrew. Françoise continued cursing under her breath. Frank took a couple of deep inbreaths through his nose. The train rumbled on.

'Passengers for Avignon and Toulouse, change please,' called the controller thirty minutes later. Frank noticed a flicker of a smile on his face as he and Françoise disembarked into the darkness. *He must be in the know.*

They had to clamber across the track to catch the next train. Françoise struggled with her bag until Frank could not bear it anymore and helped her. It was ridiculously heavy. What's in here, Sten guns? thought Frank. A blast of steam sounded and the train groaned. He ran alongside, heaved the bag aboard and pulled Françoise on in the nick of time. Just like the fur-clad German lady, Françoise demanded the controller find them seats.

'Okay, follow me,' said the controller. He slid open the first carriage door he passed and looked inside. 'There are two seats in here.' Françoise and Frank stepped inside the dark compartment, but Frank sensed her pause momentarily.

Looking around at the sleeping bodies, a terrible realisation came over him. The four bodies were wearing Luftwaffe uniforms. A crew on their way to Toulouse. Retreating from the carriage would be too suspicious, so Françoise took her seat. Like a gazelle tiptoeing across a crocodile-infested river, Frank followed her and sat by the window.

Dawn broke. From between Frank's fingers, flashes of the Mediterranean Sea shot past before the train turned inland up the Carcassonne valley, slowing for its final approach to Toulouse – the gateway to the Pyrenees. The Luftwaffe boys, who had slept all the way, left in a hurry. Françoise followed cautiously and then Frank, his mouth like sandpaper. He was exhausted.

The exits were all covered by Germans or gendarmes. Unable to talk to each other, Frank followed Françoise's lead, certain he was going to feel a hand on his shoulder at any moment. Françoise marched purposefully towards the meekest-looking gendarme who, putting his arm out to stop her, received a piercing earful.

'How dare you stop an elderly woman like me!' she shouted. 'Do you think I'm a terrorist? Can't you see I'm struggling with my bag already?'

Frank knew a cue when he saw one. While everyone crowded around Françoise, he casually strolled out of the exit like a railwayman coming off duty. He had no idea where he was but, fighting the urge to leap for joy, he continued to the far side of the square, turned down a side street and stopped to watch the station exit.

Passengers emerged slowly. Must be a thorough search, thought Frank. Eventually Françoise materialised, with none other than the gendarme himself carrying her bag. She was still remonstrating with him while he desperately hailed a fiacre, a horse-drawn carriage, to take her away.

Françoise clocked Frank and ordered the cabby across the square. She looked at him without a flicker of recognition as they went past. Frank sprinted down the street after her, whereupon the carriage stopped. 'Would you like a lift?' said Françoise.

Twenty minutes later, deep in the outskirts of the city, Françoise told the cabby to stop. She paid him and walked off up the street, Frank following. Once the carriage was out of sight, she turned and went in the opposite direction, whispering to Frank as she passed him, 'I'll walk ahead. When I point at a door, wait outside it.' He did as he was told.

Standing beside the large iron door where Françoise had gestured, Frank heard the scraping of metal bolts being slid back. A tall, red-headed woman in her mid-fifties opened the door. In a thick Irish accent, the woman said, 'Will you be waitin' here while I go in the house and let you in the side door?' She disappeared back into the house.

It was the first proper English Frank had heard in a week. A side door creaked open and he stepped inside. The house was a higgledy-piggledy mess of half-chopped onions, open tins, discarded knitting and dirty dishes. The furniture was crammed into the low-ceilinged room and an array of weird and wonderful paintings lined the walls.

Where the hell am I? Where's Françoise? Frank's eyes raced around the room, stopping suddenly on a strange-looking person standing in the far doorway. The tall, lanky figure lumbered towards him with an outstretched hand.

'How,' he said.

Looking up at the lanky figure's face, Frank saw a man who could be aged anywhere between eighteen and forty.

'How,' said the figure again, clenching Frank's hand with one of his long, pipe-cleaner arms. He was easily north of six foot and had a deeply tanned, lightly scarred face with youthful blue eyes and a razor-sharp jawline.

'Frank Griffiths, RAF,' said the Welshman, suddenly aware of his small hands. This guy had a certain swagger, even if he was too big for the room. He wore a blue, zip-fastened golfing jacket, jeans and enormous black boots. He looked like a gardener or maybe the odd-job man.

'Oh, you're English! Thank god, I got someone to talk to,' said the figure loudly, realising his new acquaintance was not French. 'Haven't had a proper conversation in weeks.' He spoke in a thick New York accent and already Frank could tell he was at odds with every element of clandestine life.

'Who won, the Yankees or the Cardinals?' asked the American.

'I'm afraid I haven't a clue,' Frank replied. 'Is that baseball?'

'Whadya mean, "Is that baseball"?' the New Yorker roared. 'I can't get news of the World Series out here.'

He strolled over to a crowded windowsill and picked up a radio in one of his bucket hands.

'Joe Manos, by the way. Eighth Air Force. You know Bury St Edmunds? That's where we flew from. Goddamn boring place. Impossible to get passes for London. How'd you end up here?' he added as an afterthought. It was a shock hearing the staccato New York accent.

'I was shot down near Annecy,' said Frank. 'Lost my crew but managed to get to Switzerland and now here.' Joe had switched the radio on and was trying to tune it.

'Gee, sorry. You were the pilot?' he asked over the radio's crackling. Frank nodded.

'That's cool. I'm a tail gunner. Joined up for the war, but I'm gonna stick with the Air Force though. I love it,' said Joe smiling, revealing a full row of healthy teeth.

'How did you end up here?' asked Frank, enthralled by this young, seemingly carefree American.

'My Fort [*Flying Fortress*] got hit raiding Le Bourget near Paris. Two FW 190s attacked us head-on. Didn't realise my crew had baled until I spoke on the radio and no one replied. The bell had been ringing, but ya can't hear a thing as a tail gunner. I'm gonna tell 'em that when I get back.'

Joe told the story as though it was such a minor inconvenience, it was almost not worth the breath.

'Yeah! This is a good one,' he shouted suddenly, as the radio picked up Tommy Dorsey's 'In the Blue of Evening'. Joe rocked his head up and down for a few moments.

He then resumed his story. He recounted to Frank how he landed in a park, folded his parachute under a bench and, thinking he was to become a prisoner, walked to the nearest bar and ordered a beer, in English. The barman took one look at him, a six-foot-four nineteen-year-old American, and summoned his Maquis comrades. They gave Joe French clothes and took him in.

'That was July 14th, and here I am still in France. Been in this place a week. Everything takes freakin' ages 'round here.'

Frank listened spellbound. It was like meeting an alien. Joe fit almost every stereotype the snobbish RAF held of Americans. *Overpaid, oversexed and over here.*

'How old are you?' asked Frank.

'Nineteen,' said Joe. Frank was thinking about what he was doing at that age, when the tall Irish woman entered the room.

'Ah, Joe, what did I tell you about that radio? If you must be listenin' to it, keep it away from the window, will you?' Joe stood up and lolloped away. He was an absolute beanpole.

'Frank, is it? Pleased to meet you. I'm Thérèse,' she said, tackling the washing-up pile. 'I've told Joe to shift his stuff. Françoise says you're a squadron leader. And you're older.'

She spoke quickly and efficiently and although clearly Irish, the names Françoise and Thérèse came out in a perfect French accent.

'He's a bleedin' pain,' she said, rattling the dishes. 'Won't do a thing I say. Blasts that radio and winds the cat up constantly. I can't wait to be rid of him.'

Even stooping at the sink, Thérèse was taller than Frank. Her long red hair and pale skin made her country of origin easy to place. She wore thick black glasses, which made her eyes look swollen and a tatty woolly jumper covered in cat hair.

'Can I help?' asked Frank. Thérèse turned and gave him the look of someone who did not get asked that question very often.

'Yes!' she cried, launching a dishcloth his way. 'Start with these.'

As the pair worked, Thérèse told him a little of her life and war working for the Allies. She had been in the Resistance since the very beginning but, as a six-foot, red-headed Irish woman, was too distinctive for espionage. Befriended by Dissard, she ran Françoise's safehouse in Toulouse instead, hiding, feeding and conditioning escaping airmen for their arduous trek over the mountains into Spain.

Toulouse, close to the Pyrenees and a hub of the Resistance, was the perfect place for a safehouse. Most locals seemed to think these eccentric, middle-aged women were a couple of spinsters. But in reality they had harboured hundreds of highly valuable airmen, and the safehouse was a vital launch-pad for men taking the 'Chemin de la Liberté', France's most famous – and most brutal – escape route through the heart of the Pyrenees.

'Most of them are good as gold, but there can be a fair bit of waiting to be done,' explained Thérèse, wringing out her cloth. 'That's when they cause me problems. I know how to handle it, though. Would you be wantin' any pepper with the stew? Got some on the black market yesterday.' Frank nodded and sat down at the table. Thérèse called for Joe and ladled out three bowls of stew.

Joe strode towards the table and flung himself down in a chair. 'Hey, what's this rank squadron leader in our army? Theresa's naggin' me to move my stuff.' He made no effort to pronounce her name.

'Major,' replied Frank.

'Gee, that's rank. Better shift my things,' Joe said. He fell on his stew like a soldier emerging from the siege of Stalingrad, clearing his bowl in minutes. Then he tried to turn the radio on, but Thérèse was having none of it. They had a short row and he stalked off to his room, leaving his chair untucked. Frank, more open-minded than most, found himself seriously disliking this American.

Noticing his drooping eyelids, Thérèse insisted that Frank go to bed as soon as he had finished lunch. He was exhausted from the night's tense train journey.

Sliding under the blanket, he caught himself wondering whether this was all real – his chain-smoking escort, the compartment full of Luftwaffe aircrew, the tall Irish woman and the loutish American teenager.

CHAPTER 7

THE MOUNTAINS BECKON

By Frank's fourth morning at the safehouse, 26 October, he knew the drill. After descending the stairs, he would turn straight back around and climb them on his tiptoes. Then repeat it twenty-four times. Thérèse made each of 'her' airmen do this twenty-five times before she would serve them a meal. It was her way of getting them fit for the mountains. Frank's calves burned with the effort, but he knew he must take it seriously. His period of recovery in Switzerland had left him very unfit.

Joe, however, did not enjoy taking exercise.

'I don't need this crap,' he muttered, walking up the stairs normally, pretending to do the exercise. 'I can handle the mountains no problem. I grew up in westside Manhattan. I'm tough.' The pair walked into the kitchen, Frank rather gingerly, and sat at the table.

Frank got on better with Joe than Thérèse did, but his brash manner infuriated him at times. It also scared him. After being in France for such a long time, Joe was fearless. But the sheer bravado of his habits – like listening to illegal BBC broadcasts on the radio, or wandering around the streets when he should be keeping his head down – could get them both arrested. Frank had mixed with folk from all walks of life, but Joe was testing his patience.

Joe did at least have a bit of respect for Frank. Even if he was a stuck-up, aged Brit with bad teeth, Joe knew he was an experienced squadron leader who had flown a staggering list of aircraft, including some cool American ones. If there was one thing Joe loved other than baseball, it was aircraft. From polar-opposite backgrounds, this gave them something to talk about.

'Say, Theresa, when are we outta here?' Joe called.

She set down two bowls of watery porridge and looked at him gleefully. 'Soon. Françoise is comin' today to tell you the plan. That could be her now,' she said, leaving to check who was knocking on the courtyard door. Joe began wolfing his porridge while Frank rubbed his calves.

Thérèse burst back in, her eyes wild and worried. 'Germans! Quick, into the back room the pair of you! Don't come out till I say.' The men scarpered but Frank, slipping on some water on the floor, crashed to the ground on his bad shoulder. Terrible, exquisite pain overcame him as he swallowed his scream. Joe turned around and picked him up as if he was sack of potatoes and carried him into the back room.

A few minutes later, Thérèse opened the door to the room. 'All clear! Only the bleedin' grocery boy, the Germans happened to be askin' him for directions just after he'd knocked on the door . . .' she trailed off. 'What the devil happened?' she asked, seeing Frank wincing while Joe stood by. 'This small incident put my arm back weeks,' wrote Frank.

Françoise arrived with Mifouf in tow, who was wearing a red coat. It was a mangy looking cat at the best of times and somehow the coat made it seem even more pathetic. Joe fell about laughing and teasing Mifouf while Françoise, who had clearly knitted the coat, raked him with fearsome French curses, not a word of which he understood.

She put a cigarette in her holder and lit it, staring menacingly at Joe.

'Tomorrow we will travel to Perpignan,' she said, wheezing slightly from the verbal barrage she had just unleashed. 'From there you'll start your journey over the mountains. You're with me,' she said gesturing at Frank, 'the American is going with another escort.' Joe looked uninterested. 'Don't talk to each other. Don't acknowledge each other. These papers will get you through the controls.'

Frank studied his new identity. He was to become Monsieur Henri Sylvestre. Joe's cover was less convincing. Some of his more boyish features made him firmly of the age that would have seen him called up for forced labour in Germany. His alias – Edouard Machot – was an off-duty railwayman, one of the few jobs protected from the labour draft.

'We leave at eight a.m. tomorrow,' said Françoise, daring Joe to crack a joke, ask a question, or do literally anything.

Wednesday, 27 October, dawned. 'At last we were to be on our way again,' recalled Frank, who was keen to get into the mountains and countryside where he did not feel so trapped.

'Hey, Theresa!' called Joe, walking down the stairs. 'I ain't doin' your exercises this mornin'. We hittin' the mountains today!' A large quantity of bread awaited them, and even a little butter that Thérèse had managed to procure on the black market.

A moustachioed Frenchman arrived, touched his beret, pointed at Joe and then at himself. He did not speak a word of English which, being Joe's escort, was just as well. Françoise and Mifouf completed the party. They rose to leave and Thérèse rushed forward and hugged them tightly, muttering encouragement in their ears.

It was a beautifully crisp, autumnal day outside as the quartet waited at the tram stop that would take them to Perpignan train station. Joe and the silent Frenchman stood at one end and Frank and Françoise the other. The tram arrived and there was a scrum to get on. 'The French do not understand queuing,' observed Frank.

Piling into the carriage, Frank and Françoise found themselves tucked up against a fully uniformed German NCO. The soldier was sitting on one of the few seats and asked the frail-looking Françoise if she would like his seat.

'Ahhh, monsieur!' she cried. 'I wouldn't dream of taking your comfortable seat. You are a passing visitor in our beautiful country so please enjoy your holiday!'

Her words were somewhat lost on the German and luckily he did not see the smiles ripple around the carriage. She can't help but dig, thought Frank. Germans are like red flags to a bull for her.

At Perpignan station, Joe's escort bought three extra tickets and slipped them over. Two long queues snaked back from a pair of gendarmes checking papers. Frank chose the longer, hoping the police officer would be less thorough in his check, which he was. Loitering on the other side of the barriers, Françoise and Frank watched Joe approach. Surely he's going to be caught, they both thought.

Towering above the crowd of French locals, Joe was painfully conspicuous. The way he walked, the way he slouched his shoulders, even the angle he held his head looked different to everyone else. Perhaps the thing that made him stand out the most was when he smiled or yawned and revealed a set of healthy teeth. One thing Joe did have on his side was an air of utter disregard. If anything, he was enjoying himself.

It was still half an hour till the Perpignan train arrived, so the trio tried their best to melt into the busy platform. There was a sprinkling of Luftwaffe boys about, and a few NCOs, most of whom looked uninterested. Apart from one particularly lanky, bespectacled man taking an interest in Joe. The six-foot-four teenager scowled back, daring the German to challenge him.

Glancing over his newspaper, Frank clocked six Anglo-Saxon-looking types kicking their heels. They kept glancing at a young lady with a suitcase, who was doing her best to remain innocuous. Frank was certain they were RAF and sure enough, when the lady got up and strolled to the other end of the platform, the six men followed like a flock of sheep. If that lanky NCO had any initiative, thought Frank, he could have seven birds with one stone. I wonder what route they're taking over the mountains?

The train arrived and there was a terrific mêlée to get onboard. Joe, seeing Frank was struggling with his dodgy arm, plucked him from the crowd and forced themselves into the carriage, elbowing locals out the way. There was nothing subtle about him, but Frank was increasingly reassured that Joe was on his side.

The unlikely pair surged down the corridor until a controller appeared and pushed them into a compartment. It was a friendly steer and he was clearly in the know, realised Frank. The controller appeared later with Françoise and Joe's escort, who took the last seats in their second-class compartment, which had filled with French women.

One of them, a toothless, thin woman of about fifty, had a cage with a live hen inside it on her knee. She babbled at Frank, who shrugged and deflected as best he could, with Françoise taking care of the rest.

'Will you hold my chicken, please?' the woman asked, thrusting the cage into Frank's lap. She took out some bread and a hardboiled egg. He was happy to accept, thinking it rather a good disguise.

Françoise looked relaxed. As a general rule, the poorer people were, the more anti-German they were: they had less to lose from not collaborating. From the packed compartment, Frank caught glimpses of the soaring peaks of the Pyrenees as they ran down the Carcassonne Valley. *Spain.* For the first time in weeks, he felt more excitement than fear.

But there was still the control in Perpignan station to get through, hopefully the last before Spain. The quartet surrendered their tickets and walked towards the exit, bracing themselves for a Françoise hissy fit. But no one was there. They walked straight out of the station into the cool Mediterranean air of Perpignan.

Rounding a corner in pursuit of Françoise, the two airmen came face to face with Joe's escort.

'See that man reading a paper ahead of you?' he asked. Frank and Joe nodded.

'Follow him. Goodbye. Good luck. Don't shake hands.'

In Toulouse, I am keen to find out more about Françoise, my favourite character in Frank's escape.

On a busy retail high street, I find 40 Rue de la Pomme, the location of the dress shop Françoise ran before the war. An off-white, marble plaque streaked with black reads:

'Françoise', heroine of the Resistance, head of an escape network.
'Françoise', from 1943 to 1944, organised with members
of her network the clandestine passage to Spain
of more than 700 Allied aviators and resistors that she
disguised, hid and transported beyond the Pyrenees.

I head to the Departmental Museum of Resistance and Deportation, where I find an impressive tribute to the disproportionately large role women played in the Resistance. Amongst several placards to heroic women there is one for Françoise, summarising her role in three sentences.

I visit the grand Monument à la gloire de la Résistance just down the road from the museum. De Gaulle's famous speech invoking the Resistance Spirit, given in exile in London, June 1940, is emblazoned in thirteen sentences.

In the Jardin des Plantes, one of Toulouse's finest parks, I find statues of Jean Moulin and François Verdier, two male Resistance heroes. Moulin, a national icon, was betrayed and mercilessly tortured by Klaus Barbie until he was beaten to death. Verdier also endured torture before being shot in a forest.

Both statues rightly stand near the centre of Toulouse, where their inscriptions are read by hundreds of people every day. Moulin – the fifth most popular name for schools in France and the third most common for streets – has a museum dedicated to him, appears on commemorative coins, and is the focus of two French films. He features highly on the French school syllabus.

But ask a child about the name 'Dissard' and they are likely to look at you blankly. I discover she does have a statue, but it is sixteen kilometres outside of Toulouse's centre. Similarly, the Rue Marie-Louise Dissard is tucked away in the outskirts. Perhaps her greatest legacy is a school named after her in the western suburbs of Toulouse. Moulin has four.

The last place I go in search of Françoise is the city's cemetery, where I know she is buried.

The Cimetière de Terre-Cabade is not an attractive place. Covering eighty-two acres, it is a vast sprawl of grey, concrete tombs crammed inside crumbly walls in Toulouse's gritty east. I have no idea where Françoise is and there is no map. After an hour of wandering the hot, dusty paths searching for the name Dissard, I give up. With 28,000 tombs, Françoise is a needle in a concrete haystack: her legacy a footnote in Toulouse's history.

I resume my journey in Frank's footsteps and catch the train to Perpignan. It is a glorious journey east down the Carcassonne Valley and I spend most of it looking at the Pyrenean mountains with a sense of excitement and foreboding. For once, I am certain this is the same view that Frank enjoyed in October 1943. At 2,784 metres, the snow-capped Canigó Mountain towers above the rest of the eastern Pyrenees, while the Mediterranean flashes past on the other side of the train.

Like Frank, I will be crossing these mountains on foot. Unlike him, I will be carrying a heavy backpack on my shoulders, sleeping rough under a small tarpaulin and I have no guide.

I'm twenty-two, I think, what could go wrong?

The man with the newspaper strolled slowly through Perpignan, turned into a shady park and sat on a bench. He signalled at Frank and Joe to join him.

'I'm Antoine,' he said, his face buried in his paper. 'Don't look at me, just listen. Which one of you speaks French?' Frank realised his modicum of schoolboy French had made him the translator. Joe, who had been in France four months, had learned two words – *servez-vous*. Help yourself.

'Okay, here's the plan,' murmured Antoine, turning an unread page of newspaper. 'You two will stay here until four p.m. I'll come back for you then and lead you to my uncle's farm in the mountains. It's about forty-five kilometres away, but we can catch a bus for the first twelve.' Frank glanced at his watch. He had four hours to wait with Joe.

'Walk around a bit so you don't look weird,' continued Antoine, 'and I'll see you at four.' He folded his newspaper and sauntered away. The two airmen had not yet seen their new contact's face, but watching Antoine leave the park, they both saw a tall, slender man with an athletic gait. Leaves stirred on the floor as he swept passed them, rounded a hedge and disappeared.

Frank and Joe took out the food that Thérèse had packed into their pockets. 'How I bless that woman's foresight,' wrote Frank, 'we had prunes, sugar, chocolate, all highly nutritious foodstuffs.' While eating, Frank noticed some words scratched into their bench. *Per Ardua Ad Astra!* It was the RAF motto, meaning 'Through Adversity to the Stars!' He took heart from the fact he was not the first RAF airman to take this route. Joe gobbled everything he had, not saving anything for later.

'C'mon, let's walk, I can't sit around for too long,' he muttered to Frank. There was not a lot to see in Perpignan, so the duo spent the next three hours watching the German troop movements.

Antoine returned at 3.30 p.m. He was early. This time he looked straight at the pair as he spoke. He was young and clean-shaven, with thin lips, a wide mouth and a pronounced Adam's apple.

'We can't get the bus,' he explained. 'The Germans have put a guard in the station. We'll have to walk the whole way. Sooner we get started the better.'

Great, thought Frank, I've had enough of this communal travelling. Joe looked nonplussed. He did not like exercise and walking was dull.

'Follow me as far behind as possible without losing sight,' said Antoine, who was almost as tall as Joe. 'My uncle will meet us on the outskirts of town. Ready?' He looked around the park for danger. Sycamore leaves pirouetted earthward and a pigeon pecked its way towards their bench. '*On y va.*'

It was 27 October and the watery autumn sun made for perfect walking conditions. Leaving the suburbs of Perpignan, Frank and Joe saw a figure holding a raincoat acknowledge Antoine and set off in front of him. That must be 'the uncle', Frank thought. There was very little traffic about, only cart-loads of German soldiers heading into Perpignan from their out-of-town billets. Unlike the locals, who could spot a foreigner a mile off, the Germans paid them no interest.

The pace was nothing like the earlier stroll through Perpignan. With the uncle leading, Frank strode purposefully to keep up and, unused to exercise except for Thérèse's regime, his heart beat steadily inside his chest. He seemed to be taking two steps for every one of Joe's. Looking straight ahead, he could see the snowcapped peaks of the Pyrenees looming ominously on the horizon, like a dog baring its teeth.

Unknown to the airmen, the uncle and Antoine had worked out a fail-safe system. Walking 200 yards ahead of Antoine, the uncle would drop his coat if he could see trouble around the next bend. Antoine would then halt, with Frank and Joe doing the same 200 yards behind him. As the uncle lived near the French/Spanish border, he had the correct papers and would go and investigate the problem. Only when the uncle returned to pick up his coat and continued walking, would the procession continue.

But the system only worked while it was light. Dusk was falling and with every passing minute Antoine had to get closer to the uncle, as did Frank and Joe to Antoine. Eventually, Antoine gave up and joined Frank and Joe.

'He'll shout if something happens,' whispered Antoine. 'If any cars come now, jump in the ditch and hide until they pass.'

At 8 p.m., after four and a half hours walking, Antoine hissed something to his uncle, stopped and climbed into the ditch beside the road. The uncle appeared from the gloom. He was wearing a sort of full-length shawl and rope sandals. He shook hands with Frank. The uncle's hand felt like a jumble of toothpicks wrapped in leathery skin, but the grip was firm. He produced a bottle of wine from a battered haversack.

After five minutes' rest, the march resumed. It was a dark, moonless night and Frank could feel the road getting steeper. *We must be in the foothills.* Long silences ensued as the quartet trudged on. Joe's boots struck the road heavily, causing deep thuds between each stride. Antoine moved silently. Frank's rhythmic breathing was only interrupted by Joe's spitting and an owl hooting in the distance.

'Aaagghh!' came a scream from ahead of them, followed by a splintering crash of twisting metal.

As one, Frank, Joe and Antoine launched themselves into the ditch and strained their eyes against the darkness. Two men – the uncle and another – were yelling angrily. He is being arrested, thought Frank, scrambling up the far bank ready to flee into the night.

A hand grabbed his belt from down in the ditch and yanked him backwards.

'It's okay!' whispered Antoine furiously, 'they're speaking Catalan!' So what? thought Frank, adrenaline coursing through his body. A few minutes passed and then, still crouching in the ditch, the trio watched a man limp past wheeling a bicycle. The uncle whistled from ahead.

Joining him, the uncle explained he had shouted as a warning to the bicycle, which he could hear coming. Not having a light, the cyclist had ploughed straight into him. As for the speaking of Catalan, apparently it was a reliable indicator of anti-fascist/pro-Ally sentiment.

The uncle cursed and chuckled and led the trio from the road into some scrubland. He delved again into his haversack and pulled out a cooked goose and another bottle of wine.

'That was the last road you'll walk on in France,' said Antoine. 'From now on we'll be in the *maquis*. Make sure you don't lose the man in front. Hold onto him if you can't see.' After two or three glasses of wine, Frank felt great. The vegetation and darkness felt like a safety blanket – like the bushes behind Ma Baraque, or the fog on the Swiss border – affording easy escape should disaster strike.

At 11 p.m., the march resumed. Antoine led with the uncle, Frank and finally Joe following. How on earth does Antoine know where he is going? thought Frank. The 'path' had rapidly disintegrated into a tangle of gorse and heather, broken up by occasional boulder-strewn gulleys. 'We were contour chasing mostly,' recalled Frank, 'but occasionally Antoine got fed up and cut straight across a valley through thick undergrowth.'

The only respite came when Frank insisted on stopping to drink from streams. Lapping at the icy water, he could feel fatigue collecting steadily in his limbs. Thousands of feet above them, the snow-covered peaks glowed dimly while waterfalls cascaded down the mountainside.

At 1 a.m., the quartet rested beside the gates of a large chateau.

'Half an hour more,' Antoine muttered. 'There's a railway line ahead and then we're into easier going.' He spoke to Frank directly, who was beginning to fall off the pace. 'A railway line in this country,' wrote Frank, 'I had the impression we were at the uttermost ends of the Earth.' Despite flouting Thérèse's exercise regime, Joe was as fresh as a daisy.

Slipping over the railway line and down into a valley, the spiky scrub gave way to the fields and hedges of cultivated country. A small farm materialised ahead of them. Antoine led them through a door into what Frank thought was a stable, but after switching on the light turned out to be a kitchen. *Chairs!* After ten hours walking, it was exquisite to sit down. Frank's head soon began to bob as sleep overtook him.

The uncle appeared with bowls of potato soup and copious draughts of wine. Pulling themselves closer to the heavy wooden table, the four men fell on their soup underneath a single naked bulb. Two sleepy sheepdogs watched them with half-open eyes. Mice scurried in the shadows. The cracks in the stone floor were lined with mud and hair. The air was thick with the smell of farm animals.

Antoine gestured to a ladder leading to a loft where Frank and Joe were to sleep. It was filled with freshly mown hay. 'The comfiest bed I ever had,' recalled Frank.

Hours later he found Antoine standing over him, a bowl of warm milk steaming in his hands and sunlight streaming between the wooden planks of the loft's walls.

The day of crossing the frontier had arrived.

Armed with a small tarpaulin, a camping Jetboil, a canteen, a bivvy bag and a roll mat, I set out from Perpignan on foot, seventy-nine years to the week after my great-grandfather.

The narrow streets are awash with the smells of bakeries and last night's beer. I march south-west past several bus and train stations, rucksack straps fastened, pockets full of Haribo, feet unblistered.

On nondescript pavements and empty bike paths, I navigate through a sea of industrial parks, parcel depots and ring roads. Beyond the featureless light industry, the mighty Pic du Canigó looms. At 2,784 metres, it would have drawn Frank's eye as it does mine, but I have the advantage of knowing my route lies at least thirty kilometres further east over the Pic de les Salines, significantly less daunting at 1,333 metres.

Thundering traffic has replaced the horse-drawn carts that Frank saw, but the roadside ditches, gouged out by heavy rain and snowmelt coming off the Pyrenees, are still two to three metres deep in places.

After five hours, the flat tarmac gives way to gravel tracks sloping steadily uphill. It is still a barren landscape. Gorse blankets large swathes of the hillside. The occasional cluster of cypress trees or a conifer plantation flecks the hillside with a darker shade of green. I crunch past dried-out sheep skulls, crooked church towers and waterless river gorges, the Pyrenees refusing to come nearer.

Frank would have climbed this ridge in darkness, unaware it was a mere foothill in his journey. Sometimes it is better not to know what is coming. Sadly, this does not apply to me. I know this is the lowest point in a band of hills protruding from the base of Mount Canigó into the Roussillon plain. To get to the farmhouse where Frank stayed, I need to go straight over this ridge and drop into the Vallespir valley beyond, surrendering all the elevation I have gained today. Here the real climb to Spain begins, but that is tomorrow's concern.

I yomp on into the dusty furnace and arrive at the tiny village of Llauro. It consists of a few houses, a goat farm and a shaded bar carved into the hillside. I slake my raging thirst with a delicious cold beer. The temperature has not dropped below thirty degrees yet. I have covered thirty kilometres, just over half what Frank did, but already the heavy pack is sapping my back and legs. Watching the condensation droplets slide down my pint, I look back at Perpignan, a distant blemish on the land. My hamstrings twinge menacingly as I rise from the table.

A gentle breeze stirs through the olive trees as I continue to climb steadily. Blobs of orange sandstone jut out of the hillside, too steep and infertile to support plants. I pass remote, ramshackle vineyards with signs reading 'keep out' or 'private', despite their total isolation. Other than goat farming, vineyards seem to be the only way for locals to make money off this wretched piece of country. But I can see why Frank felt secure. It would be very easy to slip away into the contours of dense vegetation if a German patrol passed by.

I can feel blisters developing on both my heels, and my shoulders feel bruised from the weight of the heavy backpack. My right knee is also causing me to limp heavily, but finally the contours ease and I reach the top of the ridge. It is 6.30 p.m. and darkness is descending. My smartwatch says I have covered 50,000 steps, with a fair amount of elevation too.

I leave the track and enter a magical cork oak forest in search of a clearing to sleep in. The floor is a blanket of crisp, brown leaves and the silvery oak trunks twist upwards like a witch's fingers. The oaks, having had the bark of their lower halves harvested for wine corks, look like women whose skirts have blown up in the wind and are twisting in embarrassment.

I suspend my tarp and cook my ration-pack meal, giggling at how much my legs hurt. My niggling knee is the major concern, an injury capable of derailing the whole trip.

At 8 p.m. it gets dark. In my quest to save weight I have no lights, so all I can do is go to bed. For hours I lie listening to the stirrings of the forest. Fatigue burns in my legs like an ember. Dead leaves crackle. Mosquitoes whine.

I don't dream.

CHAPTER 8

EIGHTY MILES TO FREEDOM

'Do not go outside today,' warned Antoine, as Frank sipped his bowl of steaming milk. 'All the farms around here are watched by the Germans. They have observation posts on all the ridges with telescopes trained on us.'

'Hey, I'm tryin' to sleep here,' grumbled Joe. Antoine ignored him and folded a map out on the hay. The loft was snug and the smell of fresh hay and milk wafted deliciously in the air.

'This is us,' Antoine said pointing at a forested bend in the River Tech about three miles west of the medium-sized town of Céret. Frank noticed Antoine's fingertip was well within an area of the map he had shaded and marked *Zone Interdit* (Forbidden Zone).

'And here's where you'll be going over the border tonight.' Antoine dragged his finger over hundreds of contours, stopping and double-tapping his finger on a thick black line running along the highest ridge, labelled *France/Espagne*.

Twelve miles to freedom, thought Frank. Twelve miles until I can see Ruth and Tessa again. Twelve miles until I can go home.

'I won't be coming with you tonight, just my uncle and my young cousin,' continued Antoine. 'At the border they'll hand you over to Paul and he'll take you into Spain. Paul lives right on the border and knows the mountain better than anyone.'

'Gimme some of that,' muttered Joe, reaching out for the bowl of milk, a strand of hay stuck to his cheek.

'We'll leave as soon as it's dark – about seven,' said Antoine. Frank checked his watch. *Nine hours' rest.* 'We'll bring your meals up here. You can wash in the cattle shed down there. It's nothing special, I'm afraid . . .'

'Thank you, Antoine, that's marvellous,' said Frank.

'Yeah, cheers, Antoney,' added Joe.

'Oh and Frank,' murmured Antoine, as he placed his feet on the first rung of the ladder. 'Do you think you might give me and my cousin an English lesson, please? Just as we've got the day and he's really keen. It's no problem if you're tired.'

'Of course!' beamed Frank, relishing the chance to give something back to his hosts. 'I've checked my diary and I have no plans. You know where to find me.'

No sooner had Antoine got to the bottom rung of the ladder than he was he climbing back up with his young cousin Pierre. After ten weeks of being told what to do, it felt strange being in charge for an hour. 'The lesson was very simple and considering the lads had taught themselves, they did very well,' reflected Frank. 'It was satisfying to see someone else struggle with a language for a change!'

Just as the lads were leaving, Frank had an idea.

'Pierre, wait! Have this,' he said, holding out his pocket French/English dictionary he had bought in Geneva. 'I won't be needing it in Spain. Keep practising. You'll be better than Antoine soon.'

The rest of 28 October passed in a flash. It was Frank's seventy-third day in mainland Europe. He tried to sleep, but his watch seemed to be burning a hole into his wrist. He paced the loft instead. Peeping between the planks of the loft, he saw the farm was nestled in a heavily wooded valley awash with sunshine and birdsong, like a hot August day in England. Shame we won't get to see any of it, he thought.

At 6.30 p.m., Antoine reappeared and asked for Frank and Joe's francs and their *cartes de travail*.

'No way!' protested Joe. 'I'm holding onto mine as a keepsake. Don't know if I'll ever be back in France.'

An argument ensued as Antoine and Frank pleaded with Joe to give up the very things that proved he had come from France. Eventually he tossed the card on the table in a huff. Bloody American brat, thought Frank. Tight-arsed Brit, thought Joe.

After a nervy last supper, Frank, Joe, Pierre the young cousin and the old uncle stepped outside into the gathering gloom. Ahead, jagged black shapes cut holes out of the starry sky. The Pyrenees.

'*Bonne chance*,' said Antoine, shaking their hands. Frank was sad he was not coming. Antoine watched the six-foot-four American teenager, a 31-year-old British pilot, an elderly Catalonian farmer and a fifteen-year-old boy stroll across the lawn until their mismatched silhouettes melted into darkness.

Barely ten minutes had passed when the quartet came to their first obstacle: a fast-flowing river. It was waist-deep and had bits of snow and ice floating in it. The men stripped off their lower layers, linked arms and began wading, gasping as the water crept up their legs.

Frank was through the worst of it and taking his last few strides to the far bank when his foot slipped on a rock and trapped itself in the riverbed. His weight, combined with the flow of the river, twisted his knee sharply and he cried out in pain.

'Night marching can be enjoyable,' said Frank, 'if you are sound in wind and limb. But it is agony if you are carrying an injury.' The uncle bound Frank's knee with his handkerchief, which he had dipped in the icy river as a form of cold compress. With mutters of encouragement from the others, the quartet began climbing the steep, rocky mountainside in earnest. When they were not on all fours, they used large sticks to tap the side of the path where it dropped away steeply, like a blind man would a pavement. It was totally different to the previous night's march through the rolling, arid foothills.

An hour into the climb, Frank slipped on some scree and began sliding towards the edge of the precipice. Using his good shoulder, he clung to the side of the path but was unable to pull himself up. Thankfully, the next man in the line was Joe, who scooped him up with ease.

'No time for tea breaks now, old man,' he said, dusting Frank off with a couple of solid pats.

'He was strong as a bull,' remembered Frank. 'If it came to a pinch, I think he could have carried me the whole way.'

At 9.30 p.m., after two-and-a-half hours' walking, the uncle halted proceedings. He spoke quietly to Pierre, and Frank could tell it was about his slow progress.

'Don't worry,' interrupted Frank, 'look, I'm going to take these. Good for pain. I'll walk faster.' He showed them a small tin marked 'Fatigue Tablets'. He had swiped them from his RAF escape kit before Victor and the Swiss authorities requisitioned it.

He popped one in his mouth, took the bottle of wine from Joe and had a few hearty swigs. The bottle made its way around the circle and ended back up with Frank, who drained the last two inches. I haven't come this close to turn back now, he thought.

The scramble continued. After about twenty minutes the fatigue tablet took effect. Pervitin, a potent methamphetamine, increases alertness and confidence while reducing appetite and the need to sleep. 'All weariness left me and I felt fully confident,' recalled Frank. 'My knee was bad and had swollen considerably, but didn't seem to hurt anymore.' Every time the party had to cross a stream, Frank bathed it in the icy water, numbing any remaining pain.

Climbing was fine, it was descending that made Frank cry out in agony. The uncle was clearly not taking a direct route up to the border, but cutting across valleys and ravines, bashing through thick undergrowth and sending branches sweeping backwards, scratching Frank's face. 'We were in one extremely dark patch when to my amazement the uncle struck a match,' he remembered. 'It was just as well, because we were about to cross some stepping stones over a stream. I realised the stones were at the top of a waterfall. One slip and we would have had it.'

Safely across, the uncle called another break and sat everyone down in a pitch-black clearing. It felt like the ends of the Earth. The old boy produced another bottle of wine and the remains of the goose they had eaten the night before.

Then it happened.

Enveloped in the total blackness of a forest high in the Pyrenees, gnawing on a goose leg at the top of a waterfall with a bottle of wine in hand, Frank began hallucinating.

'It was 1.30 a.m. and it was not my knee so much but my thirst assailing me,' Frank wrote. 'I've met others who've crossed these wretched mountains ... they too have seen strange things when experiencing this thirst.' [*Maybe the powerful methamphetamine – a form of speed – had something to do with it.*] 'My hallucination took the form of eight or ten pints of shandy with great heads of froth going round and round the perimeter of a Catherine wheel.'

With every step, the amphetamines strengthened their grip on Frank's central nervous system. 'I was in a peculiar mental state at the time. Long periods would pass when I didn't seem to remember anything, or I would wonder why I was following the man in front of me. Then I would wake up and get a tune on the brain, like "And nightly pitch my moving tent a day's march nearer home."'

The uncle turned around, holding his finger to his lips to silence the humming.

'We are close to the Boche now,' he whispered. 'The border is two kilometres away, but we have to cross a track first,' pointing into the darkness. 'The Germans patrol the track, so no more noise at all. After the next stream, we'll wait for Paul at the rendezvous.' The party moved out silently.

Arriving at the meeting point, Frank lay down. It was 3.10 a.m. and he was dog tired. At 1,300 metres above sea level, they were a stone's throw from Spain. Visions of sitting in a Spanish café sipping *café con leche* overcame him and suddenly the Gestapo seemed far away. He fell asleep.

At 3.30 a.m., he awoke to find the uncle whispering Catalan to a new figure, Paul, who had just arrived at the rendezvous.

'Pierre and Jacques will go back home now,' Paul whispered. 'I'll take you over the road and up to Spain. It might take a while.' So the uncle's name was Jacques, thought Frank.

'*À la Victoire*,' murmured the uncle, melting into the brush with his son Pierre. How that old boy could walk, Frank thought. They might be home before daybreak.

Joe, Frank and Paul moved out. They were in less wild country now, darting from thicket to thicket on a flatter plain lit moderately well by moonlight. 'We could hear the German patrols stamping about and rattling their equipment,' Frank explained. 'By remaining still and listening carefully, it was possible to tell where they were.'

Paul seemed concerned. 'If they have dogs,' he hissed, 'run for wild country. Try and cross streams to throw them off your scent.'

'I'd rather run for the safety of Spain,' Frank ventured.

Paul scoffed silently. 'The Spanish guards will send you straight back over the border,' he said. 'If the Germans hear us they'll open fire . . . not at you,' he added hastily, 'but to wake the Spanish guards up.'

For the second time since being shot down, Frank inched his way towards the edge of France.

Moving two or three hundred yards at a time, constantly listening for patrols, the trio arrived at the road and lay in some gorse bushes. 'We could now see the top of the mountain which Paul said was the frontier,' recounted Frank. 'We climbed steadily all the way to the top, passing right over the peak and making no effort to cut over the shoulder.'

At the summit on the frontier, Frank's eyes gazed out over the twinkling lights of Catalonia. It was the first country he had seen not in blackout for four years. He felt the warm winds of Spain blowing lightly between the gaps in the rocks, filling his lungs with promise. It was 6 a.m. and the tiniest hints of daylight were collecting on the horizon.

'Welcome to Catalonia,' said Paul.

'Yeah, boy!' mouthed Joe silently, pumping his fist. Frank grinned giddily.

'If anything goes wrong now,' said Paul, 'scatter and keep walking south. Avoid roads and villages and only walk at night . . .' Frank and Joe were not listening.

'Ready?'

In my clearing in the cork oak forest, a pack of wailing hounds wakes me at dawn. I had made camp near some kennels, and the kennel boy must have been feeding them at 6 a.m. Soon every dog within ten miles is howling and the cockerels are giving it the beans too. Blinking in the half-light, I slither from my sleeping bag, eat half a Snickers bar, pack up and walk off into the thick, cool air.

If I was to keep to Frank and Joe's pace, I would need to reach Spain this afternoon, about twenty kilometres away. The challenge was in the elevation, not the distance. After a downhill start, I faced 1,200 metres of climbing through forests and boulder fields. I make it my goal to reach the frontier by nightfall.

My problems, however, begin much earlier. Descending into the Vallespir valley, with twenty kilos on my back and no breakfast, my knee starts playing up majorly. I want to retrace Frank's journey as faithfully as possible, but I do not plan on damaging my knee like him in the process.

In the town of Céret – 'the jewel of Vallespir valley' – I stop in a café for croissant, coffee and ibuprofen. I realise that not only am I replicating Frank's knee injury, I am also copying his reliance on pills to help get me over these wretched mountains.

There is another reason for my stop in Céret, to meet Marie-Laure Saqué. She is the daughter of Pierre, the young boy to whom Frank gave his pocket French/English dictionary. She is also the granddaughter of Jacques ('the uncle') and the niece of Antoine, Frank's athletic guide who met him in Perpignan. The Saqué family still own the farmhouse where Frank and Joe were taken after their first night's walk.

Despite only connecting for the first time less than a week ago, Marie-Laure has agreed to travel 500 kilometres from her home in Lyon to meet me. But she is late.

With the clock ticking and Spain beckoning, I text her and ask if she is still coming. The moment I press send, a ping goes off behind me. Turning, I see a group of middle-aged women sat around a table looking like they are waiting for someone. One is looking at their phone expectantly.

'Marie-Laure?'

'Adam!'

The link is made. As we had only emailed, neither of us had any idea what the other looked like.

To roars of laughter and much cheek-kissing, we introduce ourselves. Marie-Laure is short, has dark, greying hair, and a wonderfully warm smile and playful demeanour. Not speaking each other's language, she is shy at first – a fair reaction to meeting a total stranger who looks and smells like he has just slept rough in a forest after walking forty kilometres.

After pleasantries and more coffee, Marie-Laure switches positions with her friend Leslie, who is translating. With enormous brown eyes, she scans my face for my reaction as she thumbs through a photo album of her family, pausing and explaining slowly in French who they are. Pierre, Antoine and 'the uncle' are there alongside other family members, their lean, tanned, attractive Catalonian faces smiling for the camera.

It is like talking to an old friend. Marie-Laure is a hoot, gasping and laughing as I tell her about Frank, what happened to him next and about my walk so far. At the mention of Antoine, Pierre and 'the uncle', she swells with pride. I scribble desperately as she talks about her predecessors, all too aware of the time racing past.

'Will you come to La Pouillède for lunch?' she asks hopefully.

'What's that?' I reply.

'The farm your grandaddy stayed in! You didn't know the name?'

I did not. This was too good an opportunity to pass up on. Spain could wait.

'Shall I buy some baguettes?' I ask. Marie-Laure looks offended.

And so, nearly eight decades after Frank arrived exhausted and in pitch darkness, I visit the farmhouse. Tucked in a forested bend of the river Tech in the shadow of the Pyrenees, La Pouillède is a heavenly, timeless place.

The two-storey stone building, with wooden window shutters and a terracotta roof, is surrounded by pot plants, flower beds, cacti and clusters of alder, horse chestnut and bamboo. Near the farmhouse, in the centre of the gently sloping lawn, a stately holm oak tree stands, casting a ring of shade on the lawn. In it there is a wooden table groaning with bread, cheese, wine, grapes, dips, chutneys, charcuterie, onion pie, tangerines, pizza, quiche, olives – all of it homemade or local. After my Snickers breakfast, I feel like weeping.

I am ushered to the middle seat and plied with food and wine. Conversation sparkles. Twelve of Marie-Laure's friends join us, total strangers, enthralled by this story. All of them in middle age, they probably remember Antoine, Jacques and Pierre. I realise Marie-Laure is not even with us for most of it; she is in and out of the house with plates of food, pastries, tea and coffee, hosting effortlessly.

'Hi everyone,' calls a voice at the end of the table. It is one of Marie-Laure's friends, an extravagantly dressed man in jeans and a purple top, with a greying Afro.

'I think we can all agree this is a pretty special moment – to have Adam here, this weather and this lunch – it's amazing.' He reaches for his plastic cup of wine. Birdsong booms around the garden. 'What Marie-Laure's family did is just incredible ... to risk their lives for people to go over the Pyrenees, wow.'

'To Frank!' he says, holding his cup aloft, smiling.

We all drink, feeling like we are part of something much, much bigger. I glance across the table and see tears rolling down cheeks. I feel I must say something about the Saqués. They were the ones risking torture, deportation and death, after all.

But I cannot think of anything. 'Thanks' feels like an insult.

What do you say when you are sitting outside the farmhouse that sheltered your great-grandfather from the Nazis with the very people who risked everything to get him back to his (my) family? One hour ago, I thought I was meeting Marie-Laure for a coffee and a photo.

While our glasses are aloft, I realise I will never forget this moment. These French people, most of whom I do not share a language with, raising their glasses to my great-grandfather! A normal man from North Wales whom none of them ever met. The sunshine, the wine, the fatigue from the walk, the lack of sleep, the beautiful countryside and the birdsong. It is all too much.

Thankfully, Marie-Laure suggests we go and see the loft that Frank and Joe slept in. It is wonderfully cool in the farmhouse. It looks unchanged since Frank's visit; the door he thought was a stable door, the ladder up to the loft, the barrel of wine in the corner.

I wander through the garden to the River Tech, just as Frank, Joe, the uncle and the young Pierre did all those years ago. I tell Marie-Laure I want to see it, because it is where Frank twisted his knee. But she is adamant that he and Joe left La Pouillède on horses led by the uncle and Pierre. She says her grandfather did not want the aviators' feet getting wet before marching all night.

Could Frank have misremembered in his fatigued, drug-fuelled state? I am sure he would not have forgotten twisting his knee in a river, but perhaps it was at a later crossing. Yet there is no mention of horses in his book and as he was a lover of horses, I find that unlikely. Perhaps the horse story passed to Marie-Laure related to another party the Saqués helped to cross the Pyrenees.

Wending my way between towering bamboo patches and ivy-clad alders, I arrive at the meandering Tech, a wide, boulder-strewn river on its bones after weeks of drought. Originating on the French/Spanish border 2,500 metres above sea level, in high water Le Tech crashes out of the Pyrenees before surging east down the Vallespir valley and eventually spilling into the Mediterranean between Saint-Cyprien and Argelès-sur-Mer. This is what it would have been like when Frank crossed it, be that on foot or horse.

I remove my shoes and bathe my blistered feet in the cold water. I wade out to somewhere very close to where Frank twisted his knee, wiggling my toes in the gin-clear water and stumbling on slimy rocks. Sunlight sparkles on the water's surface, illuminating overhanging leaves.

It is 4 p.m. and if I am even going to come close to Spain, I must leave.

I extricate myself from these good people and try, insufficiently, to thank Marie-Laure for everything she has done. She waves it all off like it is nothing. Wandering away from La Pouillède, I pinch myself about what has just happened.

'Wait!' shouts Marie-Laure. 'I have the dictionary!'

Back under the shade of the holm oak, on a table covered with a floral tablecloth, she gently lays out a tiny, black book with *Collins French Dictionary* embossed in gold letters in the top left corner. Marie-Laure opens the crinkled, yellow pages with the delicacy of a surgeon. There in the front cover, scrawled in faded pencil, is '*English man Griffiths*' in Frank's handwriting.

This was the dictionary that Frank gave to Marie-Laure's father, Pierre, in the loft. After all these years she still had it, a symbol of her family's heroic bravery and a direct link to that day in October 1943. I realise the hairs on my forearms are standing up, but it is less at the sight of this tattered little dictionary and more at the manner Marie-Laure is handling it, the way she is looking at it. To her, this dictionary is irrefutable proof that her family were on the right side of history, evidence that she is descended from heroic, gallant people.

As we flick through it, the French members of the group begin to laugh. I do not understand. Marie-Laure explains that her father Pierre had underlined the rude words in the dictionary. If that is not proof Frank gave it to a twelve-year-old boy, I don't know what is.

I set off for the second time up a steep road that soon peters out into a footpath. Whether it is the long lunch, the convivial atmosphere or the wine, my knee has stopped hurting. Sweat pours off me as the temperature remains in the high 20s late into the evening.

Steadily I climb, weighed down by the mountains of food Marie-Laure has stuffed into my rucksack and pockets. Juniper shrubs, rhododendron and a variety of ferns cling to the rocky hillside. At 6.30 p.m., I come to a stone monument marked with a Croix de Lorraine. It reads:

In honour of the passeurs who from June 1940 guided men
through these paths to their freedom, often with their lives at risk.
They contributed to the liberation of France.
Let's not forget them.

I make camp at the Font de la Fontfreda, a fountain beside a small car park situated 1,096 metres above sea level. The Vallespir valley begins to fill with mist, concealing Céret and the farmhouse. The ridge I climbed on day one, one of several, now looks like the first in a set of waves approaching the Pyrenees.

I climb into my sleeping bag on a bed of leaves and earth. Sleep comes quickly this time, but I find myself waking time and again in a panic, fumbling for my pathetic headtorch only to reveal a fox standing ten or so metres away, eyeballing my ramshackle tarpaulin.

The forest comes alive in the darkness. Every snapping twig sounds like a bone breaking, every stirring leaf is a snake hissing. After midnight, the wind starts. Like a whisper at first, it rustles the treetops softly as leaves tumble from the sky. But in seconds the whisper rises to a growl, then a roar, as branches crack and trunks groan and it feels like the forest floor is about to be ripped up.

Then, as quickly as it started, a pregnant silence descends on the forest. The trees sigh, fall still and stand firm, ready for the next gust.

CHAPTER 9

A CRUEL CROSSING

Hallucinating, hobbling, Frank descended on Spain, freedom within his grasp. As the wine and the amphetamines wore off, the pain in his twisted, swollen knee intensified.

'It nearly made me scream at every step,' wrote Frank, 'but I didn't want to take another fatigue tablet as we should be asleep in an hour.'

Paul the guide and Joe were getting antsy. The sun was creeping over the horizon, lifting their safety blanket of darkness. It would be light soon, but the Catalan and the American could not speed Frank up. Joe tried to help, but propping his enormous frame under Frank's armpit only compounded matters. The teenager did not understand why Frank could not go any faster.

'C'mon Frank, so close, buddy,' he implored. But Frank did not want to hear it.

Every step felt like someone bashing his kneecap with a hammer. Shut it, you lippy Yank, he thought. Useless tea-sipper, thought Joe. Over a particularly rocky section with high gorse bushes, Frank looked up to see he was alone. He limped around for a minute or so, hissing for Paul. Dawn had broken and Frank, walking on a bed of pine needles surrounded by birdsong, felt like he was dreaming.

'*Hssst*,' responded Paul, who was standing ten yards away at the entrance of a tiny stone barn encircled by prolific gorse. 'I'll go get some food. Have a sleep in this barn.'

Frank collapsed on the hay-covered floor and was asleep in seconds. A few hours later, Paul shook him awake. He had returned with brown bread and hot milk. Sunlight was streaming through the small window onto Frank's face. The pain in his knee had subsided to a dull, throbbing ache. He felt nauseous and empty.

Slowly, Frank tuned into Paul and Joe's conversation.

'No one expected England to hold out,' said Paul. 'Being a collaborator was the sensible thing to do. I thought Pétain was the saviour of France.' Sitting cross-legged on the hay, he looked how Frank imagined all Pyrenean guides to look – wiry, tanned and hard. 'That was before I went to Germany in the labour draft. I spent a year working for the Germans ... terrible ... the hours, the food, I swore never to go back. When I came home for a week's holiday leave, the Germans had occupied Vichy. I changed my identity and started working for the Allies.'

Conversation drifted to Spain and the route forward, but Paul knew very little of what lay after the *Zone Interdit*.

'Apart from Germany, I've never left these mountains. I'm going back to my farm on the border tonight. My friend Manuel will come at 6.30 p.m. and lead you south for about twelve kilometres. That should take you out of the *Zone Interdit*. Once you get past Figueres, you shouldn't be stopped. Just keep walking till you get to Barcelona.'

Eager to alert the British authorities, Frank took out the pencil, paper, envelope and stamp Thérèse had given him (originally intended to write to his wife once he was in Spain) and wrote a letter to the Consulado Britanico, Barcelona:

29th October 1943
Dear Ambassador,
    I am Sqn/Ldr Frank Griffiths, an RAF pilot shot down
15th August near Annecy. I have just walked into Spain with

an American tail gunner, Stf/Sgt Joe Manos. We are in the
foothills of the Pyrenees in the northern part of Catalonia and
our plan is to walk to Barcelona. If all goes well, we should be
there in about four days. Please do keep an eye out for us and
if possible, tell my wife I am alive. Her address – WAAF Ruth
Griffiths, Gibraltar Farm, RAF Tempsford, Bedfordshire.
Thank you.
    Yours sincerely,
    Sdn/Ldr Griffiths

He tucked the letter away in his pocket, with the intention of posting it in the first letterbox he passed.

At 3 p.m., after another few hours' kip in the barn, Frank was awoken to Joe's cries. 'What the hell? Jesus, get the heck off me!' yelled the American.

Bolting upright, Frank almost toppled over laughing as he saw Joe being snuffled by three large pigs.

An elderly woman with a stick rounded the nearest gorse bush. She was Paul's grandmother and she had brought sustenance for the men. Driving the pigs to new grazing was her cover. All four went into the barn, where the woman laid out an enamel chamber pot filled with soup, a bag full of Spanish omelettes with chopped ham, and some apples and grapes. She had also lugged a litre of wine up the hill. All this stuffed in her clothes and bag.

'I drank far too much of the wine,' recalled Frank, 'and passed out and slept like a log for another three hours, waking up with a blinding headache.' He awoke because the wizened old woman had returned, this time with bread and some dried meat.

The men split up the rations and then Paul got up to leave. It had been a short but vital acquaintance. Frank and Joe watched as he effortlessly strode away up the mountain, melting into the gorse. They turned and watched the final brushstrokes of the sunset in silence.

Manuel, young, skinny and smiling, arrived. Immediately the trio set off into the twilight. The first two hours were downhill through rough undergrowth. Frank was painfully aware how much faster Joe and Manuel would be without him. But by 8.30 p.m., the slope evened out and Frank was able to make greater speed as Manuel led them down a series of winding paths.

'Don't worry, the guards will all be asleep,' explained Manuel at Frank's look of concern when Joe started whistling. 'All we have to do is avoid villages and roads and there's no danger.'

At 11.20 p.m., the trio came to a fairly large road and, after checking the coast was clear, darted across.

'That was the border of the *Zone Interdit*,' said Manuel. He pulled out a small map. 'See this band of hills south of us? Keep walking until you reach them. There's a farm here by this track.' He pointed at the map. 'You can sleep there and there might be some food supplies. Whatever happens now, you shouldn't be sent back to France.'

Manuel folded his map away and looked seriously at Frank and Joe. 'If anything does happen, you must not speak a word about where you crossed the mountains. Terrible things will happen to us. Franco likes Hitler much more than Churchill.' He grasped both men's hands, wished them luck and set off back to his anxious mother. Frank did not ask his age, but he could easily have been in his mid-teens.

For the first time since staggering away from his burning Halifax near Annecy seventy-four days ago, Frank was back under his own steam and responsible only for himself.

Until now he had exclusively been in the care of others, relying on their kindness and bravery to take him in, and their skill to keep him hidden and transport him around. But from now on, every decision would be his own. Every footstep would be of his own accord.

There was just one problem. A six-foot-four problem.

Joe Manos.

Frank and Joe were an unlikely pairing. At thirty-one, Frank was twelve years Joe's senior, but six inches shorter. As a squadron leader, he was several ranks above Staff Sergeant Manos, but the American and British armies did not react well to taking orders from each other.

'Above all else,' explained Frank, 'I was a countryman and I realised only too well that Joe was totally inexperienced in country lore.' This was indisputable. Joe had barely left New York. Further, Frank desperately wanted to see his wife and child again. Joe wanted to enjoy his time in Europe. He did not know if he would be coming back.

Will he work with me? Frank thought. I can't let his carefree attitude get us caught. He's a teenager, won't he let me make decisions?

I hope he doesn't try bossing me around, Joe thought. I ain't letting this old man slow me down. I don't need an English officer who can't even walk telling me what to do.

The arguments began immediately.

'Joe, can you slow down please?' Frank would ask, only for Joe to cast a pitying glance over his shoulder, roll his eyes and carry on walking. 'I couldn't help but be amused at my condition compared with Joe,' reflected Frank. 'Joe, the big lazy hulk of a man who Thérèse could not force to take exercise and I thought would never get fit enough for the mountains, was as fit as fiddle, whilst I, who had taken great pains to get fit, was lame and exhausted.'

Both had agreed on getting to Barcelona 160 kilometres away. But they could not agree on how to get there. Frank thought he could walk it in four days, but only with sleep and food.

'I say we find somewhere to sleep now,' he suggested, 'and then we can walk all day tomorrow. Manuel said it was safe to move in daylight now. We don't know this area anyway; we'll get lost very quickly in the night.'

'Nah, I don't like it in daylight . . . let's push on,' replied Joe. 'We're safe in the shadows. I can go all night, especially if these shoes don't fall apart on me,' in reference to his GI boots that were falling to pieces. 'I wanna go till the sun comes up and then thumb a lorry to Barcelona.' There was a conviction in his voice that Frank had heard before and dreaded. He acquiesced.

They pushed on into the brush, down the track that Manuel had pointed out, until a small farm appeared. It was just past midnight.

'Joe, I have to sleep. My knee is giving me jip and I won't make it all night.'

'Nah, c'mon man, it looks shitty. You know I can't sleep in these places.'

Frank ignored him and limped up to the nearest of several barns. *Please be filled with straw.*

He stepped inside. Something rustled, then growled. Frank struck his lighter and saw a large stack of hay with a young, scared-looking sheepdog standing guard. He held his fist out for the dog to smell, but rather than calm the animal, it erupted with barks and tore past him into the night. Frank hobbled to the doorway and looked around for Joe to tell him he had found a bed. But he had vanished.

Some minutes passed before the American re-emerged, looking white and shaky.

'Is that rabid thing gone, old man?' he asked.

Frank could not believe it. The fearless American, who had

not been scared one ounce by German soldiers and Milice officers, was frightened of dogs.

'It's gone. Come look at this,' Frank replied.

Joe took one look and turned to leave. 'No way, old man. Ain't sleepin' on that stuff with things bitin' me. Let's bounce.'

'Please Joe. I really can't go on . . .'

'C'mon, you'll be alright, I'll carry you if it gets real bad.'

'It is real bad, I'd be fine if I could just sleep,' said Frank, his temper wearing thin.

'Don't start orderin' me round now, old man,' replied Joe. 'Not my fault you can't walk. Rank means shit out here.' He started to walk away. Frank looked longingly at the dry, warm straw and then back at Joe's large, stooped back bobbing away into the darkness.

'Do you want to lead then?' he called. 'Be my guest. I'm sure this is just like New York.'

Joe turned quick as a flash and Frank knew he had made a mistake. There was no point arguing with someone like Joe Manos – the more you did, the less likely he was to agree and the more likely you were to antagonise him.

'Yeah, I fucking do actually. Not like you're gonna get us anywhere is it, old man? Can't even frickin' walk.' There was no stoop in Joe's spine now and Frank could see a glint in his eyes in the moonlight. 'I'd be better off without you slowin' me down anyway. I'll see ya in Spain.'

Joe turned and swaggered off into the brush, hoping that Frank would follow him. Frank stood there watching, hoping Joe would stop and come back.

Joe's lanky frame cut a pathetic shape against the rolling Pyrenean foothills. For all his faults, Frank knew he was as strong as a bull and could probably carry him if things got unbearable. If there was any nastiness to come, Joe was the man he wanted by his side. Reluctantly, Frank hobbled off in pursuit of the teenager.

In truth, Joe had slowed down slightly and was relieved when he heard the old man's shoes on the gravel behind him. Both being stubborn, they said nothing, but Frank noticed Joe had lessened his pace. Unfortunately for Joe, walking in this god-forsaken countryside at night was near impossible. Every track he took seemed to peter out into impenetrable gorse. Frank could not help feeling a wave of joy each time Joe was forced back by the prickly undergrowth, muttering terrible curses. Every cell in his body wanted to scream, 'I told you so!'

Eventually Joe stumbled across a medium-sized road and for the first time in an hour, he spoke to Frank.

'Where do you think this goes?' he said, dropping the customary 'old man'.

'Looks like it heads south-east,' said Frank, consulting his map, 'to the town of Figueres.'

'That on the way to Barcelona?'

'Yes, but—'

'Then I'm takin' it,' Joe announced.

Something about walking on the road was worse than in brush. The relentless pounding of concrete had even less give than gravel and without gorse thickets blocking the way, Frank lost the sporadic breaks his knee needed. Gradually, his leg muscles started twinging with cramp. Fatigue was bedding in and after a few miles, he knew he must stop soon or face collapse.

'Joe,' called Frank to the shape ahead of him, 'I can see a farm up there and I'm going to try and find somewhere to sleep.' His voice was perfectly calm and reasonable. 'My knee – it's too painful. You can go on without me if you like.' Joe said nothing, but he did not carry on walking.

Shuffling into a barn, Frank climbed a ladder to the hayloft and struck his lighter. Several large black shapes scurried into a stack of dried peas at the far end. 'What was good enough for rats was good enough for me,' remembered Frank. He climbed into the stack of peas and made a nest for himself.

'Ain't they gonna give us away?' asked Joe, gesturing to a row of hens perching on one of the beams. Thankfully he was still on the ladder and had not seen the rats scatter.

'No,' Frank replied. He fell asleep. But after just five blissful minutes, Joe shook him awake.

'Hey, there's rats here. I can hear them. I ain't stoppin' here no longer, let's go.'

'Please, Joe, I just need an hour, then I'll follow you.'

Joe relented, climbed down to the doorway and tried to sleep on the floor. Again, Frank fell into a fitful sleep, but was woken by a tugging on his pocket.

A rat had crawled inside his pocket and was nibbling the meat Manuel had given him. He whammed his fist down hard on his pocket and the rat squealed and dashed off. Frank decided to join Joe on the floor, carrying down some pea stalks to cover them both, as he could see Joe shivering violently.

'After that I had a good hour's sleep,' recalled Frank, 'but at 3.30 a.m. Joe woke me and said he couldn't stand the cold any longer and we had to "push off".' Frank took pity on the shivering teenager. He felt better for having slept, some of the giddiness had gone, but his swollen knee trembled with pain. They headed back to the road.

'Of course, we shouldn't have used the main road,' wrote Frank, 'but that's what you do when you're fatigued. Take risks.'

The hellish march continued, Joe leading, Frank twenty yards behind. Whenever a car passed, they both jumped into the ditch. Tiny splodges of light were appearing in the sky as they trudged past a sign reading 'Figueres – 10'. Detouring up a hill to avoid a village, the pair realised their climb had been pointless, for a river lay across their path to Figueres and the only bridge was in the centre of the village.

Risking capture for the sake of dry feet, they marched through the town and over the bridge, Frank forcing himself to walk normally. Mercifully, a hut marked 'Control' was empty. Although they had not said it, Figueres had become the goal of both men. It was only four miles away and Frank hoped desperately he could make it before dawn broke. He envisioned sleeping all day in the hot sun on a quiet riverbank somewhere, bathing in its refreshing water when they got too hot.

The awful concrete road snaked its way towards Figueres. Frank and Joe shuffled silently past farmers milking in the pre-dawn gloom, as sleepy-eyed locals riding carts into town overtook them. It was light enough for it to be pointless jumping into the ditch now.

Frank was suffering. The lights of Figueres were blurring as his vision played tricks on him. He ached to the marrow of his bones. Even Joe had started offering sympathy and encouragement, but his words fell on deaf ears.

Just outside Figueres, Frank reached his limit. He had been summoning strength he did not have, and he felt he was causing long-term damage to his knee. Turning off the road, he slumped against a large stone wall and finished the meat the rat had chewed earlier, not caring whether Joe joined him or carried on.

'I was so utterly fatigued,' Frank recollected. 'I knew I would pass out if I walked any further. Joe seemed as fresh as a daisy and could not understand why I couldn't go any further.'

The pair sat for an hour, Joe keeping watch as Frank dipped in and out of sleep. A loud bugle sounded from behind the wall that Frank was sitting against.

'The hell was that?' said Joe, jumping to his feet with enviable ease.

'Must be a military barracks,' suggested Frank, 'we need to get out of here.' He rose wearily. 'You can do what you want, but I'm going into Figueres to see if I can jump a freight train to Barcelona. If not, I'll buy a passenger ticket. No more walking.'

Joe grumbled something but followed.

The outskirts of Figueres were pleasantly deserted, but the market was busy and the whole town looked as though it was celebrating Frank and Joe's arrival. Flags hung from every window, bunting criss-crossed the streets and bullfighting posters were plastered across every wall. Frank noticed some stalls had bananas and oranges, the first he had seen in four years.

At the train station, Frank approached the friendliest-looking old man he could see and asked, '*A qué hora es el tren por Barcelona?*'

The old man shook his head. '*Solo Girona. A 9.30.*'

Girona it was then. With forty-five minutes to kill, Frank and Joe wandered into a small park outside the station and tried to look inconspicuous while sunning their cold, aching bones. A sparrow sat on the bench next to them, ruffling its wings and shaking its head. Frank spotted a post-box and popped his letter to the British Consul into it.

At 9.15 a.m., the pair walked into the station. Frank bought two tickets to Girona at five pesos each. There was no friendly look, no wink of encouragement as the man clipped their tickets. Sunshine was bathing the outer half of the platform, so Frank and Joe, still defrosting from the night's march, went and stood in it.

Craning his neck so the sun reached down his collar, Frank knew he looked out of place but did not care. He closed his eyes and felt heat seep into his pores.

From somewhere in the blissful darkness, Joe whispered, 'This guy's got his eye on us.'

Frank opened his eyes and saw how the platform had filled with people, some in the uniform of the Guardia Civil, Franco's fascist, paramilitary police force.

But Frank could also see their train approaching and he knew they would be on board in minutes. He tried to look unbothered as it steamed into the station, the controller taking an age to open all the doors.

As the carriage doors opened, Frank felt the crowd compress around him, scrambling to get good seats. I'll be safe in the middle of this melee, he thought. He took a step forward to board, reaching out for the handrail. The crowd jabbered away in Spanish and the train's brakes hissed.

Joe's hand fell heavily on his shoulder. What does he want now? Frank thought, turning to face him.

But there was no Joe.

Instead, an unsmiling officer of the Guardia Civil stared back, one hand on Frank's shoulder, the other on his holstered pistol.

At the Font de la Fontfreda near the Spanish border, I wake to the sound of feet thumping the earth. Emerging from my sleeping bag, I realise my camp is metres from a path now being used for a trail-running race. The leaders are thundering past in the cool morning air, their thighs pumping like pistons, lungs panting like steam engines.

Breakfasting on cold pizza, quiche and tangerines, I prepare for the final push to Spain just a few kilometres away. Had I stuck to Frank and Joe's pace, I would have been waking up on the other side of the border. But as their crossing point over the Pic de les Salines is only a few hundred metres' climb in elevation away, I hope I might catch up with a good day's hike.

The going is challenging but enjoyable, mostly through dense beech forests with silvery trunks wrapped in patchworks of lime-coloured lichens. The forest is broken up by large fields of jagged boulders, the gaps in-between them filled with heather, moss and ferns. A long, dry autumn has left the mountain's waterfalls and streams toothless.

Crossing these mountains in the dead of night, however, would have been a very different beast with the streams full, the amphetamine hallucinations kicking in, the threat of capture looming and a seriously gammy knee.

After an hour's pleasant trekking, I reach the shoulder of the mountain and a small, third-rate road running west along the border. Was this where Frank lay in the bushes listening to the German patrols marching up and down? I stroll across a small clearing, past a few volunteers standing next to an enormous pile of orange peels they had handed out to the trail runners. Like Frank, I clamber right up to the peak, where thick shards of rock stand like giant razor blades.

I brew a celebratory cup of tea and wash it down with the wild boar saucisson, goat's cheese and crackers that Marie-Laure gave me. The Griffiths family are once again being helped by the Saqués to cross the Pyrenees.

I take my first steps into Spain. Immediately it feels different. The mixture of deciduous trees in France gives way to conifers, while the trail, now blanketed in sweet-smelling pine needles, is even drier and dustier. I have entered the Pyrenees' rain shadow, a phenomenon that occurs on the leeward side of mountains when descending air warms up and dries out, resulting in less precipitation. Walking here feels vastly more Mediterranean than the French side not one mile away.

The atmosphere too is different. As I plod downhill, shots ring out through the forest as hunters add wild boar to their larders. A scraggly mongrel begins following me, barking pathetically. Walkers acknowledge me with '*Buen día*', instead of '*Bonjour*'.

A few kilometres into Spain, I make a serious navigational error. Rather than keep to the trail following the Rinadal stream, I stray west and get lost in a series of dead-end paths. Eventually, with the sun beating down, I surrender and take the bumpy track to a town called Maçanet de Cabrenys. It is not the route Frank took and it is not even particularly short, as it snakes too far west and the vegetation is too thick for me to cut a path between switchbacks.

But the going is decent and the view of the Boadella Reservoir, snatched between ash and pine branches, is impressive. The only catch is the nagging pain growing in my legs. As usual I have begged for the uphill to end, only to find the downhill is more painful.

A convoy of 4×4s pass me, boar and deer carcasses hanging limply on their roofs. The occupants, always old and hard-looking, are dressed head to toe in camouflage, but with orange high-vis vests. Twirling cigarettes in their moustachioed mouths, they hold a hand aloft and smile at the dusty, limping Brit being followed by a barking mongrel. *Mad dogs, Englishmen, midday sun . . .*

The dusty track turns to actual road as I enter Maçanet de Cabrenys. It is 4 p.m. and there is not a soul about. The shops are all closed, the roads devoid of cars and the streets deserted. I am hot and bothered and want a break, so I sniff out the town's bar. In a beautiful, cobbled square, the Bar la Pau appears like an oasis. I enter through its large wooden doors into a dancing hall ringed by an interior balcony and lit by three enormous windows at one end, like those of a church.

A few men playing cards fall silent as I trudge in, barefoot and stinking, and approach the bar. I think for a moment there may be a shoot-out, but a young bartender appears and saves me from the locals' hostile stares. '*Cerveza, por favor*.' She opens a freezer door behind her, takes out a frosty pint glass and fills it with a local Catalonian beer. The top inch of the pint forms a slush immediately. With a pack of crisps under each armpit, I return to the shady square and drink deeply, whimpering softly.

Figueres, however, is still a depressing twenty-seven kilometres away. I know there is no way I can catch up with Frank and Joe, but every step I take today, I will not have to take tomorrow. Spirit buoyed and head significantly lighter, I press on south-east down the steep-sided Rinadal valley, giggling like a schoolboy after his first alcoholic drink. Eventually I reach the western edge of the Boadella Reservoir and make it about halfway along its banks when an attractive bridge catches my eye.

It is flat, grassy and has a view up a steep gorge where a trickle of water tumbles out of some Pyrenean foothill into Boadella. Exhausted, I slump against the crumbling bricks of the bridge's walls and whip up a meal in my mess tin – Ben's Mexican Rice with boar saucisson chunks.

Darkness falls quickly. The orangey triangle of sky above the gorge fills with jinking bats. I realise, tucked in my sleeping bag, this is the first day in years I have not looked at my phone even once. Sad, but true. It died the night before. Lying on my back, I watch the twilight give way to a starry canvas, wondering if Frank had been able to enjoy the night sky on his night march to freedom.

The night passes fitfully. The tinkle of the stream thirty metres below makes me need a pee and I am convinced every crackle from the forest is a wild boar stomping over the bridge.

With Marie-Laure's supplies exhausted, I pack up my sleeping bag and tramp off in the direction of Figueres. The air is beautifully cool as I stroll along a bed of pine needles in silence, hankering for coffee and croissant. After passing an upturned BMW motorbike on the track, clearly too heavy for its owner to right by themselves, I find a café in the town of Darnius.

It was somewhere near Darnius that Frank and Joe were left to go it alone. Reading between the lines, they argued bitterly as Joe, significantly junior to Frank in rank and age, tried to blaze his own trail through these thickly overgrown foothills in the darkness.

I cannot imagine what Frank would have looked like. Limping heavily, with torn clothes, a scarred face and wild hair, he must have looked like a zombie. I imagine he had deep, deep lines in his face, bloodshot eyes and the pained expression of a man suffering a 'come down' off a potent methamphetamine, not to mention the severe lack of sleep for three nights.

Arriving in Pont de Molins, I know I am close. There is a large bridge in the centre of town, almost certainly the one Frank took at dawn, slipping past the sleeping guards. I pick up a footpath alongside the E15 – the main motorway from France to Spain – which, if I drove, would have taken me from Perpignan to Figueres in fifty minutes, as opposed to four day's hard walking.

The flat coastal plain of Figueres unfurls before me. Loud, dirty trucks thunder past as I stop to pick pomegranates and chew on the seeds. In the gritty outskirts of Figueres, the pain dogging my legs eases and before I know it, I am standing in the centre of town admiring a blue-and-yellow water fountain and a homage to Salvador Dalí.

Paella and wine await.

CHAPTER 10

SPANISH PRISONERS

'Follow me, please,' said the Franco policeman on Figueres train station platform.

Frank and Joe filed in behind the bulky frame of the officer, who parted the crowd boarding the train with a wave of his hand.

'Aviators?' he asked.

Frank nodded. '*Inglés*,' he said, and '*Americano*,' gesturing at Joe.

The man looked impressed and signalled for them to follow. After ten minutes he turned into Figueres police station. A group of men in plain clothes sat around a table playing cards.

'I want to speak to the British consulate,' said Frank firmly. No one replied.

He repeated himself.

'*Mañana*,' the officer replied half-heartedly. He took Frank and Joe downstairs, ushered them into a cell and closed the door firmly. The bars of its small grille rattled down the corridor.

No one knows I am in here, thought Frank. He had heard of airmen being imprisoned in Spain for months, even years. The thought of doubling or tripling his three-month stint in Europe filled him with dread. He had already missed nearly half of Tessa's life. It was her first birthday in two months. *That letter better reach the British Consul.*

Even Joe, who feared nothing but dogs and rats, was rattled. He leaped to the door and gripped the bars of the grille, pulling on them like the collar of a man in a fight.

'Ever heard of a trial?' he yelled through the grate. 'I'm never complainin' about the USA again.'

Frank took in his new surroundings. The cell was filthy. Measuring five feet by eight, it was made entirely from stone and there was not so much as a bench to sit on. It had no window; the only light came through the grille in the door. In one corner stood a broken-down lavatory with several dark stains running out of its base.

After an hour the officer returned. 'Follow me,' he said to Frank, leading him downstairs to a dirty cubicle. He jammed Frank's hands into a putrid smelling ink tray to take his fingerprints. With the ink still wet, he was then led to a back room downstairs. A close-cropped, brutal-looking Spaniard sat waiting for him.

'How did you enter Europe?' he demanded.

'I crashed on the fifteenth August in the Milan raid, but escaped to Switzerland,' Frank half-lied. 'I want to speak to the British Consul. I've been locked up with no trial.'

'Yes, yes, we are contacting the consul,' came the reply. 'But how did you come to Spain? What was your route over the Pyrenees?' His manner was aggressive. 'What aircraft were you flying?'

Frank babbled nonsensically about his route, before telling the Spaniard he was flying a Halifax on the Milan raid.

'No, it was a Spitfire,' the interrogator said.

'No, Halifax,' insisted Frank.

The Spaniard wrote down Spitfire. He was not very intelligent.

'Tell me your route over the mountains.'

'I can't, we crossed at night-time. I didn't know where I was.'

'That's impossible, you arrogant English think you can fool us . . .' Frank pulled out a small pocket compass. The Spaniard stared as if he had never seen one before. After several minutes' explanation, he finally understood and called for all his colleagues to come and see this marvellous instrument. Frank was sent back to his cell, but Joe was gone.

An anxious hour passed, the first he had spent alone in weeks, until the guard returned and took Frank back to the interrogation room.

'You were not on the Milan raid on fifteenth August,' the interrogator began. 'We checked. So why are you lying to us? Do you think we Spanish aren't intelligent enough to check?' Frank, who was still shaking from his cold cell, tried to hide his fear, but he was sure he was going to be roughed up.

'Tell me how you came to Spain,' the interrogator continued. 'Your American boy already has, so there is no point in lying anymore. If you tell me, you can have a bed. You can sleep.'

It was standard interrogation procedure that the RAF were trained for.

There's no way Joe has told them anything, that's for sure, thought Frank. Could I make up a route over the Pyrenees without endangering Antoine and his family? His bones still ached and fatigue clouded his brain. If he could just sleep, he could work out what to do. He had to sleep somehow . . .

'How did you enter Spain!' roared the interrogator, standing up and banging a fist on the table. It had a peculiar effect on Frank. The physical action triggered some competitive response within him. A stubbornness forged in the Dee Estuary came alive. I'm under this man's skin, he thought. He's not going to break me. I don't think he's even going to hit me.

'I told you I walked over the mountains, but it was at night-time, I didn't know where I was.'

'Lies! We know you are a squadron leader and that you were carrying arms for the French Resistance. Why won't you admit it? Typical English arrogance. You will lose this war because of it,' lectured the interrogator.

Blimey, they know all that, thought Frank. The Spanish must be in cahoots with the Germans to know that. So much for their neutrality.

'How are you a squadron leader at only thirty-one? The RAF really are desperate. No such thing would be allowed in Franco's great Air Force.' On and on the interrogator went about ranks in the Spanish Armed Forces, Franco's strength of character and why Russia was a menace to the world. He was so interested in his own lecture, he forgot to continue questioning Frank.

By dusk the interrogation was over. Frank and Joe were ordered to form up outside the police station.

'Where are we going?' asked Frank.

'To a nicer prison,' said one of the guards. 'Move.' Marching at gunpoint, Frank could not help thinking about the party of chained prisoners he saw being marched across the French border town of Annemasse to the Pax Hotel, to face Barbie and his Gestapo colleagues in the dungeons.

Two huge walls loomed out of the half-light and Frank recognised the building immediately. It was the fortress he and Joe had rested against on their way into Figueres, the one he thought was a barracks. 'Each wall, fifteen feet high and five feet thick, had an armed guard at each corner. We passed through three sets of great iron gates on the way in and I had a feeling it was going to take some getting out of,' he recalled.

The duo were marched into one of the central buildings, along a corridor and into cell number seven, where they joined five elderly Frenchmen. Like the police station, the cell was all stone with a lavatory in one corner and a stone basin in the other. The floor was thick with grime and the air heavy with the smell of drains. There was no bench or newspaper, but there was a window way up on the outside wall. The last of the day's light was filtering between its iron bars. It was a pathetic amount of light, but it was vitally important, for it allowed a prisoner to keep a track of time.

The Frenchmen seemed to have accepted their fate and were sitting down in the grime. Frank joined them and felt the penetrating cold leap up through the concrete. He put his head in his hands and tried to think, but his mind was utterly fatigued from three nights' marching and hours of interrogation. He seemed only to focus on his aching bones and the filthy hole he found himself in.

Gradually the sun set, extinguishing what little light the prisoners had left, until they sat in pitch darkness. 'I had the feeling one might easily die in such a place with no one any the wiser,' wrote Frank.

The door flung open and the cell filled with harsh light. A shaven inmate stood in the doorway.

'Up. Everyone out. Hurry if you want a blanket,' he said. Joe barged his way out and everyone followed. Several men with shaved heads bossed the inmates into a line and began a thorough search. They were obviously senior prisoners trusted by the Spaniards to help run the prison.

Frank's searcher, the large Frenchman who had opened their cell, discovered his last few items from his escape kit but, strangely, he popped them back where he had found them. He gave Frank's arm the slightest pat. It was a clear signal and it felt terrific. *He's one of us.*

After the searching, each man was issued with two blankets and a hunk of bread, both from the Red Cross. 'I did not appreciate the Red Cross until Figueres,' said Frank. 'I do not know how I would have survived without them.'

Back in the cell, Frank attempted to get comfortable for the night. 'I will never forget that stinking floor. There was not enough room for us all to lie down, but I managed to get in a corner as far away from the lavatory as possible. This was fortunate for as the night wore on, it soon became apparent that the old men suffered from weak bladders. The consequences of this in utter darkness in an over-crowded cell are best left to the imagination.'

Frank and Joe tucked up against one wall and were able to sleep sporadically, turning over every forty minutes to relieve their aching backs. The night was filled with fierce scuffles as the other inmates trod on each other on the way to the lavatory. Through the window, sentries called to each other every fifteen minutes on the perimeter wall.

Friday, 29 October, was Frank's first morning in prison. The cell door was kicked open. It was the prison governor checking that all prisoners were present. His assistant followed, handing out bowls. Behind him some orderlies were dragging an enormous black cauldron of coffee down the corridor. The inmates were allowed to take one ladleful each. The pot was almost certainly never washed and the coffee stank.

'It tasted foul,' Frank recalled. 'Only extreme thirst enabled me to drink it.' His cellmates, who had been inside longer than him, fought to get their ladleful first, which resulted in much of the putrid liquid being spilled.

'Showers! Everyone out,' called the governor's assistant, walking down the corridor banging on every door. All fourteen cells emptied into the prison yard, where some communal showers stood.

'Strip and shower!' came the order. It was the first time Frank had seen all the prison's occupants and it was a grisly sight. Ranging widely in nationality and age, most had the huge, bloated tummies of malnourishment, sunken eyes and shaven heads. Their skin was peppered with red blotchy bites, festering impetigo scabs, and one man even had several deep scars criss-crossing his back. He was a Polish soldier who had been captured at the very start of the war and whipped by the Germans after attempting to escape.

The shower was freezing but refreshing. Afterwards, Frank was marched to the prison doctor's room where he was inoculated, then the barber's room to be shaven. 'It was the most luxurious place in the whole prison. There were chairs!' observed Frank.

Under a large portrait of General Franco, the prisoners had their heads shaved. It was a convivial atmosphere. The barbers, who were also prisoners, talked openly about their hatred of Franco and held their razors to his throat each time they passed the imposing painting.

With Frank's abundant locks hacked off in tufts and smoothed over with a razor, he got up to join Joe and the rest of the men filing out.

'Joe, what are those scars on the back of your head? Did you get them when you baled out of your Fortress?' he asked.

Joe turned around and grinned. 'Nah, they used to throw bricks at me when I was a kid living on thirty-third street. Reckon they wouldn't mess with me now.'

Frank agreed. Joe was a terrifying sight. He had appeared tough before, but now his six-foot-four frame was complete with a scarred, shaven head. He looked like a hardened criminal.

Despite their battles in the Pyrenees, Frank could feel them growing closer in prison. Joe knew he needed Frank's smattering of French and Spanish, as well as his status as a Brit and an officer. Frank knew he needed a big bloke who could fight. Like typical men, they had gone from hating each other to

The grave of Frank's crew members two days after the crash. The young men were buried in Meythet Cemetery, half a mile from the crash site.

Thousands of locals visited the airmen's grave in the aftermath of the crash, burying it with flowers and crosses. This cross commemorated the one crew member whose remains could be identified, Robert Peters.

Hélène Bastin, aka Pépette, proprietress of 'Ma Baraque' in her younger years.

'Ma Baraque', the restaurant-*cum*-brothel where Frank was hidden in the loft while he recovered from his injuries.

Mimi Pallud (*left*) and her brother-in-law, André. Mimi hid Frank in her house, Le Petit Coin, on the condition she tell her neighbours he was a lunatic who had escaped the local asylum.

Josette Pallud, Mimi's six-month-old baby who reminded Frank of his own baby, Tessa, at home.

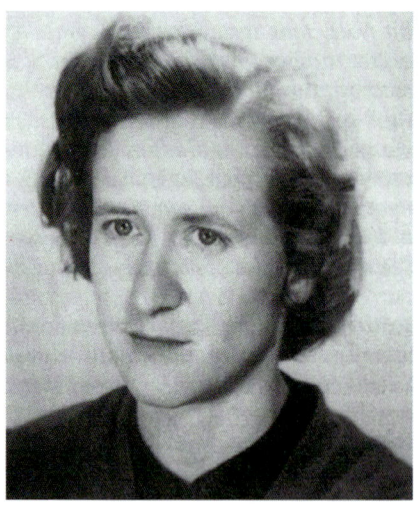

Colette Périès-Martinez, the 22-year-old French woman who walked with Frank to the Swiss border.

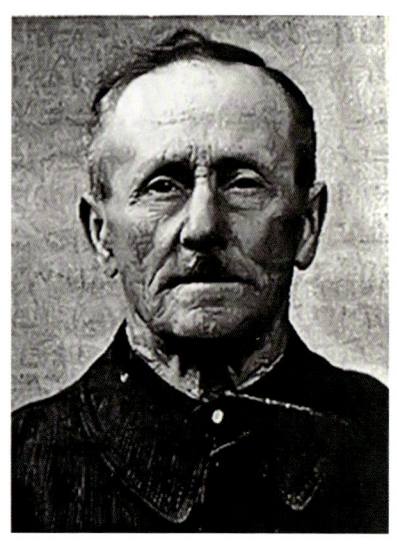

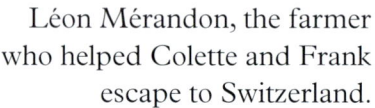

Léon Mérandon, the farmer who helped Colette and Frank escape to Switzerland.

The Swiss–French border passing Léon Mérandon's farmhouse (*on the right*).

Joan and Felix Plottier, the couple Frank stayed with in Switzerland. The Griffiths and Plottier families became close friends after the war and remain so to this day.

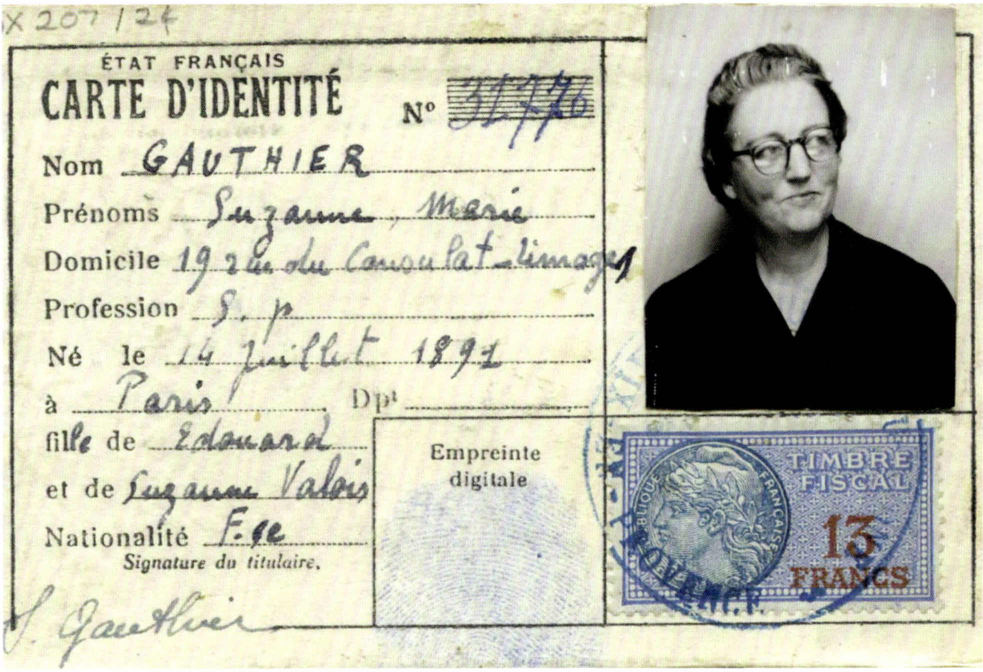

ÉTAT FRANÇAIS
CARTE D'IDENTITÉ   Nᵒ ~~3~~

Nom *GAUTHIER*

Prénoms *Suzanne, Marie*

Domicile *19 rue du Consulat Limoges*

Profession *S. p*

Né le *14 Juillet 1891*

à *Paris* Dpt

fille de *Edouard*

et de *Suzanne Valois*

Nationalité *F.se*

Signature du titulaire.

S. Gauthier

Empreinte digitale

TIMBRE FISCAL **13 FRANCS**

Thérèse Baudot de Rouville, the red-headed Irish-French woman
who ran Françoise's safehouse in Toulouse. (Suzanne Gauthier
was one of her many *nom de guerres*.)

Marie-Louise Dissard,
'Françoise', the chain-smoking
62-year-old who couriered
Frank across France to Toulouse
under the Germans' noses.

Joe Manos, the 19-year-old American who hiked over the Pyrenees with Frank.

Antoine Saqué, the 28-year-old Catalan who guided Frank and Joe over the Pyrenees into Spain.

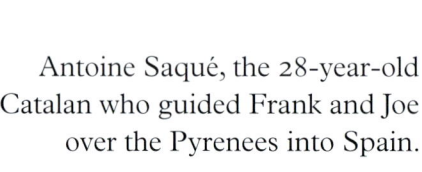

Figueres jail, or *Castell de Sant Ferran*, where Frank was imprisoned after crossing the Pyrenees.

Retracing Frank's escape in 2022.

With Marie-Annick and Samuel
Fontaine, granddaughter and great-
grandson of Angéline Fontaine.

With Josette and Nico,
daughter and grandson
of Mimi Pallud.

With Bernadette and Laëtitia
Mordal, granddaughter and
great-granddaughter of
Léon Mérandon.

With Marie-Laure Saqué at
the farmhouse where the
Saqué family hid Frank.

Frank returns to Gibraltar 79 years later.

close comrades without so much as a word said. They knew
they were in this together.

Back in their cell, the two men sat shoulder to shoulder on
their blankets until dinner time. Like the coffee, dinner was
dragged along the corridor in a cauldron. When it reached the
cell door, a mêlée broke out as the men fought to get their
ladleful. 'The strange thing was that although you were mad
with hunger, when the soup arrived you would be overfull by
the time you had drunk it, yet half an hour later you would be
hungry again,' said Frank.

'Oi, you two, come to the door now and I can transfer you
to my cell with the American,' said the governor's assistant
from the corridor. Frank and Joe needed no second invitation.
They slipped across into cell six, the governor's assistant on
their tail.

'André,' said the assistant, extending one of his bony hands
and closing the door behind him. He was tall and lean, but
with a pot belly like a cartoon character. I must get out of here
before that happens to me, thought Frank. 'I've been here for
two years,' André said. 'I was on my way to join the Free
French when they arrested me. How did you two end up
here?'

Frank and Joe explained their story briefly, wary that André
could be a stoolpigeon.

'They gave you two years just for leaving France?' Frank
enquired.

'No, not just that. When I came over the Pyrenees in 1940,
I stupidly brought my father's revolver. He'd used it in the
First War, said he wanted me to have it and that it was my turn
to fight, the fool.' He had a gaunt, steely face and already
Frank could sense his command of cell six.

'Anyway, when I was arrested, the Spaniards took one look
at the revolver and gave me three years for smuggling arms

into Spain,' continued André. 'They'll lock anyone up. Gives them bargaining power with other countries. That's why you two are in here.' André gestured to their new surroundings. They were a great deal more hospitable than where they had just come from.

For a start, there were only six men in their new cell and not eight, with the bonus that all were young and had some form of military training, essential if six men are to live harmoniously in a cell measuring fourteen by seven feet. It was less grimy too, and the lavatory did not leak. As head of the Red Cross stores, André held sway in jail. Like all long-term prisoners, he had contacts on the outside. Frank later learned he received a small allowance from the British Consul each week, which he used to help feed British prisoners. Even in jail André was contributing to the Allied effort.

Cell six also held Clement Carlotto, another Frenchman who had fled France, an Italian pilot called Ricardo, a Belgian bee farmer pretending to be an Englishman called 'Henry Brown' and, finally, the American Pete Seniavski.

Pete, a waist gunner, was still in his uniform having been shot down on the Schweinfurt-Regensburg raid on 17 August – one of sixty Flying Fortresses to go down that day. Having been knocked out on landing, Pete regained consciousness in time to avoid several German farmers hunting the downed airmen with shotguns and rifles. Unbelievably, he made it to Spain in eight days, almost entirely on his own and without a word of French or German.

After a few hours in cell six, a guard arrived with two tatty mattresses. 'For the Englishmen,' barked the guard as he thrust them into the cell, looking at Frank and 'Henry Brown', the Belgian. 'We found that by putting them end to end,' Frank recollected, 'we could all lie with our hips on them and thus stop the intense cold from striking through the concrete floor.'

André guessed they had probably come from the British Consul.

Does someone know I'm in here? thought Frank.

The next morning, 2 November, Frank made a crucial discovery. The unmarked tube from his escape kit was not in fact burn ointment, as he thought, but condensed milk. 'We had a smear of milk on the tips of our fingers for breakfast. It was grand; for it took away the awful taste in our mouths which collected overnight.'

It was his first full day in cell six, and already a routine was establishing itself.

First the inmates purged themselves of the bugs that descended from the ceiling in the night to feast on their flesh. Each bug, trapped between the men's fingertips, was ceremoniously squashed on one wall, where their blood (recently the prisoners' blood) was being used to write 'De Gaulle' on the whitewash.

Coffee followed, before a 'wash' in the prison yard and ten minutes to stretch their legs. Frank learned that the bullet-hole riddled wall was in fact the 'execution wall', though André assured him prisoners were rarely shot.

After that the hours were whiled away sitting on the mattress in cell six talking, chiefly about food. 'How our minds kept harping back to that eternal subject,' remembered Frank. The prison ration of two ladles of cabbage soup per day and a quarter pound of Red Cross bread every other day was woefully insufficient. 'I was so hungry, I swore I would never complain about food in the mess again. I was once a mess secretary and I only wish I could have put a few of the chaps who used to write complaints about only having their eggs fried on one side and similar rubbish in Figueres jail.'

Comradeship grew quickly in the cell. Clement was receiving thirty-five pesetas from the Free French Organisation, and this combined with André's money from the British Consul meant the pair could buy items from the staff canteen like bananas or figs, albeit at an extortionate rate. 'I was much struck by the *esprit de corps* in the cell,' said Frank. 'If anyone had any food, they made no attempt to eat it secretly, but shared with the rest.'

Occasionally Frank's mind wandered home. Closing his eyes, he transported himself out of his hellhole and into his and Ruth's cottage in Malvern. What was she doing right now? He pictured her feeding their baby Tessa. He saw her giggling and burbling nonsensically while he pulled silly faces, her face screwed up in laughter. The vision warmed him, for he knew that whatever the Spanish did to him, they could not take it away.

The last 'fixture' of each day occurred at sundown, the singing of Franco's song in the prison yard. Shuffling from their cells with swollen bellies and shaved heads, the scraggly procession of inmates were encouraged (at gunpoint) to 'sing the song loudly', particularly the ending: '*Viva Franco! Viva Franco! Viva Franco!*'

Never one for tradition, Frank sung 'Viva Spanko!' loud enough for his cellmates stood around him to hear. Soon they were all at it. It was one of the few good moments of each day, belting out the nonsensical words as the sun set, a final smile before another cold, scratchy night.

Thirst was a constant problem. 'The orderlies seemed to make a point of not giving us water so they could charge us for a glass when they pleased.' The system, so obviously a scam to shaft the malnourished prisoners, caused deep resentment between inmate and guard.

On Frank's fourth day in jail, he banged on the cell door for several minutes, eventually attracting the attention of a guard.

'*Agua, por favor, señor,*' he pleaded.

His throat was scratchy and swallowing uncomfortable. The guard pretended to take pity and returned with a glass of water, holding it through the flap in the door for Frank to take. But as Frank reached out, the guard jerked his hand and chucked the water in Frank's face, cackling with laughter.

But what the guard had not seen was Joe sitting beside the door. He instinctively grabbed the guard's hand and forced it back against the door, spraining his wrist in an instant.

'That'll teach you, you fascist piece of shit!' he shouted. Days of internment with no way of fighting back had embedded a restless fury in Joe.

The guard yelled something in Spanish and footsteps filled the corridor. Keys began turning in cell six's lock. Joe, however, was laughing and shouting at the guards to bring it on. He was desperate for action; he looked like a madman.

'Joe, just take it, don't fight,' implored Pete, as the key turned. 'They'll shoot you.'

The door flew open and several guards bundled Joe out into the corridor, where for the next ten minutes he was kicked and punched. The thuds rained down until Joe, laughing maniacally and screaming, 'Is that all you've got, you fascist bastards?', fell silent.

Maybe he's unconscious, thought Frank, fearing worse. The cell door was opened and Joe flung back inside. He was bruised and bleeding but smiling.

'Too many to fight by myself. Bastards thought they had me on the ropes when I went quiet. That was nothing compared to some of the beatings I got on thirty-third street.'

Despite Clement's money, André's clout and the two mattresses, Figueres jail was a punishing place, even capable of sapping the morale of an optimist like Frank. 'The constant hunger after the trip over the mountains put me in very low spirits,' he recalled. 'It wasn't so bad during the day when we were talking, but during the night it was horrible. I began to believe I was never going to get out.'

On Frank's fifth day in jail, André told him the prison governor had received instruction for all British and Americans to be put under the surveillance of the Spanish Air Force somewhere other than Figueres. He did not know where, and it could be another prison, but Frank could not help feeling a tremor of hope. Perhaps it was somewhere he might be fed three meals a day, not one bowl of soup. Perhaps there would be beds, no lice, and somewhere to walk around outside when he pleased. Perhaps he could write to his wife.

Pete, the other American in the cell, seemed to have been left off the list. Frank and Joe tried to console him, but he was not having it. 'He was in a very low state and began banging his fists on the wall,' Frank related. 'I was afraid his mind was going. Few people realise how utterly depressing a prison can be, particularly Spanish.'

Pete was still cursing when Frank and Joe were summoned by the governor to the prison office. 'I felt on top of the world,' said Frank. 'Just to get a look at the outside world after that stinking cell was incredible.' His piercing hunger seemed to leave him. Images of beds with sheets, of personal space, of water whenever he wanted it, drifted around his head.

But the escort transferring Frank and Joe had not arrived.

'Where are they?' asked Frank.

'I don't know,' replied the governor.

'Well, when will we be going?'

'Tomorrow, maybe. Perhaps next week. Not my decision.'

'But we were told today,' said Joe. 'Doesn't anything happen on time around here?'

'Guard! To the cells, now. Go.'

Frank and Joe were taken away and locked in a new cell – number 13 – far away from Clement, André and their precious mattresses. 'We spent the next seven-and-a-half hours pacing up and down that cell,' stated Frank. 'We had no blankets and it was too cold to sit on the floor. We were both very thirsty and we kicked a lot on the door to try and get water, but to no avail.'

Having been so close to leaving Figueres, cell 13 hurt. Hope had needled Frank. 'I reached the depths of my depression around two in the afternoon. Was I ever going to reach England? It seems strange to write about it now. I don't know how I could have felt so depressed, but disappointment had upset me. I had rather a lovable family in England and I felt that I was never going to see them again. It was now three months since I had crashed and it seemed such a long journey home.'

As the afternoon wore on, it became obvious no escort was coming. 'I began to give up all hope. I could understand why the prison guards were so keen on removing from one's possession anything that might be useful for the purposes of dying by suicide.'

The cell grew dark as the last of the day's light faded away. Frank's legs ached to the bone from so much pacing, but to sit down was to freeze. The outside of his fist was bruised from pounding on the door. His throat was parched from shouting. His stomach twisted with hunger. He prepared for another night in this wretched hole. How many more were to come?

Slowly, the temperature fell, bringing quiet across the prison. Frank rubbed his hairless scalp and closed his eyes. Helplessness filled his mind. He massaged his eyes for a while, wracking his brain for positivity, but he knew when he opened them it would be the same bare walls to greet him. The same grimy, freezing floor. The same infernal bugs.

From somewhere behind his eyelids, footsteps echoed. Keys jangled. Lock mechanisms clicked. *Are they opening our cell?*

The door opened. A grey-uniformed policeman with a holstered revolver stepped inside.

'You two, let's go,' he said.

Figueres jail, or Castell de Sant Ferran to give it its proper name, is still the same crushing place where Frank spent the most miserable week of his life.

Like Frank, I approach it from Figueres on foot, a walk of about a kilometre up a gently sloping hill. The jail was originally a vast military fortress built in the eighteenth century. It sprawls across the hill's highpoint, a seemingly endless maze of interlocking, windowless walls rising twelve metres from an empty moat.

It is a pleasant 18°C, but as I walk through the imposing stone gateway and into shadow, I feel the temperature drop. There are no gates or guards now, but the walls are easily a metre thick. Even the moat is surrounded by a six-metre wall. Everything is made of stone or brick and the effect is brutal.

I can only imagine the crushing sense of foreboding that Frank would have felt as he was marched into this fortress, exhausted and limping from the mountains, with no idea if anyone knew he was in there. His description of the place as somewhere 'one might easily die and no one be any the wiser' was spot on.

Covering an enormous 790 acres and with a perimeter of three kilometres, Sant Ferran is the largest bastion fortress in Europe. Under Franco's fascist control, it became a prison for political dissidents in 1939, later airmen, and it remained a jail until 1997. It is now a tourist attraction, with a focus on its groundbreaking architecture and scale for the eighteenth century.

I stroll towards the heart of the fortress, through a series of courtyards and stone archways, flanked continuously by high stone walls with sentry lookouts. I notice parts of the prison that Frank remembered so vividly. The main yard – no longer showers and an execution wall – is filled with grass and small fences. The overcrowded cells, with their leaking lavatories and biting insects, are closed to the public. Looking down a roped-off corridor, I see a heavy red door bolted shut.

Was Frank locked up here? Was this where he and his cellmates wrote 'De Gaulle' across their cell wall in the blood of the insects that had been feeding on them? Where he sympathised with those attempting to die by suicide?

The squalor and hardship of Figueres jail stuck with those who experienced it. 'I start shivering, even now, when I see a piece of concrete,' wrote Frank, forty years after his experience of Figueres jail. To those who heard Frank talk about his escape, the impression was that he had spent most of his three months in Europe inside the Spanish jail, whereas it was in fact just six days.

I have been told he held a grudge against the Spanish for the rest of his life because of his treatment. Frank's daughter Tessa, seven months old at the time of his incarceration, supported the Red Cross for the rest of her life on account of her father's experiences.

But there is no sign to inform people of Sant Ferran's dark history in the Second World War, no mention of it on their website and no plaque to commemorate the incredible resilience of the inmates locked up here. Sant Ferran is a tourist attraction and needs to make money, hence the focus on the vast underground water supplies or the 500-horse stables.

It seems wrong that without knowledge of Frank's story and a great deal of research, Sant Ferran's average visitor would spend a day exploring the fortress and leave without a clue of the degrading treatment prisoners suffered here as pawns in a vast diplomatic game between Franco, Hitler and the Allies.

Having explored most of the former jail, I walk around the dusty, litter-strewn perimeter wall, thick with weeds. To the north, the Pyrenean foothills rise towards France, and I spy the route of Frank's hike and now mine.

Frank was a man who had lived on a boat for six years, who was happiest outside and embraced individuality. He had survived a devastating plane crash, crossed France under the Germans' noses and completed a brutal hike over the Pyrenees at night, only to be locked up by the Spanish in a cramped cell with seven other identically shaven inmates. He was a man blessed with reserves of mental fortitude, but pushed to breaking point.

I leave Sant Ferran hoping not to go back.

CHAPTER 11

GOODBYE TO JOE

The policeman led Frank and Joe down the long corridor, into the prison yard and out of the thick stone entrance into fresh air. 'I could have cried for joy,' Frank remembered. Smelling something other than the stale, filthy prison air was exquisite.

In town, Frank asked the escort if he could buy a hat. Joe still had the beret Thérèse had given him, but Frank felt conscious of his hairless scalp. The escort, a jolly sort, agreed and led the pair to a hat shop.

'Hold up,' called Joe, eyeing a fruit stall off down the street. '*Uno momento*, yeah?' he said to the escort, disappearing into the throng of people. The guard did not seem to care. Even though Joe could have run away, there was little point as he would probably end up back in jail.

Disappointingly, the hat shop had nothing that would fit Frank. That did not matter. Joe had returned with three dozen bananas and three kilos of figs. Frank could not bear to watch him eat it through the shop window. He rushed out, tore upon a banana and chewed vigorously, savouring the sweet, creamy flavour, so wonderfully different from the cabbage soup and stale bread they had existed on for the last week.

The smiling guard tapped his watch and the trio continued to the train station, the location where they had been arrested six days earlier. Frank and Joe barely drew breath as they inhaled figs all the way to the platform.

A tall, pale man in a light suit emerged from the platform crowd.

'You'll be Squadron Leader Griffiths?' he said, in a perfect English accent. 'I'm Smith-Ferrers, the consul's secretary. We got your letter yesterday. Sorry we couldn't get you out sooner.' Frank could have wept. It was such an incredible relief to be able to talk to a fellow countryman.

'I'll be taking you to the Governor's office in Girona. He will arrange for you to stay there before transferring you to the Spanish Air Force,' continued the secretary. 'In your letter you mentioned crossing the Pyrenees with an American . . .?' said Smith-Ferrers, looking at Joe.

'Staff Sergeant Joseph Emanuel Manos, sir,' said the American teenager, bunches of bananas in one arm. '331st Bomb Squad, 94th Bomb Group. Been in France since four-teenth July, Bastille's Day.'

'Excellent,' replied Smith-Ferrers, 'well, if you'd both like to—'

'Who won,' Joe burst out, 'the Yankees or the Cardinals, sir?'

Smith-Ferrers smiled. 'I believe it was the Yankees. Four games to one. Lots of your people have been asking me that.'

'I knew it!' shouted Joe, pumping his fist. 'DiMaggio or not, I knew we could do it!'

Joe was still jabbering when the crowd began to surge. The Girona train was arriving.

Smith-Ferrers raised his voice to be heard. 'There'll be a grand dinner for you tonight in the hotel and beds, of course. I'm not sure how long you'll have to wait in Girona, the Spanish Air Force take an age to do anything . . .' Frank was not listen-ing. He was still registering the words 'grand dinner' and 'bed'.

On the train, Smith-Ferrers led Frank and Joe to a first-class carriage where they sat on a seat for the first time since having their heads shaved in the prison barbers. As the train clanked out of the station, Frank watched Figueres jail slide out of sight and thought of the poor wretches left inside.

A final jerk of the train's brakes woke him in Girona. After disembarking, Smith-Ferrers led the pair across town to the Governor's residence. They were stopped twice by men in the street for handshakes. It seemed their lack of hair was not a source of embarrassment, but a badge of honour. 'As soon as you have beaten Germany, we too will be free,' muttered a passer-by.

It was a similar story in Girona's Grand Peninsula Hotel. The head waiter was a communist sympathiser and liked anyone with no hair. He piled huge portions of paella onto Frank and Joe's plates. It was the first time they had eaten a meal off a table since the first night in the Pyrenees at the Saqués' farmhouse. Omelettes and fruit followed, with various side dishes that Smith-Ferrers kept ordering. 'We made absolute pigs of ourselves while he sat back and smiled,' recalled Frank.

As soon as the meal was finished and neither Joe nor Frank could stuff in another mouthful, fatigue hit with a vengeance. They were dead beat, and a week of early nights had changed their body clocks. Climbing into bed with fresh sheets and plump pillows was a wondrous moment for Frank, but sleep would not come. His back and shoulders were used to the stone floor of Figueres, not a soft mattress. Despite the crushing fatigue, his brain refused to drop off, so he climbed out of bed, lay on the floor, and slept like a baby until the morning.

The next morning, 5 November, Smith-Ferrers announced he was returning to Barcelona.

'You're in the Spanish Air Force's hands now,' he explained. 'They will be interning you in a camp in Alhama de Aragón, right in the middle of Spain.'

'How long will we be there?' asked Frank.

'I'm afraid I'm not sure. I'm sure you've realised what the Spanish are like by now. It could be weeks or months. I wouldn't count on being home by Christmas.'

For Frank and Joe, who had spent three and five months in Europe respectively, it was frustrating news. To escape Nazi-occupied France, cross the Pyrenees at night and secure release from a filthy jail, only to be interned in another camp, was maddening.

The luxury and relative freedom the pair found themselves in Girona after the horror of Figueres did help, however. They had arrived in the middle of the Fires de Sant Narcís, a ten-day festival celebrating the patron saint of the city. 'There was fireworks and dancing in the street . . . a band of clarinets and trumpets playing Catalonian songs . . . but there was not a great deal of joy about them.'

Catalonia was the rich province of Spain and, as was becoming painfully obvious, on the losing side in the recent Civil War. Girona was crawling with Franco's forces – police and the army – keeping a close eye on the population, and men like Frank and Joe. Whenever they walked the streets, usually from café to café to play chess and drink coffee, a Franco policeman would tail them. Likewise watching football, bull-fights, or visiting Girona's magnificent cathedral.

If Frank wanted a break from Joe, he would head to the hotel's library. One day he noticed the words: 'No money, no hair, when the hell do I get out of this place?' carved into a desk. Underneath, he scrawled *Per Ardua Ad Astra!*, the RAF's motto. It had made him smile when he spotted it on a bench in the park in Perpignan.

Twelve days after arriving in Girona, a man telephoned the Grand Peninsula and informed Frank they were to leave at 9 a.m. tomorrow for Barcelona.

'Next morning we were ready, but of course no escort arrived,' Frank related. 'This was Spain and to expect anyone to arrive on time was ridiculous.'

Eventually a large black car with a Union Jack fluttering over each headlight arrived. The driver raced the sixty-five miles south to Barcelona and pulled up at another luxury hotel. But there would be no two weeks to explore here, as the pair were to leave for Zaragoza at the early hour of 8.30 a.m. – 'early for Spain'.

Naturally, the escort was late. He had been at a party the night before and was unable to get himself up in time to take them to the station. As Frank and Joe had now missed the train, they would need new permits from the local Governor, General Moscardo. He arranged a permit for the express night train to Madrid. With a day to kill in Barcelona, the airmen wandered the prosperous streets of the city, marvelling at the shop windows laden with produce. 'Our minds were still harping back to food and on the slightest excuse we would go into a café and eat something. The spectre of starvation in Figueres was still with us.'

At 10.30 p.m., the night train departed Barcelona. 'This was the Madrid Express, the main train of the day and the best train in all of Spain,' wrote Frank, 'and its maximum speed was 20mph.' Their escorting officer explained the civil war had left the railways in such a dire state, all trains were limited to this speed.

The train inched its way up onto the Aragón desert plateau, arriving in Zaragoza at 3.30 a.m. Sleeping on the compartment floor, Frank and Joe were roused and told to disembark, as there had been a change of plans. Instead of going straight to the camp at Alhama de Aragón, they would meet up with another group of airmen in Zaragoza before being driven to the camp.

And so Frank and Joe spent another frustrating day waiting. They were joined by about twenty other aircrew, 'Lancaster
boys, most of whom were without their hair.' A bus arrived at
dusk to take them the last 100 miles to the camp at Alhama,
right in the centre of Spain and the Aragón desert. 'It consisted
of miles upon miles of Sweet Fanny Adams,' recounted Frank.
'Sometimes we would sweep past mule trains with the drivers
wrapped in blankets muttering "*mucho frio*" [very cold] to
themselves. That was it.'

It had taken forty-eight hours to travel 300 miles from
Girona to Alhama, but finally the bus arrived at the camp.
Except there was no barbed wire, guards or watch towers in
Alhama, only an enormous hotel.

'With a hundred miles of desert all around, we were not
likely to run away,' Frank observed. As the men sorted themselves out in the hotel foyer, a small, well-dressed Spaniard
approached Frank.

'*Señor Griff?*' he enquired, in a thick Spanish accent.

'*Si*,' said Frank, shaking hands.

'*Bienvenido*, aviator, to my hotel. I am Rodrigo. A man in
Madrid, he just called – General Moscardo – and said you will
be most big chief officer here.' He had not even glanced at
Frank's bald head, as he was so accustomed to skinhead guests.
'He said to make you the boss.' Rodrigo took out a scrap of
paper and read slowly: 'Commanding Officer, Allied Forces,
Alhama de Aragón.' Frank could see where this was going.

'So you are boss of men while here. Please, I have many
airmen in hotel, and their actions are often very bad. They get
drunk, break things, bother my staff and make chaos. They
go . . . how you say . . . *loco*. Please, you must handle them. *Por
favor.*'

Frank looked at the motley group of ragged airmen milling
around the foyer. He imagined trying to control these hairless

young men, mostly fresh from stints in jail and hazardous journeys across Europe, not to mention surviving being shot down in the first place.

To make matters worse, Rodrigo had been instructed to give 100 pesetas to each man by their respective embassies in Madrid.

'A fatal mistake when brandy was five shillings a bottle,' reflected Frank.

He had been asleep for only minutes on his first night in Alhama de Aragón when a policeman burst into his hotel room, crying, '*Mucho vino, commandante, mucho vino!*'

The breathless policeman, with fear in his eyes, gesticulated wildly that there was a fight going on and that Frank better do something about it. He was white in the face and sweating. Frank rose from his bed and woke Bill, a large Canadian pilot with whom he was sharing a room, and asked him to help.

The trio set off down one of the many corridors of the vast hotel. Frank assumed they were heading to the exit and into town, but the policeman had stopped at the beginning of a new corridor.

'*No continuaré,*' he said crossing his arms, motioning for Frank and Bill to continue. Nothing could persuade him to carry on. '*Peligroso.*' ['Dangerous.']

'Brace yourself,' said Frank to Bill as he ventured down the echoey corridor. He prepared himself for blood and violence, hoping no one had picked up any weapons. But as he walked, Frank noticed he could not hear any signs of fighting – no thumps or shouts of abuse. In fact, all he could hear was muffled jazz music and a deep, growly sort of noise. *Was someone being throttled?*

Frank and Bill rounded the corner and came face to face with the source of the trouble. A flabby Canadian taking turns with an American to chunder into a lavatory. 'I had expected at least a dozen chaps to be locked in mortal and deadly combat,' said Frank. 'This however was a situation which, through previous experience, I could easily deal with.'

After fifteen minutes of mopping up sick and enforced water drinking, Frank and Bill eventually got the drunks into their room. The policeman was waiting outside, his stance indicating he expected some sort of bribe, which Frank duly handed over. He later learned the policeman had been called to a bar in town where the airmen had gotten rowdy, but on arriving, the drunks had stopped fighting each other and chased him instead. Returning to the hotel, the Canadian and the American had shared a tin of spam which, combined with the half bottle of brandy they had consumed, did not sit well.

Next morning, Frank arrived at breakfast feeling sheepish. He had promised the hotel manager he would try to control the men, but clearly he had failed miserably.

'It is the same every time,' began the manager, 'you English cannot control yourselves.' Frank prepared for a lecture, but noticed Rodrigo was smiling. 'I have had several hundred aviators through my hotel. When the Russians drink, they cry. When the Spanish drink, they fight. When the Italians drink, they sing. But when the Anglo-Saxons drink, they just go around smashing things.'

After breakfast, Frank went for a walk around the strange little town of Alhama de Aragón. Strolling across the dusty, reddish earth in the cool morning air, he saw what a desperately poor place it was. It existed thanks to geothermal springs, which were hot all year round and attracted tourists who believed that bathing in the warm water afforded healing powers.

Rodrigo's enormous hotel, a short stroll from the springs, hosted these tourists through the summer before closing for the winter. Now it was crawling with young Allied airmen, dashing from lake to hotel in towel-togas with brandy in hand. How do I control these men? thought Frank. I haven't any hair or uniform to instil discipline.

A party of roughly thirty fresh faces arrived at lunchtime. They had been released from various prisons across northern Spain, barring some French Canadians, who had reached their embassies without being arrested and imprisoned. Sadly, there was no outranking man to replace Frank as *comman-dante*, but there were some more officers who seemed fairly steady.

One, a popular American called Hank, started a huge game of craps after lunch. In what was a massive stroke of luck for Frank, Hank and another officer called Boucher were excellent card players. And they had not been drinking. Steadily they won all the other Americans' money. By dinner time, some of the men had not a peseta to rub together. With no money, the aviators could not buy alcohol. Hank and Boucher held the purse strings, nipping much of the carnage in the bud.

Frank spent another three days in Alhama, longing to continue the journey home. Although out of immediate danger, his mind would not rest until he was on the plane home. Any shift in Franco's governance, or any rebalancing of the delicate geopolitical position that Spain found herself in, might land Frank back in jail. Although the war was going relatively well for the Allies in late 1943, Hitler could still exert significant pressure on Spain to slow up the passage of airmen, or reincarcerate them. Spain remained a fascist country and although officially neutral, favoured Germany far more than Britain.

On the evening of 23 November – Frank's ninety-ninth on the continent – a lorry arrived from Madrid and a British embassy official stepped out. He carried with him a letter from the Spanish government authorising the release of all British internees.

'You will leave by lorry tomorrow morning for Madrid,' read the official. 'Madrid will be your last location before you get the train to Gibraltar. You'll be back in Britain before the week is out.'

Frank looked at his watch. It was Tuesday.

He would be spending the weekend with Ruth and Tessa.

Leaving Alhama for Madrid meant saying goodbye to Joe.

As Frank strolled through the interminable corridors of the grand hotel looking for him, he wondered what he was going to say. Despite their differences in age, rank and nationality – not to mention their hatred of one another in the Pyrenees – Frank knew this was the end of a unique relationship. Joe was the only person on Earth who would truly understand what they had gone through.

Frank found his room and knocked.

'Fuck off if you haven't got any money,' came the reply from within. Frank opened the door, revealing several bored airmen sprawled across the room.

'Joe, a word?'

'Oh, hey old man – I mean, sir,' Joe said, looking around at his company. 'Sure.' They stepped outside together.

'Hey, Griff,' began Joe, 'don't suppose you could lend me a couple pesos just to get me back in the game? I'm a good player. I just got unlucky with Hank, I'll—' Frank waved his words away.

'I'm leaving tomorrow,' he said. 'We all are – the Brits, I mean – to Madrid, then home. I don't know why it's taking longer for you lot.'

'Oh yeah, right . . . I see,' said Joe sensing this was goodbye. 'I mean, we'll see about that, hey?' he said, smiling. '*Mañana*, right, how many times did we hear that in this damn country.' They both laughed.

'Well, I'll see you around, Griff,' said Joe, shuffling his feet. 'I mean, old man,' he added, flashing a smile that said: 'I know you hated that name.'

They shook hands briefly. 'Thanks, Joe,' Frank said earnestly. 'We had a couple of tight spots on that trip. It was good to have you.' Good to have you? thought Frank. Is that all you can think to say?

'Hell, we were always gonna make it! Don't know whadya talking about, old man,' joked Joe, reaching for the door handle. 'Now if you'll excuse, I gotta get back to my financial negotiations. Figured I could get the boys to pay me to provide entertainment to them – you know, run around the hotel naked, or shove one of the waiters into the spring or something. See ya later, old man!'

Frank and Joe met just once more in their lives in 1978. Since then, there had been no contact between the Griffiths and Manos families.

I make it my mission to put that right. After months of searching, I am overjoyed to finally locate one of Joe's sons in Sacramento, California, who is also called Joe Manos.

We video call one rainy afternoon in April 2024.

'Hey, Adam, how are ya?' asks Joe Jnr in a soft Californian accent, as our call connects. It is 8 a.m. on the west coast of America and sun is streaming into Joe's home office, illuminating his smiling, clean-shaven face and full head of grey hair. His skin is tanned and healthy and he looks younger than his seventy-one years.

'Hi Joe, I'm good, thank you. How are you?' I reply, rain pattering against my window.

'Doing great, thank you.'

'Thanks so much for talking to me, especially at eight in the morning.'

'I get up early on the west coast, so it's the middle of the day for me,' Joe Jnr jokes. He speaks in a beautifully cadenced voice. I learn he is retired but still busy running a golf club, advising various business associates and spending lots of time with his family. I sense he has been successful in his working life. He is married with two children.

We come onto his father. The first thing Joe Jnr says is, 'My dad was really a private guy, especially when it comes to World War Two, like many of the veterans. His best friend – the right-side waist gunner – was killed when they were attacked, so he watched him die. I know he had nightmares about that for years, my mom told me.'

'I had no idea they were best friends,' I say, trying to imagine my nineteen-year-old self having to leave my best friend's body in an aircraft while I jumped out.

We turn to Joe's early life.

'Dad met my mom [*Dorothy*] in New York, they both grew up there. Mom is still alive aged ninety-eight, it's incredible. They were dating, nothing serious. After the war when he came back, they got married. I think he was still travelling around Europe as part of the Air Force after the war, so they got married in 1952, the year before I was born.'

'Do you know much about your dad's childhood?'

'He had two brothers, both older. His dad passed when he was young. There was a doctor he somehow became connected with, who became almost like a father figure. His mom died in 1950, I think.'

Frank had written about how Joe's harsh upbringing in New York had made him so tough, but the discovery that Joe had lost his dad in his childhood, and that he probably spent his adolescence competing with two older brothers, shed further light on the incredible resilience of the man.

'His eldest brother died in a plane crash – he was in the Air Force as well – a captain,' continues Joe Jnr. 'He died post-war in a training exercise. The other brother was killed in the war too.'

As I scribble notes into my shorthand pad, I realise that by age of twenty-four, Joe had lost his dad and both his brothers. By twenty-six, he had lost his mum too. Perhaps she died of a broken heart.

'And so he joined up straight out of school and got posted to England?' I ask.

'Yeah, pretty quickly. Think they had to wait for an aircraft to get built first.'

'Did he ever talk about his time in England?' I enquire, knowing Joe had been stationed just outside Bury St Edmunds.

'No, not really. The war was just a chapter he compartmentalised and put on a shelf,' says Joe Jnr, gesturing. 'He never talked about it.'

We turn to the raid on Le Bourget on 14 July 1943, the day Joe saw his best friend die, before parachuting into France.

'I know there were a lot of nightmares from that time,' says Joe Jnr. 'He'd just been shot down and he didn't know if he was gonna get shot while he was coming down in his parachute. It's just amazing. If he hadn't escaped the aircraft or the Germans had shot him while he was coming down, I wouldn't be here!' Joe Jnr chuckles in disbelief. 'Crazy.'

I probe gently for what happened next, aware Joe did not talk about the war.

'It must have been then when Dad got separated from his crew,' Joe Jnr explains. 'When I saw a YouTube video of Dad [*recorded as part of a series on Second World War Escape and Evasion in 2016*], that was the first time I'd ever heard him talk about getting shot down. I was just blown away. You know, when he says, "Then we were driving around France with the underground." I was like, oh my God, why would you go driving around on the streets if you could be arrested at any point and thrown in jail!'

I tell Joe Jnr the story of his father landing in a park in Paris, walking to the nearest bar and ordering a beer.

'That wouldn't have been Dad,' says Joe Jnr, laughing, 'he was a very logical thinker. Like it said in the video, he parachuted into the cornfield, buried his chute and then thought he saw a German, so he hid. Somehow he hooked up with the French underground and a farmer told him to hide and he'd come back for him. Dad didn't know if it was a setup, but luckily it wasn't.'

I tell Joe Jnr about the weeks that followed, in which his father was hidden and fed by the local farmer, on the condition that he helped collect the harvest, shoot rabbits and play chess with him in the evenings.

Joe Jnr is not surprised. 'Following the war, Dad was so thankful to the French underground that he sent the key group of folks care packages for years.'

I ask what he was like as a person, as a father.

'He was matter of fact,' explains Joe Jnr. 'There's right and there's wrong and if he saw something that . . . whether it was an officer or someone else . . . if he thought it was wrong, he'd call them out. He'd say, "That's baloney." I could see younger Joe, especially with the New York upbringing, kinda getting in someone's face if they were being stupid.'

I raise the story of Joe slamming the Spanish prison guard's wrist against the cell door after he threw water over Frank.

'Wow, yeah. I'd say that's almost uncharacteristic of Dad. I mean, I could see him doing it, but in his later life he was pretty reserved. I guess if he was locked up, though. I'm sure – being young – he was pretty animated and forthright in his beliefs for sure. Being a parent to me and my upbringing, there was right and wrong and you didn't cross this line. He was a man of few words, but when he said them, you stopped in your tracks.'

Joe Jnr continues, 'He was a great family man over the years. I remember him teaching me how to swim in Guam, he had me jumping off the pontoon. You can see in some of the pictures I've got when he was younger, he had a moustache; he was a good-looking guy.'

I talk of Frank's admiration for Joe's physical resilience and youthful stamina, despite his hatred of exercise.

'He was always in good shape. Very fit. I remember he'd come home from work and before he had his one beer he'd do his workout. His sit-ups, push-ups, all the different calisthenics he did. That was his routine. It came from the military, I guess. Even when he retired, he'd bike and walk for miles every day.'

Again, this surprises me. Are we not talking about the man who refused all exercise in Toulouse under Thérèse's regime? Perhaps he had loathed exercise in his teens, but practised it in his twenties, thirties and forties, before giving it up again in his fifties.

I ask about Joe and Frank meeting in 1978, but Joe Jnr knows nothing. He and his wife had moved away from the area by then, but he is surprised his parents did not take a photo or write something about it.

'Did he ever talk about Frank?'

'Not to me,' says Joe with a wry smile, as though he was expecting the question and wanted to be able to give a different answer. 'I'm sure he did to his flying buddies, but yeah, it's sad, Dad was very private on that stuff, so it's just one of those things.'

Like Frank, Joe had lived an extraordinary, long life. They had both survived traumatic events in the war and dealt with the mental repercussions in their own ways. Both had lost their closest friends. In Ruth and Dorothy, both men had found their lifelong partner, but did not know if the war was going to allow them to spend their lives together.

CHAPTER 12

LIGHTNING STRIKES TWICE

'Next!' bellowed the truck driver taking Frank and his fifteen RAF compatriots from Alhama de Aragón to Madrid. Frank stepped forward, collected his ropey blanket from the man and climbed into the back of his open-topped lorry.

It was a complete joy to be leaving Alhama. Looking back at the hotel, Frank watched the gaggle of Canadian and American airmen who had come to wave them off, whooping and cheering crazily. He chuckled as some mooned the truck. Their bums were soon slapped by opportunist pals and a scrum of headlocks and flailing limbs ensued. *God help whoever is put in charge of them.*

It was 100 miles to Madrid, a journey made exceptionally uncomfortable by Spain's war-torn roads and freezing temperatures. It was 24 November and a biting northerly was blowing down off the Pyrenees, across the desert and into the back of the lorry.

One hour into the journey, Frank spotted a biplane approaching from the north. As it neared, he identified it as a Bücker Bü 133 Jungmeister, a German aircraft from the 1930s – the Luftwaffe's equivalent of the Tiger Moth. The freezing airmen watched more in interest than in fear, as the biplane picked up the lorry's path and descended to a dangerously low altitude. Surely he's not going to? thought Frank. But moments later, the Bücker's gun opened up and bullets whistled through the air.

With absolutely no means of returning fire, and nothing but the lorry itself to hide behind, the escapees were vulnerable. But bizarrely, the Bücker backed off after only one strafe and the lorry arrived safely in Madrid by lunchtime.

Frank spent three days waiting in Madrid for the paperwork for the next leg of the journey to arrive. He was to catch the overnight train to San Roque, the nearest train station to the Gibraltar border. The 500-mile journey was expected to take sixteen hours and could be delayed by anything up to six hours. But progress, no matter how slow, felt better than more interminable delays.

For the first time in a month of travelling across Spain, Frank arrived on time in San Roque. An English army officer was waiting for him. Racing off for the border, Frank soon saw the mighty Rock of Gibraltar, a shuddering reminder that he really had made it. It was a sight he thought he might never achieve at points on his mammoth journey south-west across the Iberian Peninsula.

'We drove past the Spanish border guards and across to Gibraltar,' Frank recorded. 'We were quite overcome by the sight of an English policeman in his ordinary English uniform. Many of us had to swallow twice and I often wonder if that policeman realised what an impression he made on evaders and what his uniform really stood for.'

Exiting the bus, Frank set foot on British soil for the first time in 103 days. It was 28 November 1943. A little over three months had passed since he took off from Tempsford on Operation Pimento.

A staff officer greeted them.

'All flying is cancelled today, lads, too much weather about,' he said. 'You'll be on the first aircraft home tomorrow evening. Overnight flight up the Bay of Biscay. The enemy should be in bed.'

The hours, pleasant as they were in Gibraltar's officers' mess, ticked by sluggishly until finally the evening of 29 November arrived.

Darkness had already fallen across Gibraltar's runway when Frank left the mess in search of the Warwick aircraft that would be taking him home. Several people had gathered beside the twin-engine aircraft. Frank was amazed to see a woman he had met in Geneva some two months earlier, as well as a Luftwaffe officer in full uniform. With six crew and nine passengers, it was going to be a tight squeeze in the Warwick.

'Sorry, everyone,' called Captain Kelsey, as he approached the Warwick, 'we've been delayed four hours. Cloud is too thick. Hopefully it'll disperse enough for us to get away later tonight. We'll make the final run over the Bay of Biscay in daylight if it does.' Frank went for a sleepless snooze in the mess.

At 2 a.m., Kelsey declared the flight was on. Everyone piled into the Warwick and, using the entire length of Gibraltar's sea-ended runway, it roared into the air, setting course for the Atlantic. There the captain would turn north for the Bay of Biscay, north-west for the Celtic Sea and finally east up the Bristol Channel, before descending into RAF Lyneham, Wiltshire.

'What a joy it was to lie back and sleep and not have to worry about navigation, fuel consumption, and so on,' remembered Frank. After a few whiskies in the mess, he was buoyed, his thoughts full of home and of Ruth and Tessa. Soon the drone of the engines faded and he fell into a happy sleep.

CRACK!

Frank jolted awake. It was daylight outside. Was that an explosion?

One of Kelsey's crew appeared in the fuselage with parachutes in his hands. *You've got to be kidding me.*

'What happened?' Frank shouted at the crewmate, the smell of burning thick in the air.

'No idea, we didn't see any enemy aircraft,' replied the crewman distributing parachutes. 'Something's on fire, though.'

'Everyone listen!' he shouted. 'Something's burning. Get ready to jump. Wait for my command!'

A mixture of panic, fear and bitter rage clouded Frank's mind. He had already survived a horrific crash and spent three months escaping Europe. He was not about to do it all again.

It was 7 a.m. The Warwick was over the northern part of the Bay of Biscay – well within range of a Junkers 88 – but where was it? The sea, too, was clear of ships. One of the passengers began jettisoning the escape hatch. Frank prepared to jump.

Kelsey's crewman returned. 'Captain says the instrument panel is behaving and she's holding 8,000 feet. Keep your chutes on for now. Does anyone have explosives in their luggage?'

He began tearing up the floorboards and rummaging through the luggage compartment. But he found nothing. Frank could sense the aircraft was performing normally, indicating no engine failure. Gradually, heart rates fell as the crew rushed around the Warwick eliminating the possible causes of the explosion.

'What the bloody hell was that all about then?' asked Frank incredulously half an hour later, as the crew distributed sandwiches and flasks of coffee.

'We thought you asked for an alarm call, sir,' said the airman.

An hour later, the Scillies appeared out of the starboard window, followed by Cornwall, Devon and South Wales. Kelsey lowered the aircraft over Somerset, skirted south of

Bristol and began the final descent into Lyneham in northern Wiltshire.

After seven hours flying, the Warwick's wheels met British soil. For Frank, the danger was over. There were no obstacles left to negotiate. He was home.

As the aircraft slowed, he readied himself to stand.

But the aircraft jolted violently, slamming Frank back down into his seat. A terrible scraping noise filled the fuselage. Had the landing gear broken?

The aircraft began to spin, pinning the starboard passengers to the wall as the portside passengers fell into them. Coffee flasks flew about the fuselage, smashing into the aircraft's metal body. The Luftwaffe officer began shouting in German over the din.

Don't let me die now, thought Frank. I can't die now.

Several chaotic seconds passed before the Warwick's scraping spin halted some two to three hundred feet off the runway. While the occupants picked themselves up off the floor, Frank shot to the escape hatch, kicked it off, leaped from the aircraft and bolted across the airfield.

Later he learned that the explosion over the Bay of Biscay was the Warwick being struck by lightning.

The strike had burned away the latches holding the aircraft's nose cone in place. For most of the journey it was held in place by air pressure, until the air pressure decreased sufficiently on landing for it to drop off, dislodge the landing gear, and bookend Frank's three-month escape with another crash-landing.

Like Frank, I begin the final leg of my journey with a train from Madrid to San Roque, the nearest station to the Gibraltar border.

Gibraltar, I discover, is not the easiest place to enter. You cannot simply get a train from Spain into Gibraltar, or a bus, or even a taxi, unless the driver has their passport with them and is willing to queue for hours. Years of dispute between the Spanish and British governments have meant the border is very much 'hard'.

My plan is to catch a bus from San Roque train station to La Línea de la Concepción, the closest bus stop to Gibraltar. Then I will walk across the border, passing through passport control as some 15,000 people do every day for work, 10,000 of them Spanish.

There is just one problem with my plan: the train breaks down. After sitting on the tracks for an hour, I begin to get nervous that I will be very late arriving in San Roque. Eventually, the train crawls into a station, and we are told to disembark and wait for a new train. After two and a half hours, a new train arrives, but it only gets me to San Roque in the small hours.

I alight with two other passengers, both of whom are picked up by friends or family immediately. I walk to the deserted bus station and begin reading the timetables. There are no buses today, I have missed the last one. I walk to the taxi rank, but it is empty. At the end of one month travelling, I do not have the money to pay for one anyway. I could walk to Gibraltar, but it is twelve kilometres, so it will take me about three hours.

I begin to worry. San Roque station is not actually in the town of San Roque, but in a small suburb of some 2,000 people. There is not a soul about, nor are there any cars on the road. I could walk twenty-five minutes to the nearest town and hope to find accommodation, but again, unless it is very cheap, there is not enough in my bank account to pay for it. I could call my parents and ask for money, but they would be asleep, and I would still have to find a taxi or accommodation.

An idea comes to me: sleep in a hedge. Having graduated a few months earlier, I remember going on nights out in cities where my mates and I did not have accommodation. Not wanting to pay for a room, we would stay up all night instead, maybe getting a few hours of sleep in a bus shelter or on a bench before catching the first train home. I decide to do this with the Gibraltar bus.

I begin walking the deserted streets looking for somewhere to sleep. I still have my sleeping bag and roll mat from the Pyrenees, and with the temperature at 18°, warmth is not an issue. My concern is the amount of comfort my quarter-inch roll mat will provide, particularly if I am to sleep on concrete. I also feel a strong need for some kind of shelter or protection, despite the fact it is not raining or windy. It is a desire born from a strange feeling of vulnerability I have not felt before. I also don't want anyone to come across me in the night and steal my rucksack.

As I explore, I see suburbia in a completely new light. Could I sleep in someone's front porch on their bench or astro turf? I decide it is too risky. I do not want to set off any alarms or wake any dogs. Should I walk out of town and find a field or a hedge? I decide against it, as I don't know what might be crawling around and I have no flashlight. My phone is now dead and it is approaching 2 a.m.

After an hour of walking, I still cannot find anywhere suitable. I head back to the station, hoping there will be benches on the platform to sleep on. Before I get there, I spot something. Right in front of the station, where I exited an hour and a half earlier, is a large concrete flowerbed rising half a metre off the ground. It is about one metre wide by six metres long and is ringed by a small, neatly trimmed leylandii hedge.

The bed is not made of earth, but small, uniform white pebbles. *Perfect.*

I climb into the raised flowerbed, lay out my roll mat inside the hollow leylandii hedge, have a final bite of my baguette and snuggle down inside my sleeping bag, pulling my cap over my face to block out the streetlamp. It is spacious within the leylandii, and no one would see me unless they peered right over the hedge. As I drift into sleep, tummy rumbling and mosquitoes whining, I chuckle at my own predicament. How very 'Frank' it was.

After a few fitful hours of sleep, I wake to a gentle hissing sound and what looks like fog right in front of my face. Jolting upright, I realise the flowerbed is lined with sprinklers. They must be scheduled to go off at 5 a.m. Misty water is now firing into my lair, soaking my rucksack, sleeping bag and roll mat in the process. I drag my stuff to a part of the flowerbed where the sprinklers are not going off, check if there are more, and attempt to go back to sleep.

This time my problem is not the sprinklers but mosquitoes. Perhaps the misty water has brought them out, for they descend on me with a vengeance, whining infuriatingly. I pull the drawstring tight on my damp sleeping bag, making as small a porthole as possible for my face. But judging by the itches flaring up on my cheeks and forehead, I am too late.

Then, at 6.30 a.m. on the dot, I hear a car stop right beside my part of the hedge. The engine is idling not two metres from where I lie. It is not moving, so I peek over the concrete lip of the flowerbed to see who it is. 'Guardia Civil' it says on the side of the white-and-green 4×4. I presume it is not illegal to sleep in a hedge in Spain and, unlike Frank, the Guardia Civil are not going to arrest me. But I am not going to take any chances.

For twenty minutes I lie motionless in the hedge, listening to the faint noise of the policemen's radio. The doors open and two pairs of feet walk off towards the station. I rise from my leafy lair, stuff my damp sleeping apparatus away, shoulder my rucksack, and set off in the opposite direction. I stop at a bench, get my final husk of baguette out of my bag and dip it in my jam pot. I have had only a few hours of broken sleep, my body aches from the pebbles, my face itches from the mozzies and I am damp all over.

That is not the end of my problems. After waiting forty-five minutes, the first bus to the Gibraltar border arrives and I get on. But the bus's card reader will not accept my bank card. I am sure there is enough money on it to cover the €2.50 fare, but without phone battery I cannot check my online banking. No matter how many times I swipe the reader, it beeps and rejects me. I dig around for some change, as a queue of grumpy Spanish commuters forms behind me. One by one, I place small bits of grubby change in the bus driver's hands until I have none left. It comes to €1.80. I look at the driver with as much sorrow as I can muster: a pathetic look of desperation. Surely, he will take pity on this idiotic Brit who looks and smells like a tramp?

Mercifully, he waves me to the back of the bus with a dismissive hand. I take my seat sheepishly among the Spanish commuters, pressing my itchy cheek against the cold window. The bus trundles off and within ten minutes I catch my first glimpse of the Rock of Gibraltar. Given the drama of the last eight hours, it is a sight I am not prepared for.

But there it is, the famous slab of rock jutting out of the ocean. A colossal limestone mountain dominating the western entrance of the Mediterranean. The same towering marker signalling the end of my journey as it had done Frank's seventy-nine years earlier. It is a terrific, hair-raising sight that I can picture vividly to this day.

Getting off the bus and walking towards the border, I cannot take my eyes off the imposing Rock. It is 8 a.m. and the sun is just rising from the Atlantic, illuminating a perfect mackerel sky. The northern part of the Rock remains shadowy and mysterious. I walk into passport control with my large ruck-sack on my back and the small one on my chest. Four queues of about twenty smartly dressed commuters advance slowly towards the desks, Spanish passports in hand.

'Hello, sir, how are you?' asks the cheery British police-woman behind the counter. It is wonderful to hear English again after a month travelling through France and Spain alone.

'Cheerio,' she calls, after stamping my passport and hand-ing it back. *Cheerio.* What a brilliantly British word. I walk out of the passport control building and come face to face with a red telephone box. This really is Britain in the southern tip of Spain.

I begin the short walk into Gibraltar, which bizarrely crosses the International Airport runway. A light Mediterranean wind is blowing in from the west. The sun, a great, orangey ball, has just risen above the horizon, silhou-etting the Rock in a brilliant contrast of light and shadow. After the night in the hedge, its rays are heavenly on my skin. I think of Frank warming his bones on Figueres train station platform before being arrested.

Dawdling across the runway, commuters streaming past me like water around a boulder, I try to imagine what Frank must have felt at this point when the constant threat of capture and interrogation abated after three and a half months in Europe. I try to absorb my surroundings, to screenshot this wonderful moment in my brain and not let my sleep-deprived emotions overpower me.

I know I have achieved something by getting here, but I am not sure what. I may never have met Frank, but I feel I have honoured him in some way by following him to Gibraltar. I know my family will be proud and this is a moment I will never forget.

As the Rock nears, so does the realisation that I am taking the last steps of my journey across Europe. I also know something else is ending, a tiny chapter of my life where, for one month, I lived and breathed the most arduous, daring, and terrifying period of Frank's life. An experience my generation of young Brits will hopefully never have to live through because of the sacrifices people like Frank made for us. An experience playing out for thousands of people in less fortunate parts of the world.

And I am sad. Living someone else's life in a foreign country has been pure escapism. How many people get to follow in their hero's footsteps as I have done? It is an intensely personal moment and I am glad to be alone among the crowd of Thursday morning commuters.

I reach into my front rucksack and take out the photo of Frank I have carried with me across France and Spain. As ever, Frank's mugshot looks back at me, eyes twinkling, mouth curling into a mischievous smile.

Perhaps I am not alone after all.

In a way, I never have been.

EPILOGUE

Sixteen months after my journey ended, I was put in touch with a woman called Helen Rush.

Helen's father was Flying Officer Sydney John Congdon, Frank's navigator on that fateful August evening in 1943. I knew Congdon was a superb navigator, as he had already flown a full tour of thirty missions with 104 Squadron in Bomber Command, receiving the prestigious Distinguished Flying Medal.

Transferred to Tempsford, John flew a further twenty-nine missions with 138 Squadron, taking his total to fifty-nine. This at a time when a bomber aircrew's life expectancy was roughly fifteen missions. Operation Pimento would be his last before completing a remarkable second full tour, an accolade that would have earned him a second period of leave, further medals and perhaps a promotion to a desk or training job.

I also knew he had married Mary Lake in Totnes parish church in November 1942 and that Mary was just pregnant when John was killed. I had read that John and Mary's daughter had been born in early 1944 so she had never met her father.

I had not attempted to find John and Mary's daughter as I had no leads, did not know if she had married and changed

R.A.F. Station,
Tempsford,
Nr. Sandy, Beds.

16th August, 1943.

Dear *Mrs Congdon,*

It is with great regret that I am
writing to confirm that your husband Flying Officer
S.J. Congdon D.F.M. is missing as a result of air
operations against the enemy on the night 14/15th
August, 1943.

At the time of writing no further
news has been received, but immediately upon receipt
of any news, you will of course, be notified.

During the time that Flying Officer
Congdon has been with this Squadron he has made
many friends and was a very efficient member of his
crew. On behalf of all members of my Squadron please
accept my sincere sympathy.

I trust that we shall hear that your
husband is alive and well, and express the sympathy of
the whole Squadron in your great anxiety.

Yours *sincerely.*

R.Speare n/c.

L.A.C.W. Congdon,
R.A.F. Station Durrington,
West Worthing,
Sussex.

The letter to Mary reporting Congdon
as missing, the day after the crash.

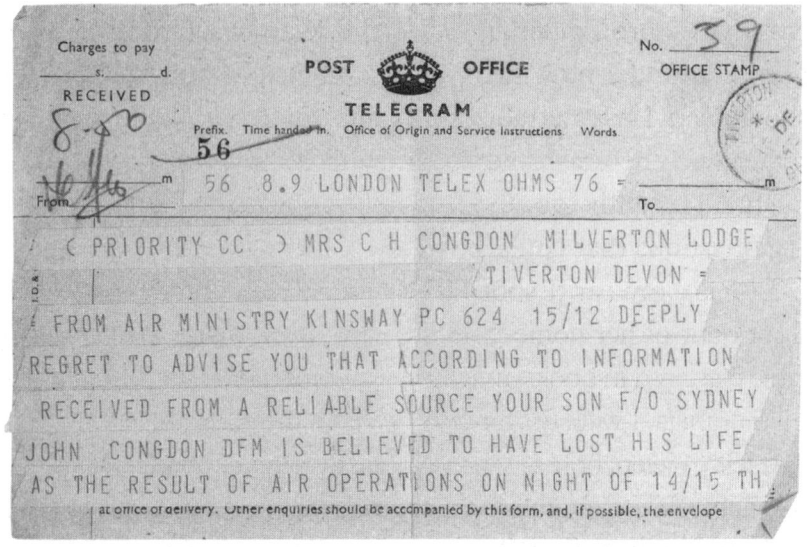

The final of three telegrams. The first two
reported and confirmed Congdon as missing.

her surname, or if she was still alive, aged seventy-nine. But I
was overjoyed to be put in touch with her.

'I can't believe it,' she wrote to me by email:

So you are Frank Griffiths' great-grandson. I am John
Congdon's daughter. I will be 80 on May 13th next year
[*2024*] – 81 years after my father was killed.

I was lucky enough to have a wonderful stepfather and half-
brother, so I had a great upbringing, though I was always aware
of my real father. My mother never forgot my father and as a
family we always kept in touch with my Congdon relations.

It would be lovely to meet up, as I may have articles which
would add to your collection and knowledge. I would love to
meet you also, because people generally don't understand
how hard it is to process all this.

We arrange to meet in March 2024.

Driving through smart, suburban Warwickshire to Helen's home, I wonder how the meeting will go and what questions I should ask. I have no idea how much Helen knows about her father and the crash that killed him. I know she has lost her husband recently too, and I do not want to ask too many probing questions that could bring up some powerful emotions.

Leaving my car, I spot Helen immediately through the glass front door of her home. She is leaning over a large dining-room table plastered in books, magazines, photographs, letters and other memorabilia. I walk up, tap a knuckle on the glass and startle her.

'Hello, Helen, how are you?' I ask, stooping to hug her as I enter her home. We chat about the weather, the journey to her house and other things that British people do when they first meet. Helen is wearing a black-and-white striped, long-sleeve top, tiny silver earrings and a thin black headband that stands out against her grey bob and fringe. Her piercing blue eyes, smooth cheeks and light makeup make her look younger than seventy-nine.

We sit at her dining room table and she begins talking me through the mountain of documents she has got out for me.

'I'm really not sure what use these will be for you, I've got so much. My late husband was such a collector. He was always interested in all this. Of course, I am too.'

Helen speaks quickly and I sense she is a little nervous. Her home is immaculate and beautifully decorated. China tea sets adorn polished wooden dressers, floral curtains flank double glass doors, and oil paintings of the English coastline hang on the walls.

We talk about how lucky it was that we were put in touch. Helen explains this is not the first time luck has allowed our families to reunite. She tells me how in 1981, when she and her husband Peter lived in Buckinghamshire, they were at a cocktail party when Peter started chatting to a retired RAF officer. Peter asked where he had served and the retired officer Group

Captain Ken Bachelor, Commanding Officer of Frank's squadron when he crashed, replied, 'RAF Tempsford.' Shocked, Peter told the man his wife's father served there too, but was killed when his plane crashed near Annecy in August 1943.

'I don't believe this,' said the officer. 'I know the pilot of the plane, Frank Griffiths. He is having a cataract operation in an RAF Hospital only thirty minutes from here. Shall we go and see him?'

Helen had met Frank once as a young girl in France when she attended a memorial at the crash site, but since then she had had no contact with him.

'It was a very emotional meeting,' said Helen, as she rummaged through some of her documents, 'even nearly forty years after the crash. I think Frank had thought lots about it. I can't imagine what he thought when I showed up.'

She found a letter that Frank had addressed to her dated 8 June 1981, days after they had met. It read:

What an amazing coincidence you should be John Congdon's daughter and that you should meet my old friend Ken [the retired RAF officer] *... I am most anxious to tell you of the last moments of your father's life because, curiously, I didn't know until two years ago what a remarkable result his very last actions had with regard to the Resistance movements and ultimately their own liberation in the Haute-Savoie region of France.*

Suffice it to say that by getting the bomb doors open and by jettisoning our two tonnes of arms into the woods just north of Annecy during those last terrible moments, he enabled most of them to be found and spirited away to be used in the Battle of the Glières [a fierce battle in which the German army crushed a major Maquis uprising]. *But I will tell you of all this later and also some of the 'ifs', such as if only we had been able to reach and land on the lake.*

Helen produced a second letter from Frank, sent a few days later from his home address in Ruthin, North Wales. It began:

Dear Mrs Rush, (may I call you Helen?)

I have now returned to the Land of Mist and Wind but at the moment it is glorious sunshine.

I can't say how glad I am that we made contact. Oddly, it took a load off my mind, for all through the years I've been questioning my decisions just before we crashed. The only solace I've had was from a Frenchman who, when I told him I wished I had landed on the lake when we had the first engine go out, said: 'But then we wouldn't have got our arms, the Resistance wouldn't have received the same boost and we would have had to wait until the Americans came.'

To me, these fascinating letters proved that John and the rest of the crew had not died in vain. Of course, Frank would have wanted to emphasise this to John's daughter, but two important facts remain.

Firstly, that two tonnes of valuable war materiel ended up in the Maquis' hands. These arms, almost impossible for local Frenchmen to get their hands on, helped the Resistance liberate themselves from the Germans in 1944, something they achieved without direct help from the Allies. To this day, the region remains fiercely proud they were first in France to do this.

More importantly, John and the crew's deaths galvanised the local population. Their fatal crash had proved to the people of the Haute-Savoie they had not been forgotten and that British airmen were willing to die for their liberation. Thousands of locals witnessed the aftermath of the plane crash and word of it spread around the region like wildfire. You only need to look at photos of the crew's graves in Meythet Cemetery from 1943, plastered in seas of fresh flowers, to see how this event touched so many hearts. Although impossible to say how many, this was the moment hundreds of people began resisting, be that by taking up arms, or simple, everyday acts.

The war materiel from Frank's Halifax, and more

importantly the motivating effect of the deaths of his crew, was partly why the Allies found the Haute-Savoie free of Germans when they arrived in the summer of 1944, and certainly why they were received so joyously. Operation Pimento – despite its tragic outcome and failure in its principal objective – did leave a mark on the Haute-Savoie's history.

On a visit to the crash site years after the war, Frank met the Mayor of Annecy and apologised to him for crashing into buildings and killing civilians. Appalled, the mayor turned to him and cried, '*Mais non! Vous étiez l'étincelle de la Résistance!*' 'But no! You were the spark of the Resistance!'

Frank's letter to Helen continued:

> *The fact that your mother married again and had a happy life and that you've got two children (John's grandchildren) does help mitigate the disaster. I've checked my logbooks and I actually did 13 trips with your father. We first flew together on 5th July. We had some leave from 28th July to 10th August and of course the last trip was the 14th. A strange time for it was just flying and sleeping at Tempsford and hardly enough time for ordinary conversation. We were so tired.*

Helen points out that, being born in May, it was during this period of leave that she must have been conceived.

It is obvious from Frank's letter that even thirty-eight years after the crash, survivors' guilt had not left him.

We go next door to her living room for tea and biscuits. There are more piles of perfectly preserved photos and documents balanced on her sofa, coffee table and floor. Sifting through the collection, I feel like I am playing top trumps with John's life, picking out the best bits for further examination. Despite the fact I have Helen's full blessing, and John died eighty-one years ago, I still feel that I am intruding on his privacy; as if I am playing God with his legacy.

John Congdon comes to life in photos spread out on the floor all around me – laughing with his young wife in the back garden, grinning on a bicycle outside the mess, staring at the camera in a solemn headshot. I look up at Helen. She is sitting beside a roaring fire, a cup of tea in one hand as she reads an old letter with the other. I wonder what must be going through her head.

She is surrounded by hundreds of photos of a man who, to all intents and purposes, is a total stranger, but is also her father. A man whom she never met, but is the reason she is here today. A man whose face she knows intimately but never saw; whose life she must have heard endless tales about, but she was never able to ask questions.

I raise the subject gently.

'I always knew who he was,' says Helen. 'My mother always made sure I knew about my real father, even if he wasn't around anymore. I don't think I understood really as a child – I thought he was just someone whom I'd never met and that was the way it was. My mother remarried when I was twenty-one months old and for a while I called Henry 'uncle'. But when my brother was born and he called him Daddy, I joined in with him. I must have been about twelve. But for my whole life, my mother made sure I knew who my father was and we always kept in touch with the Congdon family. It's amazing really that I had such a lovely, normal upbringing. My mother kept all that from me so well.'

Helen continues, her voice steady. 'It must have been so hard for her. She was so young herself, only twenty. I think she just sort of closed down that part of her life and tried to move on. I suppose she had only been married for nine months. She never went out to the crash site. When we were put back in touch with Frank, I ummed and ahhed for ages whether to tell her, because I didn't know how she'd react. In the end I told her and I think she was okay with it.

'We [Helen, her mother and stepfather] went out to the crash site in 1986. It was mum's first time visiting it, forty-three years after the crash. Those things are always difficult but I'm glad she went out. I think it was good for her. She was more worried about Henry who, although interested, found it quite difficult to process.

'I remember when she was in hospital at the end of her life, I thought to myself, right, if I don't ask her about this stuff now I never will. So I asked her about it . . . and she said that she thought he was always out there and that he'd always been watching from afar.'

Despite the topic, Helen spoke with great eloquence and candour. It was as though this was the first time she had voiced her feelings on the subject and that her words were almost news to herself as she spoke them. I could not detect any undercurrents of sadness or regret, only empathy for her young mother.

As for me, I was struggling to process everything Helen was saying. There was a violent poignancy to the story Helen was telling me, because it was so nearly the story my grandmother Tessa would have told me had her father Frank died that night too. If it had not been for those telephone wires, it would have been Tessa growing up without her biological father, or her siblings Lloyd, Mark and Rebecca.

'Have a look at this, Adam,' says Helen, gesturing me to join her by the fire. She is holding a yellowing letter. Addressed to Mrs Congdon, I assume it is another one from Frank to Helen. But the date – 2 December 1943 – does not match. Helen had not been born yet. I realise the Mrs Congdon in the address is in fact Helen's mother, John Congdon's widow. Frank must have written to her as soon as he had returned to England. Instantly, I know this contemporaneous source is more important than anything I have unearthed in two years of research. I feel slightly sick.

The first page of the letter sent from Frank to John Congdon's widow, confirming news of Congdon's death.

Helen begins reading it:

Dear Mrs Congdon,

I myself have just arrived from Gibraltar at almost the same time as your letter to my wife and it grieves me deeply to have to tell you that John was killed instantaneously on August 15th.

It is terrible to have put this in writing and I hope someday to be able to see you and tell you the whole story. I have been ordered by the Air Ministry to say nothing about the accident at the moment, but I do feel that the relatives have a right to know what happened. I think the Air Ministry are waiting for definite information from the Red Cross before they make a statement, but I think that definite proof will be a long time coming through as the Italians who shot us down are now interned in Switzerland.

I will now tell you our story in brief and trust you will treat it as confidential as the Air Ministry are very concerned to keep the work of the squadron a secret.

We left Tempsford on 14th August to carry out a special mission which involved some low flying amongst the Alps. It was a really marvellous night with a full moon and when we were flying low along Lake Annecy, John said: 'Even if we don't have any luck tonight I'm glad we've come – it's the most beautiful trip I've ever been on.' Those were his last words.

A few seconds later the Italians got us in our two port engines just on the outskirts of the town of Annecy. We were too low to bale out – only about 200 feet and as the aircraft refused to fly on two engines, despite the fact that we jettisoned everything, I sent all the crew to their crash stations in the centre of the aircraft.

Johnnie was the last to go through. He remained at his post till the last minute destroying secret equipment. Nothing is so utterly useless as a Halifax with two dead engines on one wing in the bottom of an Alpine Valley in the middle of the night. The whole floor of the valley was covered with rocks and trees and I tried in vain to get back and land in the lake at Annecy.

However the fates were against us and we flew through several trees and finally crashed on the village of Meythet. The aircraft came to rest on two houses in which Italians were billeted (we killed five Italians & one German) and all six of my crew were killed instantaneously, despite the fact that their crash stations in the fuselage were considered the safest and strongest part of the plane.

The force of the impact was so great that my part of the aircraft broke off and flew on without wings or engines across the village street. It grieves me terribly that I, the captain, should have escaped when all my crew were killed, but that is how it all happened. John and I had had some grand trips together and he'd done far more than his share in this war effort.

I managed to make good my escape with the help of the French and finally reached Switzerland where I went to hospital. On Tuesday 17th August I witnessed John and the crew's funeral from the side of a mountain near Annecy. They were all buried with full military honours and 7,000 people went to the funeral. A description of the funeral and photographs were given to me and I took them to Switzerland.

The floral tributes were magnificent and when I passed through Annecy again in October, the graves were still covered with fresh flowers. Many of the wreaths had inscribed on them, 'To our liberators', and the crowd sang God Save the King and the Marseillaise so loudly that it could be heard echoing up the valley.

Words cannot express what I thought of John – suffice it to say that we should have been a lot of worse off had we never known him.

In about a month I hope to know what I shall be doing and if possible I'll come down and see you. My wife and I are both keen to come down to Torquay again as we originally met there when I was in the RAF Hospital at the Palace and she was a WAAF.

After the war I hope you will be able to visit Annecy and see where John is buried. It is the most beautiful place I've ever seen with its lake, mountains and the snowcapped peak of Mont Blanc towering over everything. You can rest assured that the grave will be tended by the French who realise so well that John gave his life in trying to help them.

Yours sincerely,

F.C. Griffiths.

Paper-clipped to the back of Frank's letter was Mary's father's reply, handwritten in beautiful black cursive.

Once again, Helen begins reading:

Dear Mr Griffiths,

My daughter thanks you for your letter and although this is a terribly bitter blow to us all we at long last have received this information. It has come a great shock to us as owing to this lapse of time we had the belief that some time or other John would have turned up.

For you the ordeal must have been beyond words yet we are all sure that you did your best and we know that John had every confidence in you. We congratulate you on your return.

I should be pleased if you would let me know if possible why in the official casualty list your name and John's were under 'missing' but the rest of the crew 'missing believed killed', as having heard about you we thus thought that John had the same luck.

Also Mary would like to know what happened to John's personal belongings that were with him such as his watches and sundry effects. Your letter will be a great comfort to her and she wishes me to tell you how much she appreciates it.

We shall be very pleased to see you when you come down this way. Let us know when you do.

What a beastly war this is. So many lives lost for what! This must be the last time the Huns are allowed to bring such misery into the world.

Yours sincerely,

C.T.C Lake

The letter from Congdon's father-in-law to Frank.

Helen and me, March 2024.

Frank at RAF Abingdon in the 1950s.

DRAMATIS PERSONAE

In the RAF

Squadron Leader Stuart Robertson – Frank's friend whom he met in hospital in Torquay, who had received a bullet in the backside.

Frank reported: 'WAAFs were not supposed to mix with officers, but after many successful sailing expeditions on the River Dart, Stuart and I both married our respective WAAFs within twelve months.'

Following a one-day honeymoon with Daphne (Ruth's sister), he returned to operations in his Stirling bomber, but was ambushed by a German fighter one night when returning from operations over Germany. He was killed instantly in his cockpit.

He and Daphne had been married for three weeks.

Air Vice-Marshal Sir Edward Fielden GCVO CB DFC AFC – Frank's commanding officer at RAF Tempsford, and in peacetime Captain of the King's Flight (the Royal Family's personal pilot).

Having taught Edward VIII to fly before the war, 'Mouse' Fielden returned to active RAF service when war broke out. In October 1942 he was appointed CO of 161 Squadron (Special Duties) at Tempsford, flying missions in which he and his crew got to wear uniform with a scarlet lining, thanks to their association with the Royal Family. He was promoted to Station Commander of Tempsford in October 1942, before becoming Air Commodore in December 1944 and Station Commander of RAF Woodall Spa.

'Mouse' returned to royal duties after the war and was awarded a string of titles including Senior Air Equerry to the Queen, Air Vice Marshal, and Knight Grand Cross of the Royal Victorian Order.

He married Mary Angela Ramsden-Jodrell in 1940. They had two children, Mark Fielden (b. 1942, d. 1963 in a motor accident at Silverstone) and Fiona Fielden (b. 1944). Remarkably, Fiona Fielden became my great-aunt in 1969 when she married my great-uncle, Christopher Hart, giving me a second, if much more tenuous link to Tempsford.

When I asked Fiona about her father's wartime exploits and what he left behind, Fiona told me he threw his logbooks and any other paraphernalia away, as he did not think they were interesting to anyone.

'Mouse' Fielden died in 1976, aged seventy-two.

Pilot Officer John Douglas Charrot, aka 'Johnnie' – Frank's favourite navigator during his first thirteen missions at RAF Tempsford.

Finished his first tour just before Operation Pimento and was in RAF Lossiemouth when he heard the news that Frank's aircraft had been lost and there were no survivors.

In his own words: 'For forty years I believed all the crew had been killed. But one day in February 1983, my wife picked up a book in Rye library that had a picture of an aircraft dropping a body by parachute to a group of people on the ground.

'That night, I was sitting in bed looking at this book titled *Winged Hours* and turning to the back cover I found a photo of Frank Griffiths! I just couldn't believe it. After all this time my skipper was alive. I thought all the people I knew well at Tempsford had been killed. I was sure Griff was dead. He was really very lucky.

'I immediately sent a letter to the publishers and received a reply that Frank was in an RAF Hospital at Halton having a second cataract operation. The sister suggested she read his mail to him and he later told me my letter had cheered him up considerably and helped his recovery. This was good to know, because I certainly owed him a great deal.'

In France

A note on the crash – why did Frank's Halifax suddenly fall from the sky? For years he thought he had suffered engine failure, but he discovered the real reason when visiting Annecy in 1946.

'I was informed that I had been shot down by an Italian Alpini corporal with a small Beretta machine pistol, who was on guard duty at the entrance of Annecy Barracks,' Frank recalled.

The guard had let off a few pot shots at the lumbering Halifax and a lucky bullet severed the fuel pipe in the port wing, starving both engines of fuel and sealing the fate of eleven lives.

René Fontaine – the long-haired, fourteen-year-old lad who said to Frank, 'Get on my bike, I will take you to safety.'

René survived the war and ran Meythet village's garage until his premature death from liver cancer in 1969, aged forty. Sadly, the family forge where Frank was hidden in the chimney was sold and demolished two months before my visit in 2022.

John D'Aujourd'hui – René's schoolboy friend, who helped him to push Frank up the hill on René's bicycle.

Later caught by the Gestapo and brutally tortured for information about the French Resistance. Driven to Thones, Haute-Savoie, where his expiring body was thrown from a moving car on to the main square where he died, a warning to other resistors.

He is buried in the Cemetery of Morets with 200 of his Maquis companions who fought the Germans at the Battle of Glières in 1944. He was only fifteen.

Angéline Fontaine – René's mother, who tended to Frank's wounds before hiding him in her chimney.

Survived the war and continued raising her three children by herself, as her husband had died when they were young.

Hélène Bastin, aka 'Pépette' – proprietress of Ma Baraque, the restaurant/brothel to which Frank was taken on the night he crashed and where he was hidden for three days.

To Frank's delight, he was able to meet Pépette again after the war in the 1970s and say thank-you. Over lunch in Thonon-les-Bains, she told Frank that she had to flee to the mountains just a few weeks after his visit because the Gestapo were on to her.

'For two years she had the stars for her kitchen ceiling,' wrote Frank, who listened as Pépette described what life was like living with the maquisards in the high Alps on the Plateau des Glières.

But what Pépette really wanted to talk to Frank about was her grocery business in Lyon. As she spoke her hands trembled violently, and she died a few years later in 1978 of Parkinson's disease, buried with the decorations that General de Gaulle had awarded her.

Ma Baraque – the restaurant/brothel where Frank was hidden for his first three days in France.

I managed to track down Pépette's grandson on Facebook and he told me: 'Ma Baraque was burned down after the war by French people who thought Pépette was a collaborator. People who did nothing during the war except hide in their homes found the strength to burn houses and chase people without knowing what they had done at the end of the war.'

Evidently, the volume of Italian and German soldiers frequenting Ma Baraque during the war had made Pépette a collaborator in the minds of some destructive locals. If only they had known. But something did not add up. How could Frank not have mentioned this in his book, written after his meeting with Pépette in the 1970s? Surely she would have told him?

I found the answer in another memoir, *Road to Resistance*, written by George Millar. Millar was an officer in the Rifle Brigade, whose wartime escape was so similar to Frank's that I was able to corroborate large parts of Frank's story.

Millar was captured in North Africa, imprisoned in Italy and transported to Germany, where he successfully jumped from his prison train. He escaped from Germany to France and was hidden in Ma Baraque just a week after Frank, staying in the region for nearly a month before being transported south through France and Spain to Gibraltar, where he flew home.

Of Ma Baraque, Millar recalled: 'I lived most happily there, taking a huge amount of exercise with Bobby [*the labrador*], and doing as much as I could to help the brave Pépette, including playing her at ping-pong every evening at drinks time. We understood each other so well that we were like mother and son. She was an angel, an angel with a volcanic vocabulary generated in her earlier life as a singer and dancer in Lyon.'

Millar returned to Ma Baraque a month later in late 1943 and was disheartened by what he found.

'Even Pépette, who had always seemed so unruffled by danger, was edgy, and her hands were shaking terribly. She'd had two inquisitorial visits from the Gestapo in my absence and was talking about leaving Ma Baraque and taking to the *maquis*. Pat [*the local Maquis leader*] had long since gone over the Pyrenees, she said, bound for England. She had packed her most important belongings, including a picture of General de Gaulle, and imagined that the Gestapo would arrive that morning. I said that I would leave at once.'

So fleeing to the mountains was true, but what about Ma Baraque? Millar, on a tour of his escape in 1946, enquired and was told: 'Pépette took to the *maquis* shortly after you left. She went back to her place, but found it in a bad way, pretty well ransacked, who by, Christ knows.'

Perhaps Ma Baraque was not burned down, but it was a tragic end nonetheless for such a bastion of resistance.

Colonel Vallette d'Oisa – leader of the Haute-Savoie Resistance, who visited Frank when he was bedbound in Ma Baraque.

Born in Rennes in 1898, d'Oisa fought in the First World War aged eighteen, was wounded three times and decorated highly, including becoming the youngest Frenchman in history to win a Légion d'Honneur, the highest order of merit in France, both military and civil. A Captain when the Second World War broke out, he was captured during the Fall of France, but escaped to Vichy France where he began organising resistance.

Almost exactly one month after meeting Frank, on 13 September 1943, d'Oisa was arrested by the Gestapo. He was interrogated severely before being transported out of France via train. Handcuffed and with a German soldier either side of him, d'Oisa waited until his guards fell asleep to shuffle to the window, somehow open it and hurl himself out.

After stints in Switzerland and England, he returned to France and, commanding 32,000 French troops, liberated Lyon. D'Oisa then continued to fight the Germans for control of the Alpine passes between France and Italy, becoming a master of mountain warfare.

He retired as an Army Corps General in 1958 after forty-two years' service and enjoyed a further forty-two years of retirement watching his eight children grow up. Died in 2000, aged 101.

Meythet Cemetery – where Frank's crew were buried by the Italians under a hail of abuse from the locals.

Millar wrote: 'Frank's crew had been buried with great ceremony, a pyramid of flowers and the Marseillaise, brave boys. When I was in that region their memory was still honoured, even loved. Only twice I passed the graveyard gates at Meythet, but my passages were long divided, and each time there were fresh flowers, and many of them, on the aviators' graves. Frank and his crew had been the most splendid of ambassadors. I have every reason to be grateful to them.'

Eighty years after the crash, Meythet still remembers. The residents gather at the crash site every August to commemorate those brave boys killed in Frank's crash, and the innocent civilians who lost their lives too. Local dignitaries, including the mayor of Annecy, attend and make speeches, flanked by rows of French and British flags held by old boys in berets. Members of the French Armed Forces are also present in immaculate uniform, laying wreaths with notes of thanks to those who died '*pour la libération*'.

Most poignantly, the children of Meythet carry large placards bearing the faces of the eleven who died. During the two minutes' silence, the smiling, boyish faces of Frank's crew look out at the crowd, and they are remembered.

Dr Yves Raison – the elderly doctor who set Frank's broken arm without anaesthetic in Ma Baraque.

In 1979, Frank met the 'nameless doctor' and to his astonishment learned that Yves was the man who had organised the reception committee for Frank's containers the night he was shot down.

'Such was his sense of security,' wrote Frank, 'that although we had ample opportunity for conversation in Ma Baraque, he had not told either me or Pat that it was [to] one of his reception committees that I should have dropped my load had all gone according to plan.'

Immediately, Frank asked about the signal bonfires, or lack thereof, to which Yves replied: 'As soon as it was daylight after your crash, I went to the dropping zone and found the ashes of four bonfires. Whether they were lit too late or whether the wood was wet and gave insufficient flame, I never found out. I was on the run soon afterwards, and I never managed to contact my reception committee members again.'

He then told Frank why he came to be on the run.

'After setting your arm, I headed home to my apartment [*near Annecy hospital where he worked*], but found it surrounded by gendarmes and Italian soldiers. I asked one of the gendarmes guarding the stairs why I couldn't enter and was informed that I could do so as soon as they had arrested Dr Raison! So I chatted for a while to the gendarme to allay suspicion and then wandered away – for two years.'

Marie Rose Pallud, aka 'Mimi' – of Le Petit Coin, Les Goths, where Frank was hidden for three days, sleeping and eating plums in the garden.

Survived the war and in 1973 contacted Frank through the RAF Escaping Society. Frank visited Mimi in 1979 and discovered some fascinating details about his time in Les Goths.

The plan had never been for him to go to Le Petit Coin. It was a total surprise when he arrived on Mimi Pallud's doorstep. At enormous personal risk, and despite every German and Italian in the region searching for him, she agreed to shelter him.

But, as Mimi explained to Frank, there was a condition that she made the local Maquis agree to when Frank arrived on her doorstep. She said she would only shelter him if she could tell the locals that Frank was a distant relative, who had escaped from the lunatic asylum in Lyon, and she had agreed to look after him. That way no one would come knocking.

This explained to Frank, thirty-six years after his visit, why no one came to see him during his time in Le Petit Coin, when just days earlier he'd had constant visitors in Ma Baraque.

As I learned from Mimi's grandson Nico, Frank and Mimi exchanged grandchildren for years after they reunited 'with excellent exam results in French and English'. Mimi's grandchildren even attended the weddings of Frank's younger children Mark and Rebecca.

Mimi died in 1981, aged seventy-one. Josette was her only child.

Josette Buzaré (née Pallud) – Mimi's baby, who Frank held in his arms when he stayed at Le Petit Coin and thought of his baby Tessa at home.

Now eighty, she lives in Cruseilles, a town two miles from Les Goths and Le Petit Coin, with her husband, Francois Buzare. They have two sons called Nico and Domi (who made the exchange trips to Wales in the 1970s and 1980s), six grandchildren and one great-grandchild.

André Pallud – Mimi's brother-in-law, with whom Frank enjoyed conversations under the plum tree in Le Petit Coin.

Six months after Frank's visit, on 8 March 1944, André was arrested at Annecy's Town Hall for acts of resistance by the Vichy police. He was transported to the Compiègne concentration camp in the north of France. Four months later, on 15 July 1944, he was deported to Neuengamme concentration camp in northern Germany, where he was a prisoner for ten months. Then the records start to get blurry.

By the spring of 1945, the German army was in full retreat across the continent. As the frontline shifted, thousands of concentration camp prisoners were forced to march hundreds of miles deep into Germany, usually with no shoes, food, medical attention or water. These were later known as the 'death marches' and I can only assume that André was part of one.

Malnourished and overworked, he fought to survive the punishing march as the Third Reich imploded around him, but tragically he perished on 2 May, four days before the Germans surrendered and victory in Europe was declared.

He had been married for three years and was posthumously awarded the Médaille de la Résistance. He was twenty-eight.

Colette Périès-Martinez – the brilliant, 22-year-old courier who walked with Frank to Switzerland pretending to be his lover.

Colette's wartime exploits were easy to find, as she had spoken about them in 2014 when Annecy Council held a celebration of women in the Resistance. She joined the Resistance with her sister in October 1942, when her city of Annecy was occupied.

Asked why she did it, she replied, 'To be a woman was

rather a superiority in the Resistance [*applause from the crowd*], because we passed much better than the men. It was up to us to do it!'

Her role as a courier was important, but mostly she transported secret messages around the Haute-Savoie by bicycle. She would cycle up to 100 kilometres a day, on a fixed-gear bike, often up mountainous roads to places like the Plateau des Glières and La Clusaz, with written messages stuffed inside the handlebars. She joked, 'At the time of the liberation, I was ready for the Tour de France!'

Colette bucked the trend in terms of people who helped save Frank. Her father was the Mayor of Annecy and her family had money, meaning they had more to lose by not cooperating with the Germans. Several times she was nearly caught, escaping once by telling a German soldier that the man she was with was paying for her company in a hotel nearby. Colette expertly exploited her youth and femininity to help the Resistance far more than most young men could, because although bearing arms, the men had to spend much of the war exiled in the mountains.

Colette couriered an incredible twenty people into Switzerland at grave personal risk. She spoke of her friend Pierre Lamy, a fellow resister, who helped forge documents for people to avoid being deported to Germany for forced labour. Her voice quivers as she recounts how Pierre was betrayed to the Germans. They gouged his eyes out, ripped off his fingernails and marched him into a forest, where he was shot. Sexual violence often made the consequences for a woman even worse.

One other story caught my eye, the time General de Gaulle visited the Périès-Martinez house after the war. De Gaulle had come to Annecy in May 1948 to a gathering of ex-French Resistance. He ended up staying the night in the

Périès-Martinez house, peering into the cupboards once used to stash Resistance weapons and explosives. The next morning, he gave his own Croix de Lorraine to Colette's mother, who in turn gave it to her daughter.

Caring and compassionate, Colette spent the rest of her life helping people as a social worker. In 2008, she was awarded the Légion d'Honneur to go with her Médaille de la Résistance and Croix de Guerre.

Colette died in 2016 aged ninety-four.

Léon Mérandon – the First World War veteran farmer, whose land adjoined the Swiss border via 'the doghole'.

Having been injured, captured and worked harshly as a POW in the First World War, Léon's way of getting back at the Germans was by transporting documents, money, Jewish schoolchildren and a British pilot through 'the doghole'. Israel tried to bestow a 'Righteous Among the Nations' award on Léon for his actions, but he turned it down out of modesty.

He survived the war and continued farming until his death in 1963 aged seventy-six. His son Jean took over the farm and ran it until his death in 2003, at the age of eighty-six. Then it was sold.

In Switzerland

Félix and Joan Fournier, *real name* Plottier – the couple Frank spent most of his time with in Switzerland, whose flat was a hive of resistance activity.

Having moved back to their beloved France, Frank visited the Fourniers in 1946. He discovered the name 'Fournier' was a nom de guerre and Félix and Joan's real surname was Plottier.

He was told how Joan and Félix's two sons, aged eleven and

eight, had experienced a similar escape from France to
Switzerland to his own. The two boys, creeping across a misty
meadow in the dawn light, were challenged by a border guard
in German. Like Frank, the younger boy thought he had been
arrested, but seconds after bursting into tears, his older brother
pointed at the Swiss crosses on the guard's buttons.

Frank also learned that Félix and Joan's flat, so often used
to harbour couriers like Colette, was raided a few months
after he left in November 1943. Félix went to prison for three
months.

As soon as he was out, he was back up in the mountains
running arms into France for the Maquis, often carrying them
on his back on skis. While leading a party in Argentière, Félix's
group were ambushed by Swiss soldiers, who arrested them.
The Swiss government took a dim view of such activities, not
wanting to anger the Germans and be the next country Hitler
'protected'.

As the leader, Félix was sent to jail for two years. He was to
be deported after his sentence and banned from entering
Switzerland again. However, the war ended a few months
later and Félix was released. He went to Geneva Town Hall to
see about his banishment from the country.

The Swiss official, with a completely deadpan face, told
him, 'We cannot rescind the order prohibiting the entry of
Monsieur Félix Fournier into Switzerland. If Monsieur
Fournier attempts to enter our country again, he will be
arrested.' Félix was outraged, but just as he was about to argue,
the official said, 'However, there is no prohibition on our
records against Félix Plottier. Anyone entering under that
name won't be stopped.'

Frank visited Félix and Joan regularly after the war and
their friendship deepened. Félix became godfather to Frank's
newly born son Lloyd and taught him to ski. Lloyd also

remembers the contempt his godfather held for years after the war for any locals who had collaborated with the Germans. As a shop owner, he refused to do business with anyone who had collaborated.

In 1955, the families were linked by marriage. Frank's niece Jean married Tim Plottier, Félix and Joan's son, the boy who had pointed out the Swiss buttons on the border guard's tunic to his tearful younger brother. Jean and Tim had three children – Richard, Michael and Bridget – who have had six children between them. In 2015, the Plottier/Griffiths dynasty produced its third generation, a wonderful living link between two families who were thrust together by war.

Frank's account of his first six days in France – smuggled back to Britain by SOE and circulated around the War Cabinet.

Unknown to Frank at the time, his words helped to save the Tempsford Squadrons from being disbanded.

In his definitive history *SOE in France,* M.R.D. Foot wrote:

> Griffiths wrote a vivid account of his adventures in the Maquis, which Lord Selborne circulated round the War Cabinet [*September 1943*] on whom it must have made an impression; for the pilot found himself in the hands of a body of alert, well-armed, well-disciplined, uniformed young men, who evidently had the run of the side roads at least in their neighbourhood and were passionately pro-British.

Frank's words had shone a light on the French Resistance, of which very little was known in Britain. His description persuaded British authorities that the work of the Tempsford

Squadrons in arming Resistance movements, facilitating sabotage and dropping spies, was worthwhile. It disproved the argument that the Tempsford Squadrons were a waste of men and resources that should be channelled into Bomber Command instead.

The Fréjus Rail Tunnel – the destruction of which was Operation Pimento's goal.

Without the heavy explosives onboard *O for Orange*, the French Resistance were unable to destroy the tunnel. An Allied bombing mission failed to knock it out it too.

Twenty-seven days after Frank's crash, the Allies launched Operation Avalanche, landing over 100,000 men in southern Italy, mostly around Salerno. Initial success led to intense, bloody fighting as German reinforcements from France enjoyed a quick journey to Italy through the Alpine tunnels like Fréjus. They could not quite push the Allies back into the sea, but the rapid bolstering of defences made sure the British and Americans were in for a gruelling campaign as they pushed north through Italy.

In 1944, the retreating Germans drove two rail wagons laden with explosives into the tunnel and detonated them, causing severe damage.

Joe and Freddie – the SOE agents Frank re-entered France with over the wall in Annemasse.

While in Barcelona, Frank discovered the pair had passed through three weeks earlier with their hair on. They had been successfully transported to Britain shortly after. Frank never met or heard from them again, and their names were certainly noms de guerre.

Back in France

Klaus Barbie, aka 'The Butcher of Lyon' – the German SS Commander who arrived in Annemasse days before Frank re-entered France.

Barbie, directly responsible for killing 14,000 people and famous for his barbaric torture methods, had recently been awarded the Iron Cross (First Class) by Adolf Hitler when Frank crossed into Annemasse.

He survived the war and fled to South America, where despite his notoriety and status as a mass murderer, he was protected by the United States Army Counter Intelligence Corps (CIC). They valued his anti-communist stance and intelligence-gathering skills. The French government sentenced him to death in 1947, but the US ignored this and helped Barbie relocate to Bolivia, where he sold weapons and rose to Lieutenant Colonel in the Bolivian Army.

Barbie worked for several Bolivian dictators as a secret police officer, brutally cracking down on dissent and advising how to use torture most effectively. He met Pablo Escobar several times in the 1970s, guaranteeing safe supply of his cocaine in exchange for money to fund Barbie's anti-communist crackdowns.

Several pleas for him to be extradited to France were made after he was located by Nazi hunters Serge and Beate Klarsfeld in the early 1970s, but Bolivia refused. Eventually, and only after Barbie failed to deliver $10,000 worth of goods to the Bolivian government in 1983, the authorities allowed extradition to France for trial.

In a special 700-seat courtroom, Barbie was sentenced to life imprisonment, avoiding his death sentence by two years as France had abolished the death penalty in 1981. The US government made a formal apology to France for allowing Barbie to escape justice for thirty-three years.

Barbie died of cancer in jail four years later, aged seventy-seven.

Marie-Louise Dissard, aka 'Françoise' – the chain-smoking, hobbling 62-year-old who couriered Frank across France on the overnight train under the nose of a Milicien and a Luftwaffe aircrew.

Born Marie-Louise Dissard in 1881, 'Françoise' was fifty-eight when the Second World War broke out. Loath to see her beloved France ruled by the Germans, she spent her early sixties couriering airmen like Frank across France under the nose of the Milice and Gestapo. The state pension age in France in 2023 is sixty-two.

Initially Françoise worked as a courier in the Pat Line, one of two escape networks that transported downed airmen out of France. She was a master of disguise, often playing the eccentric, harmless old lady. Her dresses, described as 'extravagantly ecclesiastical', were substituted regularly as Françoise transformed from mourning widow to prostitute, from homeless woman to violin player. She operated on zero sleep, rarely ate and survived on black coffee and cigarettes.

The Pat Line's leader, a Belgian called Albert Guérisse, was arrested and executed in March 1943. The Gestapo cleaned out the network. All but one courier was caught: Françoise.

Her brilliant disguises and acting had hoodwinked the Vichy Police. In an earlier investigation into her, they had concluded she was 'mentally unstable' and not possibly up to the task of clandestine work. A Vichy police official wrote: 'She does not enjoy full command of her mental faculties and it is beyond doubt that she can exercise no influence whatever on those around her, because no one gives any credit at all to what she says.'

Despite her former leader Guérisse being horrifically tortured by the Gestapo, and the rest of her colleagues being deported to concentration camps, Françoise did not throw in the towel to save her skin.

Instead, she rebuilt the entire operation by herself.

Over the summer of 1943, she recruited hundreds of 'helpers' like Thérèse to run safehouses across southern France, while continuing to courier airmen. She travelled to Switzerland to negotiate personally with Victor Farrel, the British SOE frontman who Frank spent so much time with in Geneva, persuading him to get MI9 to fund her activities. As the only original member left, Françoise's leadership dragged the escape network from the ashes back into existence.

All this at a time when she and the rest of France's women could not even vote, open a bank account, or take a job without their husband's permission. Yet here she was, an asthmatic, frail, 'mentally unstable' 62-year-old standing at barely five foot, rebuilding and leading an entire underground movement. The Pat Line was soon being referred to as the Françoise Line, but it is the former name that dominates historical records.

Françoise personally helped 250 airmen escape to Spain. More than 500 were recorded as passing through her safehouse and 700 via the Françoise Line. With airmen taking an average of three months to train at a cost of £15,000, that means she saved the Allies £10.5 million pounds (£500 million in today's money) and 175 years of training time. Not to mention somebody's husband or father saved from Nazi interrogation, imprisonment and possible execution.

Despite her asthma and failing health, this remarkable

woman spent an average of twenty-three nights a month on overnight trains crossing France.

After the war, Françoise was highly decorated by not one but four governments. From France she received the Légion d'Honneur, a Croix de Guerre with palms, and a Médaille de la Résistance with rosette. From Belgium, an Order of Leopold II with palms and a Belgian Croix de Guerre. From Britian, a George Medal and an honorary OBE. And from the US, a Medal of Freedom with Gold Palm.

But like many war heroes, the highly decorated Françoise lived an unassuming life after 1945. She became a teacher in Toulouse and made it her legacy to lecture schoolgirls on the importance of independence and women's rights.

Frank never saw her again, but did attend her funeral in 1957, commenting that her statue in Toulouse was missing one thing, her beloved cat Mifouf.

It was then he learned why her bag was so ridiculously heavy when she couriered him across France. Not only did it contain her mangy cat, some notebooks, perfume, and several packs of cigarettes, but it was also stuffed with black market cheese from the Haute-Savoie.

The cheese served two purposes. Firstly, if she was caught, she could cover her activities by saying she was just a lowly black marketeer, a common offence in wartime France, which would warrant a mere slap on the wrist. Secondly and more importantly, the huge wheels of Reblochon were stuffed with plastic explosive!

Françoise was not only couriering British and American airmen; she was transporting bombs for the Resistance. She chose whiffy Reblochon as it masked the smell of the explosive.

No wonder she took such exception to being searched.

Joe Manos – the nineteen-year-old American with whom Frank walked over the Pyrenees.

Ever since I first heard about Frank's escape I was fascinated by the fearless, cocky character of Joe, closer to me in age than almost anyone else in Frank's escape. The loutish, six-foot-four teenager, who feared no German or Milicien, drove Frank crazy at times.

'At first, I did not like Joe,' wrote Frank in 1946. 'To say we fell out at times would be putting it mildly; for I was the product of an English public school, and Joe had been born and bred with the dead-end kids on 33rd street, New York. But I grew to respect his amazing courage and endurance.'

Joseph Emanuel Manos was born in Brooklyn on 28 December 1923, and spent his childhood in West Side Manhattan. He was sixteen when war broke out. The following year he enlisted in the US Air Force and, after training in Colorado, was sent to England as one of the first replacement crews in the 94th Bomb Group, stationed just outside Bury St Edmunds.

The USAAF, still bombing in daylight, incurred terrible losses over Europe during this time. In Joe's 331st Squadron, only two crews finished a full tour (twenty-five missions). That is thirty-nine airmen out of 300. Joe was not one of them. He was shot down on 14 July 1943 raiding a Luftwaffe airfield called Le Bourget, near Paris. Four fortresses went down after German FW 190s attacked the formation. 'Good fighters with plenty of nerve!!' as Joe recalled in his Escape and Evasion report.

That day, his squadron had been chosen as the 'low squadron', and he was in the lower element of its formation, meaning he was in one of the three lowest aircraft in the entire wing formation. Airmen called this position 'coffin corner', as they were more vulnerable to anti-aircraft fire and German fighters.

Joe was also occupying the loneliest position in the aircraft – tail gunner. Although contested, many argue the 'tail-end Charlie' position was the most dangerous, as the spherical bubble in which the tail gunner sat was exposed to enemy fighters, and the gunner tended not to wear his parachute in the cramped position. So not only was Joe in the most dangerous position in his aircraft, but the aircraft was in the most hazardous position in the entire formation.

In his own words: 'Number 3 engine was on fire. We fell out of formation. I talked to the co-pilot and he said the instrument panel was just going to pieces in front of him. The navigator was wounded. After we fell out, an FW190 came in from up high and I got a couple of bursts at him. But he raked the aeroplane.

'I didn't know the bell was ringing at the time [*signalling to bale out*]. The two waist gunners were working the gun but it exploded between them. They were both killed. The radio operator had shrapnel all up his side. I don't know why, but he baled out the waist window.

'I was back in the tail shooting and shouting "Rip it!" When I shut up, I could hear the bell ringing so I knew it was time to go. The minute I got out the aeroplane, I pulled the D-ring. I was lying flat on my back, I had a chest pack on, and it was just like lying in bed, no jolt, it just went billowing up above me.'

It took Joe over 200 days to get back to England, nearly twice as long as Frank. He remained in the Air Force for the rest of the war and flew in the Berlin Airlift. In 1952, Joe married his pre-war sweetheart Dorothy and together they were posted to Guam, where Joe tracked hurricanes in a B-17.

Joe retired from the Air Force in 1962 and got a job as a rocket technician, helping power the US's space programme. Settled in Sacramento with two children, Joe took one last job working for the local municipal power company, before retiring for good. In 1978, he sent a letter to 'Frank Griffiths, RAF, London, England'.

Frank visited him. 'Even after thirty-five years he had hardly changed in looks or manner,' he remembered. 'Looking at the lawn at the back of his house, there was a circle of worn grass round the periphery. "What caused that?" I asked him. "Oh," he said, "it's my wife, she goes in for this jogging. Me, I don't bother. So long as I can push myself away from the table after a good meal, that's all the exercise I want." The valiant attempts of Thérèse to encourage him taking exercise had obviously failed!'

Joe spent his retirement flying his Cessna 182 around California with his old flying buddies, surprising perhaps for someone who had survived such terrifying experiences in the air. In his final years, he remained an active member of the Escape and Evasion Society, played with his grandchildren and his neighbours' cats, and watched life go by from his front porch.

He died in 2017, aged ninety-seven.

The 1943 Baseball World Series – which Joe so desperately wanted news of during his time in France and Spain.

The New York Yankees reclaimed the title from the St Louis Cardinals four games to one. It was a final that would go down in history. Not only was it a rematch of the 1942 series final, but it was also potentially the last ball game for some years as the war effort soaked up manpower. As such, 68,000 fans crammed into the Yankee stadium to watch it. But none of them could have been prepared for what happened before the game had even begun.

As the teams warmed up on the field, four B17s 'buzzed' the Yankee Stadium, thundering from home plate to centre field in a low pass. Jack Watson – one of the B17's pilots – returned for an encore at a terrifyingly low altitude, clearing the flagpoles above the stadium by twenty-five feet and sending the crowd into a frenzy. The press later reported: 'An army bomber roared over Yankee Stadium so low Slats Marion could have fielded it.' The B17s were *en route* to combat bases in England, to join the 303rd Bomb Group, part of the Mighty Eighth Air Force in which Joe was serving.

As a young New Yorker who loved nothing more than flying B17s and baseball, I can only imagine what Joe's reaction would have been if he were there.

Thérèse Baudot de Rouville – the tall, red-headed Irish woman who ran Françoise's safehouse in Toulouse.

Like Françoise, 52-year-old Thérèse was considered a harmless, middle-aged spinster, when she was actually hiding up to ten highly valuable airmen in her loft, preparing them for their hike over the Pyrenees.

M.R.D. Foot, official historian of the SOE, wrote: 'Evaders often found that they had to trust themselves entirely to women; and without the courage and devotion of its couriers and safehouse keepers, nearly all of them women, no escape line could keep going at all. Most of the helpers were heart-stoppingly young, some no more than teenagers, and the lines were usually organised around a small number of charismatic and exceptional individuals.'

In the case of Françoise and Thérèse, Foot's analysis is almost spot on. Frank was totally reliant on the bravery and professionalism of these two women. Without them, the escape network would not exist. But while they certainly fitted the 'charismatic and exceptional' billing, the same cannot be said for being 'heart-stoppingly young'.

At sixty-two and fifty-two, Françoise and Thérèse had led

fascinating, colourful lives before the war, Thérèse's perhaps even more compelling.

Born in Paris on 14 December 1891 to an Irish mother and French father, Olga Baudot de Rouville (Thérèse) grew up bilingual and trained as a teacher in Belgium. The First World War saw her retrain as a Red Cross nurse, looking after the wounded in a hospital in Lille.

Her heart was broken twice in this period. Her fiancé, a French soldier, disappeared without trace and her only sibling Ludovic died of disease close to the front lines in January 1917. Little is known of what Thérèse did in the interwar period.

However, as the Wehrmacht tore across France in 1940, much of the population including Thérèse was forced to flee south. On the arduous two-week march, Thérèse saw a French couple begin shouting pro-German propaganda, suggesting France should accept its new rulers.

'It was at this moment,' Thérèse testified, 'which I shall never forget for the rest of my life, as I was seething with rage . . . It was this date I entered into the Resistance. As God is my witness, from that moment on I never left it. Every possible means seemed good to me: by my deeds, words and attitude.'

Remarkably, she rejoined the Red Cross and became a nurse in the same hospital in Lille, twenty-two years after her original stint there. She became known as 'the lady with the tea' and ran up large personal debts buying food on the black market for 'her' soldiers. With Lille firmly in German control, the injured British and French soldiers were sent straight to Germany as POWs, but not before Thérèse had loaded them with black market food and warm clothes.

Noticing her sympathy for the Allied cause, Thérèse was recruited into Pat O'Leary's renowned escape network as a safehouse keeper. For nearly two years she helped send soldiers left behind after the 'debacle' (France's defeat) south to Marseille and hopefully over the Pyrenees. But it all came crashing down when a colleague named Harry Cole double-crossed and betrayed most of the northern members of the network.

Thérèse escaped the Gestapo by the skin of her teeth. 'They searched for me in every town of significance in Occupied France,' she recalled. 'Three weeks after my flight, they were still getting on the trains in groups of ten or twelve checking old ladies and checking their papers.' Disguised as an old spinster, she made it to Marseille and linked up with Pat O'Leary himself, running his safehouse.

But O'Leary was betrayed, arrested and deported in March 1943. The network disintegrated as its members met a similar fate or fled to Spain. 'I could have left for Spain,' reflected Thérèse, 'but I decided it was unacceptable to leave the work for which I had sacrificed everything since 1940.'

Only one courier remained. Françoise.

With a fellow middle-aged woman in charge, Françoise rebuilt the network with Thérèse at its heart. At least 500 airmen passed through Thérèse's safehouse. She enforced a strict exercise routine, making the airmen climb the stairs twenty-five times on tiptoes before every meal. Rude or care-less behaviour was punished with push-ups. If the offender laughed and did not do them, Thérèse withheld the next meal from everyone, which soon sorted the problem.

When the safehouse address was discovered by the Gestapo, Françoise and Thérèse left together in February. 'I left every-thing I had there. I wanted to get away from Toulouse and start again somewhere else,' said Thérèse. She went to Marseille. But with nothing to do and no money, she spent only a month there before catching a train to Switzerland to try and enlist with Victor Farrel.

The train never made it. Travelling through the Vercors Region, the Maquis launched a major uprising against the Germans. The whole area ground to a halt. Thérèse, under the alias Suzanne Gauthier, volunteered to be a nurse for the Resistance fighters. Heavily outnumbered and lacking professional training, the maquisards fought a valiant rearguard action but were defeated. The Germans laid waste to the region, massacring entire towns and hospitals. Thérèse fled to the mountains, where she lived under the stars for seven months until France was liberated.

Eventually she returned home to Lille, but found her house totally ransacked, plundered by the Germans. She was forced to sleep on the streets while deciding what to do. Her heart settled on Britain and Thérèse wrote to several families of soldiers she had nursed in 1940 until one took her in. Unbelievably, she could not get a visa to stay. The British government sent her back to France.

Appalled at her treatment, Thérèse's old boss and head of the escape network Pat O'Leary fought for her return. He succeeded and Thérèse returned to Britain to Cockermouth, where she lived with a colleague from Lille hospital. Aged fifty-six and with no immediate family, Thérèse knew she was a guest and could not stay forever.

She decided to go to Ireland to look for her mother's family. On 3 April 1947, she departed for the Emerald Isle leaving all her belongings in Cockermouth. She disappeared off the face of the Earth.

For three decades no one knew what became of Thérèse. Rumours circulated that she had died or joined an enclosed order of nuns. But there was a third rumour, which Frank included in his book.

He wrote: 'Moved to Cork and ran a Mission to Seamen, frequently used by French fishermen. Last heard of in an old

folks' home at Concarneau, near the tip of north-west France in
1974. The RAF Escaping Society contacted her when she was in
the home and asked whether they could help her in any way. She
replied she did not wish to ask for financial assistance.

'Her wants were few, but there was one thing that she would
love to have – an electric kettle which switched itself off auto-
matically. A wish easily fulfilled, but such a small reward for
the risks she ran hiding our aircrews.'

Thérèse died three years later, just short of her eighty-
eighth birthday. She was cremated with little ceremony or
fanfare, a quiet end to an extraordinary life dedicated to helping others.

The Saqué family – who guided Frank and Joe from
Perpignan train station to Spain, accommodating them for
one night in their Pyrenean farmhouse.

The story of how Frank reconnected with the Saqué family
is extraordinary in itself.

Frank was desperate to thank the family and find La
Pouillède after the war, but as he wrote in 1987: 'One of the
sad things about escape and evasion is that to protect our
helpers, we did not wish to know their real names or to remember addresses.' Frank had even less chance of reuniting, as he
had walked at night and had no idea where he was.

Nevertheless, Frank seized the first opportunity he could to
look for the farmhouse. Flying a Dakota from Gibraltar to
Marseille in July 1945, he scoured the area but was unsuccess-
ful. 'My reconnaissance, carried out at a respectable height,
was useless. Apart from a very rough distance from Perpignan,
all I had to go on was a distinctive, sharp-pointed hill which
overlooked the farm and in 1943 could be seen through the
cracks of the hayloft door. But the area seemed too highly
populated and there was no pointed hill.'

Twelve years later, he found himself being flown over the area in a Nord Noratlas by some French pilots he was visiting in Pau. Again, the sortie failed.

'And so the years rolled around to 1986, forty-three years after I'd met Antoine,' wrote Frank. 'Unknown to me, Antoine had retired after a full career in the Armée de l'Air at the rank of Warrant Officer. He lived with his wife, sixteen hives of bees and a truffle hound in Salon-de-Provence. Homesick for his Pyrenees, he decided to attend a memorial at Tarascon to the guides and the escapers who lost their lives in the Pyrenees in the war.

'Fortunately, Antoine knew my name, as I had given a little dictionary to his schoolboy cousin with "*English man Griffiths*" written in it. He asked one of the RAF Escaping Society officials if they knew the name of a pilot called Griffiths who had escaped. After forty-three years, the contact was made.'

In June 1987, Frank visited the area and finally reunited with Antoine. 'On the last day of our tour, we dropped down an escarpment on an almost vertical track and there, to the south, was the pointed hill and hidden in the bend of the river, the farm – La Pouillède – almost the same as it was forty-four years ago. Under the tree in front of the farmhouse on this gorgeous sunny day was spread an enormous *picnique* with all the now grey-haired guides and their wives and families to greet us!'

Reading this letter after my trip, I realised I had experienced almost an exact replica of that day thirty-five years later. In the years since, Frank, Antoine and many of the 'passeurs' had died, but it felt wonderful to have honoured their memory.

Jacques Saqué, aka 'the uncle', and his wife Louise Saqué – the couple who lived at La Pouillède.

Jacques Snr, the uncle who was crashed into by a bicycle,

farmed at La Pouillède until his death in 1968 aged sixty-seven. Louise made it to ninety-two before she died.

Jacques Jnr, Pierre and Louis – Jacques and Louise's three children.

Pierre, the teenager who escorted Frank and Joe up the Spanish border and kept Frank's dictionary after their English lesson, died in 2003 aged seventy-five.

I was just too late to meet his brother Jacques Jnr and sister Louise, who died in 2019 and 2022, aged ninety-five and ninety respectively.

From Spain

Antoine Saqué – the young, athletic Catalan who guided Frank and Joe over the mountains.

Born in Agullana, Spain, on 31 March 1915, Antoine was fiercely Catalan. His family lived right on the French/Spanish border and he walked over the Pyrenees every day to go to school, instilling an intimate knowledge of the mountains in his brain and a supreme fitness in his legs.

Aged twenty-one, he joined the French Air Force but put himself on leave when France fell in 1940. From the beginning, he refused to collaborate with the Vichy government. His early Resistance work involved forging papers in Céret Town Hall, where he worked to help escapees flee to Spain. When the Germans occupied the whole of France in November 1942, Antoine upped his resistance by smuggling people out of France.

With his family farm just over the border in Spain, and his cousins' farm La Pouillède just outside Céret in France, Antoine had a perfect escape route on his hands. He recruited his uncle Jacques and cousin Pierre to help guide.

For a year the escape line (part of the Françoise Line)

passed airmen, Jews and compromised agents into Spain. Françoise Dissard was so confident in the line, she passed General de Gaulle's own nephews Pierre and Henri Cailliau through it. Antoine had no idea who they were.

Keen to fight, Antoine stopped smuggling in 1944, walked into Spain and interned himself at Molinar de Caranza camp in the hope of joining de Gaulle's forces in North Africa, which he did. He was highly decorated when the war ended.

Antoine served a further twenty-five years in the Air Force. He married his sweetheart Denise Sadaillan, who he had met before the war, but had to wait until the conflict was over to tie the knot. They had four children: Yves, Roland, Maryse and Monique. He pursued careers in accounting, beekeeping and foraging after the Air Force, and he spent much of his time as president of Veterans' Affairs in Marseille.

Unknown to me, and largely forgotten in the family, Antoine visited Frank in North Wales in 1987.

'Despite the loss of his luggage,' wrote Frank, 'his visit to north Wales was a great success, for he proved a true country-man. His greatest joy was to disappear into our local woods like a hound following a fresh scent, emerging with armfuls of toadstools all edible and delicious.' Frank and Ruth also visited the Saqué family several times in the south of France.

Antoine died in 2003, aged eighty-eight.

From Britain

Ruth Griffiths – Frank's wife, whom he met in Torquay in June 1940.

I remember Ruth well. She lived to be ninety-nine years old, dying in February 2017, when I was sixteen. Not many days have gone by in the last three years when I have not wished I had asked her more about her wartime experiences and her husband. Above all, I would like to ask her about the letter that Frank sent her after he got to Switzerland.

Of this letter, Frank recalled: 'Ruth received it four weeks later. It was highly coloured where the censors had tested it with chemicals for secret writing. She doubted its authenticity, but I did mention our wedding and one or two other things that convinced her it was me. It was the first evidence she had I was alive.' The letter sadly did not survive.

I have often wondered about her reaction to it. Ruth received a 'missing' telegram – not 'missing presumed dead' – a large distinction. Did she assume the worst, begin mourning and try to move on with her life, in the knowledge that her eight-month-old would never know her father? Or did she hold out hope and potentially make it even harder if the terrible news did come?

I remember the last time I ever saw Ruth in my grandparents' home in the summer of 2016. She hobbled around on a stick and could not see or hear much. To my shame, I remember exiting the conversation as fast as possible, as I wanted to talk to my cousins who were also at the family lunch. She died the following February and was cremated in accordance with her wishes for no fuss, no religion and no live flowers, as they would only die and go to waste.

Thinking of Ruth, I am always reminded of the saying: 'Every time an old person dies, a library burns.'

Frank Griffiths – you will probably know him by now.

After returning to Britain, Frank was given a month's leave before being posted back to Telecommunications Research Establishment at RAF Defford, his old job test-piloting. He was made acting Wing Commander in January 1944 and continued adding aircraft to his resumé, including the Meteor (the world's first jet), the Mosquito, and the Flying Fortress.

At the war's end, Frank was sent on an epic journey by Transport Command, circumventing the Atlantic in a Dakota, Hudson and Expeditor. Over three weeks, he flew from England to Iceland, Greenland (forced landing), Newfoundland, Montreal, Washington, Indianapolis, the Bahamas, the Azores, Morocco, Gibraltar, France and back to Blighty.

On his return, he was sent to the Blind Landings Experimental Unit at RAF Farnborough where, after months of test piloting and boffinry, Frank piloted the world's first blind landing.

Family members who knew Frank recall how vividly he talked about the unnerving nature of sitting in the cockpit with your arms folded as the aircraft approached the runway. Blind landings are something most readers will have benefited from, for they were the forerunners of autopilot, the system by which modern aircraft land in inclement weather every day.

Various postings in Transport Command around the world followed after the war, namely North America and the Middle East. Another epic journey in 1952 saw Frank sent to Africa to inspect the continent's runways, most having been built by the Americans during the Second World War. Flying a Skymaster, Frank left England for the Azores, Western Sahara, Senegal, Liberia and the Ivory Coast, where he headed inland across Nigeria, Chad and Sudan, turned south to Kenya, Tanzania and the DRC and finally north-west back up the Atlantic coast of Africa to Portugal, France and Britain, clocking 115 flying hours in the process.

On 1 January 1953, he was promoted to Group Captain (Air Force equivalent of Colonel), in charge of RAF Abingdon. During this tenure, the major film *Carve Her Name with Pride* starring actress Virginia McKenna was filmed at RAF Abingdon.

The film was about a young SOE agent called Violette Szabo, who was dropped into France by Frank's old squadron at Tempsford, but was captured and executed by the Gestapo.

As an ex-Tempsford pilot, Frank helped advise on set. There is a wonderful photo of the 45-year-old Frank, resplendent in his Group Captain uniform, talking to a smiling Virginia McKenna, the gorgeous actress clearly having just been subjected to one of his jokes.

Frank was retired by the RAF in 1962, but reengaged as Squadron Leader Administrative Officer in the Air Training Corps in North Wales, teaching the next generation of pilots. He retired for good in 1977 after forty-one years' service.

Frank and Ruth had three more children after his return from France: Lloyd in 1945, Mark in 1956 and Rebecca in 1960. Lloyd followed his father into aviation, becoming the postman pilot for the Hudson Bay in the 1960s, landing on water in the summer and ice in the winter. Later, Lloyd became a commercial pilot and ended his career as British Airways' Chief of Flight Operations.

To go with his DFC and AFC from Britain, Frank also won the Distinguished Flying Cross from the Netherlands and a Légion d'Honneur, Croix de Guerre with palms and a Médaille de la Résistance from France.

Frank spent retirement in his beloved North Wales in Ruthin, grazing his sheep on various roundabouts and raising money for the riding for the disabled charity. He was known as 'Uncle Frank' to many of his friends' children, as he often enjoyed playing with them more than adult conversation.

But even Frank – the seemingly unkillable pilot – could not escape old age. He died on 23 March 1996, aged eighty-six.

The following May, his memorial service was held in St Mary's Church, Llanfair. Frank's old friend, the Reverend Group Captain Arthur Reece, read a eulogy:

In many ways Griff was a pirate in the style of Drake – who too had a swashbuckling style and a great love of the sea and sailing. His energy was boundless, his keenness to fly unmatched.

One of Griff's most loveable traits was his rich sense of humour, which was probing, sometimes quirky but without barb or cynicism.

Griff was a countryman at heart and he was never happier than when he could share his knowledge with children.

There are many young and not so young here today who will remember being taught by him – to ride a bicycle or a horse, to light a fire, use a tool, sail a boat, ski, swim, gut a rabbit or pluck a pigeon, to mention just a few of the lessons he passed on.

He was not the conventional go-to-church-on-Sunday Christian – but in his books he recalls, in times of stress or danger, snatches of hymns with which he was familiar from his Christian upbringing.

Occasionally he casually or perhaps diffidently refers to prayer or praying. I visited him in hospital a short time before he died. He talked at length about all manner of things and finally, as though he had come to the point he could no longer avoid, said: 'I do believe that there is something' – and that for Griff was an admission.

Frank's ashes were spread near the summit of Moel Famau mountain in North Wales, a stone's throw from the Dee Estuary, whose hardships and beauty forged him into the man he was.

ACKNOWLEDGEMENTS

Where to begin? The list of people to whom *Operation Pimento* owes its existence is vast. I have learned that books are as much a team effort as a tug-of-war competition. My attempt to thank everyone involved here will almost certainly fail. But while my list may not be complete, it is sincere and heartfelt, and I feel lucky to have been supported by such wonderful people. Thank you, everyone.

Firstly, my parents, and in particular, Mum. *Operation Pimento* began life when you suggested I apply for that travel journalism bursary to retrace Frank's escape. I owe so much to your vision in those early days. When I returned from retracing Frank's journey and declared I was going to write a book, despite having no agent, publishing contacts or experience, you both believed in me and did not make me get a real job. I would never have been able to write this book if you had not let me live at home rent-free, eating all your food. Thank you for your unwavering support.

I should mention that I never planned to write a book. When I left for France, I had been commissioned to write one 1,200-word article for a newspaper. Which is why I must thank everyone who followed my journey on social media. I was blown away by your encouragement and interest and it played a large part in my decision to write something longer. Thanks also to the Worshipful Livery Company of Wales, who offered the bursary that made my retracing possible in the first place. I do not think it is an understatement to say that awarding me the bursary has changed my life.

I owe an enormous amount to the wonderful people I met in France on my journey. To Marie-Annick and Samuel Fontaine, to Nico and Josette Buzare, to Bernadette and Laetitia Mordal and to Marie-Laure Saqué, thank you for helping me understand your ancestors' heroics in 1943. Similarly, Joe Manos Jnr, Helen Rush and Nicola Brooks; meeting you was a pleasure and I am indebted to the source material you gave me, particularly Helen for the moving letters you gave me that finish the Epilogue.

Frank may have died thirty years ago, but it seems right I should mention him here. It must have been traumatic for him to revisit this period of the war as he did in his writing and oral history, even forty years after the events had occurred. In the 1970s and 1980s, some still believed veterans should not seek publicity from their war stories, but I am infinitely glad that Frank ignored this and committed much of his memory to paper. Thank you, Frank, you have been a pleasure to research.

No one has been more central in bringing *Operation Pimento* to an audience than Elly James, my fantastic agent. Quite moronically, I had written nearly 50,000 words before I first thought of getting an agent, traditionally the first step in getting a book published. And that thought only occurred because you reached out to me and asked if I had one. Since then, you have guided me through the publishing process like a true expert. Thank you for championing Frank's story and my writing.

A huge thank you to the Hodder dream team of Rupert Lancaster, Lucy Buxton, Barry Johnston and George Biggs. You have all been pleasures to work with, even when I was late delivering manuscripts. Not once have I detected flagging enthusiasm for Frank's story, quite the opposite in fact, as you proved, Rupert, by giving up a Sunday to come to a memorial event at RAF Tempsford to see what is left of the place for yourself.

Another truly instrumental figure behind *Operation Pimento* has been my great-uncle Lloyd Griffiths, Frank's first son. Not only did you meticulously keep and organise your father's various photo albums, documents and logbooks, but you also trusted me with them all to write this book. Your sharp memory of your father has made researching Frank a great deal easier and I have really enjoyed the times we have spent together during this project. The occasion you drove six hours to Anglesey with your father's medals for the *Antiques Roadshow*, only to step aside at the last minute for me to showcase them alone, shows how selfless you have been in helping me with this project.

I did not realise it at the time, but my teachers at school had a huge hand in *Operation Pimento*. Ms Livingston, Mr Lewis, Dr Harrison, Mr Vaughan-Smith, Ms Arrand – thank you for your encouragement at school. Your enthusiasm sparked my interest in history and English and, on the occasions I wrote something half-decent, your kind words stick in my memory even now.

Thank you to my godfather George for your advice and support, to Hannah and Erik for letting me stay in your house in France, to Katharine and George for always welcoming me with open arms, to my friends for stoically repeating 'How's the book going, Adam?' for the last two years, to Will for buying that newspaper, to Granny and Grandpop, Mark and Bec, my flatmate George, Bebsy, my sister Ella and my labrador Poppy, who would often come and nuzzle me while I wrote.

And lastly, thank you Sally, my wonderful girlfriend. We began going out at almost the exact moment *Operation Pimento* was born and I realise you have never known me without me having work to do on my book. Thank you for supporting me through the ups and downs, for always being your cheerful, joyful self, and for pretending to be interested when I blabbed on about Bomber Command tactics or the SOE or *Blackadder Goes Forth*. You have been a part of this book more than you can know.

And (really) lastly, thank you, for reading this book. If you tell one friend a story about one of the incredible people in these pages, then I have achieved my goal of paying tribute to that incredible generation of men and women. We owe them a great deal.

PICTURE ACKNOWLEDGEMENTS

First 8-page inset

Pages 1, 3: Douglas Fisher/Radar Research Archive

Page 2 (above): Harrington Aviation Museum

Page 2 (below): courtesy of The Secret WW2 Learning Network / CC BY-SA 3.0

Page 4 (above): courtesy of the Congdon family

Page 4 (centre): courtesy of the Peters family

Pages 4 (below), 5, 7: courtesy of Annecy Council Archives

Page 6: © Keystone-France\Gamma-Rapho via Getty Images

Page 8: courtesy of the Fontaine family

Second 8-page inset

Page 1, 4 (above, left), 7, 8: author's collection

Page 2: courtesy of Lionel Ferrer

Page 3 (above, left and below, centre): courtesy of Josette Buzaré

Page 3 (above, right): courtesy of Annecy Council Archives

Page 4 (above, right and centre, left): courtesy of the Mérandon family

Page 4 (below, right): courtesy of the Plottier family

Page 5 (above): Cumbria Archive and Local Studies Centre, Whitehaven

Page 5 (below): Haute-Garonne Departmental Council / Departmental Archives / Françoise Network Fund / 44 J 52-53

Page 6 (above, left): courtesy of the Manos family
Page 6 (above, right): courtesy of the Saqué family
Page 6 (below): Castell de Sant Ferran

Integrated within the text
Pages 201, 202, 209, 213, 214 and 215: author's collection

Maps and illustrations by Joanna Boyle

SELECT BIBLIOGRAPHY AND FURTHER READING

Books

Antoine, Claude, *Crash a Meythet* (Self-published, 1993).

Antoine, Claude, *Meythet* (Self-published, 2000).

Boxall, Harley, Bamford, Joe, *Devotion to a Calling: Far-east Flying and Survival With 62 Squadron RAF* (Pen & Sword, 2010).

Clark, Freddie, *Agents by Moonlight* (Tempus, 1999).

Foot, M.R.D., *SOE in France: An Account of the Work of the British Special Operations Executive in France 1940–1944* (Government Official History Series, 1966).

Griffiths, Frank, *Angel Visits: From Biplane to Jet* (Thomas Harmsworth Publishing, 1986).

Griffiths, Frank, *Winged Hours* (William Kimber, 1981).

Harding, Stephen, *Escape from Paris: A True Story of Love and Resistance* (De Capo Press, 2019).

Iredale, Will, *The Pathfinders: The Elite RAF Force that Turned the Tide of WWII* (WH Allen, 2022).

Millar, George, *Road to Resistance* (Little, Brown, 1979).

Newby, Eric, *Love and War in the Apennines* (Picador, 1971).

O'Connor, Bernard, *Churchill's Most Secret Airfield* (Amberley, 2013).

Plottier, Félix, *Guerres et Montagnes de 1915 à 1945* (Self-published, 1998).

RAF and the SOE: Special Duty Operations in Europe during WW2 (Pen & Sword, 2016).

Seaman, Mark, *Undercover Agent* (John Blake Publishing, 2020).

Seymour-Jones, Carole, *She Landed By Moonlight* (Hodder and Stoughton, 2014).

Shaw, Bob, *Top Secret Boeing* (Self-published, 2012).

Stourton, Edward, *Cruel Crossing: Escaping Hitler Across the Pyrenees* (Black Swan, 2013).

Articles

Eiroa, Matilde, and Pallares, Concha, 'Uncertain Fates: Allied Soldiers at the Miranda De Ebro Concentration Camp' (*The Historian*, date unknown).

Griffiths, Frank, 'Liverpool Days: A Short History of the Griffiths Family in Betws-yn-Rhos and Liverpool, 1816–1995' (Self-published, 1995).

Griffiths, Frank, 'Spanish Prisoners' (*Blackwood's*, No. 1563, Vol. 259, January 1946).

Holland, James, 'RAF Special Operations' (*Everyone's War*, Volume 10, Winter 2004).

Pallud, Jean Paul, 'SOE Operation Pimento' (*After the Battle*, No. 26, 1979).

https://war-experience.org/events/raf-special-operations/

Other

Keith Webb YouTube interview series with John Williamson, Bomber Command Commemorative Association, 2018.

Oral history of Frank Griffiths, Imperial War Museum, https://www.iwm.org.uk/collections/item/object/80012005

Oral history of Flight Lieutenant J D Charrot DFC, Imperial War Musuem, https://www.iwm.org.uk/collections/item/object/80027123

Proceedings of the Women in Resistance symposium, organised on 27 May, 2014 as part of the first commemoration, in the Senate, of National Resistance Day. http://www.senat.fr/notice-rapport/2013/r13-757-notice.html